ORTHODOX ALASKA

ORTHODOX ALASKA
A Theology of Mission

by

*E
99
.E7044
1992
seal*

MICHAEL J. OLEKSA

ST. VLADIMIR'S SEMINARY PRESS
Crestwood, NY 10707
1992

Library of Congress Cataloging-in-Publication Data

Oleksa, Michael, 1947–

    Orthodox Alaska : a theology of mission / by Michael J. Oleksa.

        p.   cm.

    Includes bibliographical references and index.

    ISBN 0–88141–092–6

1. Yupik Eskimos—Alaska—Missions. 2. Aleuts—Missions. 3. Tlingit Indians—Missions. 4. Missions, Russian—Alaska—History. 5. Indigenous church administrations—Alaska—History. 6. Orthodox Eastern Church—Missions—Alaska—History. 7. Russkaia pravoslavnaia tserkov'—Missions—Alaska—History. I. Title.

E99.E7037   1992

266'.19798—dc20   92-37026
                                                                         CIP

ORTHODOX ALASKA
A Theology of Mission
Copyright © 1992

by

ST. VLADIMIR'S SEMINARY PRESS

ISBN 0–88141–092–6

PRINTED IN THE UNITED STATES OF AMERICA

Table of Contents

For my beloved daughters,
      Anastasia and Ekatrina

My beloved sons,
      John and Michael

And ten special friends:
      Laurence, Nicholas, John, James, David, Daniel, Phillip,
      Jonah, Martin and Jeremiah

Acknowledgements

This book began as a research project sponsored by the U.S. Department of the Interior Village Histories Project in 1979, and evolved into a much more scholarly product which was successfully defended as a doctoral dissertation at the Orthodox Theological Faculty, Presov, Czechoslovakia, nine years later. Without assistance from Dr Lydia T. Black, Professor of Anthropology, University of Alaska, Fairbanks, and of Irene Barinoff, Seattle, Washington, the project would never have been undertaken. The inspiration and encouragement of the faculty at St Vladimir's Seminary, Crestwood, NY, was also critical in the evolution of this manuscript, the primary sources for which have already been published as *Alaskan Missionary Spirituality*, Paulist Press, Mahwah, NJ (1987). Perhaps most important of all were the cooperation and support of the parishioners of Three Saints Church, Old Harbor, and the St. Nicholas parishes of Kwethluk and Juneau, as well as the administrative and logistical support of the Sealaska Heritage Foundation in Alaska's capital, and the love and patience of my wife, Xenia.

Preface

Orthodox Christian mission has as its twin goals the "incarnation of the Logos of God into the language and customs of a country," and the "growth of an indigenous Church which will sanctify and endorse the people's personality."[1] The initial stage of any mission must necessarily be directed toward attaining the first, while a more mature and stable mission, such as that in Alaska after two centuries, must focus on the second. Outside Alaska, American Orthodoxy continues to struggle with questions of ethnicity and jurisdictional unity, so that the "incarnation of the Logos" into modern American culture has hardly begun, and among some groups, the task has been seriously questioned or even renounced as a legitimate concern. Only among indigenous Native Americans of the largest state has Orthodoxy become an integral part of an authentically American culture. Consequently, it seems appropriate that an attempt to formulate an Orthodox theology of mission should originate from the Alaskan context. If an American Orthodox missiology is to emerge, its formulation should serve not only the local Church in this country but contribute to the clarification of Orthodox theology for the entire universal Church as well.

The information about the pre-contact Alaskan Native worldview in the first chapter provides the background for the Alaskan reception of the Gospel and the basis for understanding the unique character of Alaskan Christianity today. The specific aspects of Orthodox Church history, missiology, spirituality and liturgy which attracted ancestors of modern Alaskan Orthodox Christians to the Faith, and which enabled them to integrate their own worldview with these, are discussed in subsequent chapters, together with the historical circumstances that brought Europeans and Siberians to that rather remote corner of the New World. This

1   Bishop Anastasios (Yannoulatos), "Discovering the Orthodox Missionary Ethos," (*St Vladimir's Theological Quarterly*, Vol. 3, 1964), p. 144-145.

"Aleut synthesis" of indigenous and Orthodox spiritualities emphasizes certain cosmic elements within the Biblical, patristic, and liturgical tradition that often have been overlooked or misunderstood elsewhere. Alaska has been for over two centuries the recipient of mission. This book is an attempt to transform this status, to reverse this relationship. The richness of the Alaskan Orthodox experience must enter the consciousness of the universal Church.

There is much history in this volume, however its focus is not the past but the future. Its primary purpose is to remind the Church that her mission extends beyond human concerns and issues, beyond politics, economics and even beyond "religion," as the subject is popularly understood. The risen Christ commanded that the Gospel be preached to "every creature," and St John's vision in the Apocalypse re-emphasizes the Pauline revelation that, in the end, Christ will be "all in all." The visible, created world possesses an eternal spiritual value, without which Christianity can no longer be considered "catholic," complete, whole.

The affirmation of this fundamental truth within the sacramental life of the Orthodox Church constituted an immediate link between Christianity and the religious traditions of the Alaskan peoples. Nature is not God, but nature reveals Him. Matter is not the opposite but the icon of the Spirit. The cosmos is symbolic in the fullest sense of the term, participating in the reality of its Prototype without exhausting Him. These complex theological themes might seem difficult for modern, twentieth-century secularized citizens to comprehend, but there are in Alaska Eskimo hunters and Aleut fishermen who know and understand the iconic character or Reality, and who live by it, for the Lord has seen fit to perfect praise "from the mouths of babes," and reveal His Wisdom to the "simple."

I hope that these pages may be the vehicle by which a portion of that wisdom may echo through the Church, for I am neither the creator of this vision and experience nor an adequate conveyor of it, but only one who has been blessed to witness and participate in the world of Alaskan Christianity and to have been enriched by it. I undertake to write this only in the hope that others, in other places and perhaps at other times, might also be similarly blessed by the fullness of faith as it has been "incarnate" in Alaska.

Introduction:
The Alaskan Spirit

The Beginning

The pre-contact intellectual and spiritual life of Alaskan Native peoples, as with traditional tribes everywhere, was dominated by myths and legends which contained archetypes for correct, and, more importantly, meaningful human behavior. Knowing the sacred stories of the People, as each tribe defined itself, provided each generation with the basic truths upon which survival and significance depended. The time of origins, "the Beginning," was the critical time during which the eternal paradigms originated. To know "how to" and to understand "why" were inseparable. The Eskimo stories of this type begin "*Ak'a tamaani*"—"long ago"; the Indian stories with "*Kk'adonts'idnee*"— "in distant time, it is said..." They are the sacred tales of a primordial existence and its transformation into the world as experienced today.

While the Yup'ik Eskimo of southwestern Alaska do not have a single, all-inclusive creation account comparable to the biblical book of Genesis, and lack the concept of an omnipresent and omniscient Creator, their oral tradition includes this myth of the origins of human beings:

> It was the time when there were no people on the earth. For four days the first man lay coiled up in the pod of beach pea. On the fifth, he burst forth, falling on the ground, and stood up, a full grown man. Feeling unpleasant, he stood and drank from a pool of water, then felt better. Looking up, he saw a dark object approaching with a waving motion until it stopped just in front of him. It was a raven. Raven stared intently at the man, raised one wing and pushed up its beak, like a mask, to the top of its head and changed immediately into a man. Still staring and cocking its head from side to side for a better view, Raven said at last, "What are you? Whence did you come? I have never seen the likes of you." And Raven looked at Man, surprised to see that this stranger looked so much like himself in shape.[1]

1   Fitzhugh, William H., and Kaplan, Susan, *Inua: The Spirit World of the Bering Sea Eskimo,* (Smithsonian Institution, Washington, D.C., 1984) p. 1.

Man, therefore, is created in the Creator's "image" even among the Eskimo. Raven himself is surprised by the results of his own actions. He is seen as unpredictable, and this reveals something of the Eskimo concept of the universe as well. Without a comprehensive, logical plan, the visible world is full of surprises. Anything can happen. To expect the unexpected, to live in the constant insecurity and uncertainty of the Arctic is, according to the traditional Eskimo, a basic fact of existence.

Raven himself is something of a mystery, for traditional Alaskans share this common identification of the creator with the Black Bird. While they believe that this is the visible form he most often assumes, they do not believe that all ravens are gods. Never did any tribe worship Raven or offer sacrifices to him. This circumstance is explained by the creation myth as well: Raven does not control reality. Rather, the world exists and continues in existence as the balance between spiritual forces. Each constitutive part must behave according to norms established "in the Beginning" in order to maintain the proper relationship among the various species. Any breach of protocol can have disastrous consequences.

The Yup'ik creation myth continues:

"You will be very lonely by yourself," said Raven. "I will make you a companion." Going to a more distant spot and looking now and again at Man, he made an image very like him, fastening a fine water grass on the back of its head. After the clay dried he waved his wings over it as before, and a beautiful young woman arose and stood beside Man. "There," he cried, "is a companion for you."[2]

Another parallel with the Bible is the concept that the Creator made living things from the earth and put life into them by forcing "air" or breath into them. Animals are made for the use of Man and Woman as his companion.

At that time there was neither day nor night. The Creator, Kashshakhiliuk, began to blow on a straw, and this is how the land gradually rose out of the waters and grew...The place where the first people came from was warm; there were no winters or storms, but always gentle, healthy breezes.[3]

This "eternal summer" is an Arctic hunter's image of Paradise.

The inclusion of this motif indicates that these events occurred at a

2   Fitzhugh, p. 3.
3   Bearne, Colin, *The Russian Orthodox Mission to America*, (Limestone Press, Kingston, ONT, 1978), p. 2-21.

time before the world as it now exists came into being.

> Raven thought that if he did not create something to make men afraid, they would destroy everything he had made to inhabit the earth. So he went to the creek where he formed a bear and gave it life, jumping to one side quickly as the bear stood up and looked about fiercely. He then told Man to avoid the bear or he would be torn to pieces. Raven then made different kinds of seals and explained their names and habits. He taught man to make rawhide lines from sealskin, snares for deer, but he cautioned him to wait until the deer were abundant before snaring them.[4]

The proper use of natural resources was thus established by the decree of the Creator, who recognized Man's destructive potential and sought to limit this with the creation of animals hostile to humans. Raven introduced "natural" checks and balances into the created universe to maintain cosmic order. His own ability to transform his physical appearance from bird to human reveals another fundamental traditional belief about reality, that the inner "life force" can assume many different visible shapes without itself undergoing ontological change.

Some Alaskan Indians say that when Raven first made human beings he used rock, and people were immortal. Because this was "too easy" he created them from dust, and humans became mortal, as they are today.[5]

All Alaskan Native groups believe in the fundamental intelligence of the animals with whom they share the land and upon whose capture their own survival depends, and the intimate powerful connection between the spoken word and reality. According to the Koyukon:

> The animal and its spirit are one in the same thing. When you name the animal you are also naming its spirit. That is why some animals are *hut/laanee*—like the ones women should not say—because the animal's name is like calling its spirit. Just like we don't say a person's name after they die...it would be calling their spirit and could be dangerous for whoever did it.[6]

The Eskimo call the "life force" within each living thing its "*Inua.*" The intelligent "soul" of each species possesses certain abilities which *Inua* of other species lack. The *Inua* of eagles endows them with their ability to see further and fly higher than other birds. The *Inua* of bears, which most closely resembles that of human beings, permits them to hunt, climb,

4   Fitzhugh, *op. cit.*, p. 4.
5   Nelson, Richard K., *Make Prayers to the Raven*, (University of Chicago Press, 1985), p 20.
6   *Ibid.*

swim, and walk (even on their hind legs) as people do. The *Inua* implants within each member of a species an ability to communicate with others. Speaking disrespectfully of an animal can jeopardize hunting success, for the *Inua* (or in Yup'ik *Yua*) of living members of that species may hear this and withhold themselves from the hunter. Hunting success requires being in the proper relationship with one's prey by observing established protocol, which include how one prepares for the hunt, the tools one uses, the behavior of family members, the observance of all the various procedures in butchering and consuming the skin, meat, sinews and bones, and the respectful disposal of any remains.

Traditional Eskimo hunting practices differed from those of the Indians of the interior of the state in that the former believed their behavior assured the natural reincarnation of the *Inua*, while the latter observed similar procedures to guarantee the individual hunter's continued "luck."

Eskimos encourage the recycling of names, the first children born in a community traditionally being named after the most recently deceased elder. Grandparents are "reborn" in the youngest generation, and new relationships are deliberately forged between families whose infants receive the names of newly departed members of another. Widows affectionately greet toddlers exclaiming "How is my husband today?" not only as a traditional social gesture, but as a means of strengthening a new relationship with the parents of the child. These parents may present the widow with subsistence goods saying "Your husband brings you these," in the name of the child and of her deceased spouse. The "dead" continue to support their survivors, and one's ancestors are never completely "gone."

By contrast, the Koyukon understand their intricate code of etiquette toward their prey in terms of personal success:

"Luck" is the powerful force that binds humanity to the nature spirits and their moral imperatives. For the Koyukon people, luck is a nearly tangible essence, an aura or condition that is "with" someone in certain circumstances or for particular purposes... Koyukon people express luck in the hunt by saying *"Bik'uhnaatltonh"*—literally, "he has been taken care of"...if a person has good luck, catches game, it is because Something created the world and That is helping him to get what he needs.[7]

...the environment is both a natural and a supernatural realm. All that exists in

7   *Ibid.*, p. 26

nature is imbued with awareness and power; all events in nature are potentially manifestations of this power; all actions toward nature are mediated by consideration of its consciousness and sensitivity. The interchange between humans and the environment is based on an elaborate code of respect and morality without which survival would be jeopardized. The Koyukon, while they are bound by the strictures of this system, can also manipulate its powers for their own benefit. Nature is a second society in which people live, a watchful and possessive one whose beauty is wrested as much by placation as by cleverness and craft...

...Aware of these invisible forces and their manifestations, the Koyukon can protect and enhance their good fortune, can understand signs or warnings given them through natural events, and can sometimes influence the complexion of the environment to suit their desires. Everything in the Koyukon world lies partly...in the realm we would call supernatural.[8]

According to most Native Alaskan myths, each species was not only instructed "in the Beginning" in behaviors and abilities particular to its unique design, not only were birds taught to build nests and beavers to construct dams, but each species was given its language. Human beings, like all creatures, were also given a system of meaningful sounds, each of which participated to some extent in the reality which it named. For example, there is no other way in Eskimo to ask people if they speak the Eskimo language except in terms of humanity. The question literally translates, "Can you speak like a human being?" Traditionally, Alaskans believe that wolves, bears, eagles and ducks likewise have their own ways of communicating. A century ago, this notion might have been dismissed as ridiculous, but modern research into the "songs" of Arctic whales indicates that the idea is not so far-fetched. The sacred stories also relate that the first people could understand what the animals said. However, this ability has also been largely lost since the time when "things went wrong." This does not necessarily mean that the animals cannot understand human language. The idea that one's prey might overhear all one's plans makes outsmarting it theoretically impossible.

This proposition poses another critical question: If the animals know beforehand that the hunters are coming, know before their arrival where they are and their intentions, how do the hunters ever succeed? Anyone who has seen documentary films of an Eskimo whale hunt can im-

8   *Ibid.,* p 31-32.

mediately understand the traditional answer. The bowhead whale, for example, is a huge and powerful creature, perfectly capable of escaping a small skin boat paddled by a dozen men. To catch a whale, the hunters need the cooperation of their prey. It must not swim away. It must not dive to the ocean depths. It must not attack. It must float on the surface and wait for the hunters to arrive, allow them to maneuver their tiny boat directly in front of its head, and permit them to throw their hand-made harpoons directly into its face. If, as traditional Alaskans claim, the whales are intelligent creatures who perhaps understand human language, and certainly possess ample natural power to escape their fate, how do the whalers ever succeed? The Eskimo answer is that the whales allow themselves to be killed, trusting that the People will treat them respectfully and allow them to be reborn. Very little in traditional Eskimo culture can be understood without grasping this fundamental intuition. To be in the proper relationship with creation, and thus to assure survival, is a collective responsibility. Even a wife or daughter's behavior at home can significantly influence the success of their provider, the female being the more spiritually potent sex. It is everyone's concern to maintain the proper relationships with one another, the spirits, the animals and all creation.

Koyukon women are subject to a wide range of prohibitions, the violation of which, it is believed, has a direct negative effect on their spouse's "luck." This is especially true of bears, particularly grizzlies, whose very name must not be spoken by girls or women. Men who are about to hunt a bear do not mention the bear by name, nor discuss their plans openly, since this would allow the bear to escape before the hunt began. Violation of the established protocol can result not only in temporary or prolonged loss of "luck" but even illness or the death of the offender or a relative. If a Koyukon meets a bear accidently, it is necessary to speak to it and assure the creature of one's peaceful intentions.

Eskimo art and ceremonial life cannot be properly understood without reference to the concept of the *Inua/Yua*. The decorative motifs on hunting tools, implements, serving dishes, and utensils all derive from the essentially spiritual conception of reality based on the *Inua*. The *Inua* is the basis for social relationships and events within the community, and for the practice of traditional medicine. The annual festal cycle, commemorating the determinative events of "those days," long ago, celebrates the reality of the beginning and makes it once more accessible. The songs, dances and costumes of a traditional celebration re-present, make present again, the creatures and personalities who participated in the paradigmatic deeds *aka tamaani,* "long ago." The remote past, at the dawn of time itself, is eternally accessible.

A more concrete example from Yup'ik Eskimo culture illustrates the traditional Yup'ik concept of time. In building a dwelling, the Eskimo first excavates a storage area, a basement beneath the floor, and an entrance tunnel. Post holes are also dug for the four main roof supports. After this, the floor boards are laid and the ceiling filled with drift wood, grass, and sod, leaving a central smoke hole for ventilation in the dome. The house has three levels, the *imaq* for storage, the floor level or *nuna,* and the circular dome supported by beams or *qilak.* This floor plan represents the structure of the cosmos. The world is circular, the four points of the compass corresponding to the main beams of the house. The lower level is visible only at the edges of the land, the "real *imaq*" the *imparpik,* or the sea. The vault of heaven is also called *qilak,* the same name as the rafters which support the house roof. The identical names point to an identity of structure: every house is a microcosm, a miniature universe.

Directly derived from this concept are numerous ritual behaviors traditionally performed inside or outside the dwelling at various seasons, or in the passage way, the exit or door linking the two. Young girls, for example, play with their dolls outdoors until the water fowl fly south. The dolls remain inside throughout the winter, and may be taken outside only with the springtime return of the ducks and geese. In every winter there is gestation, in every spring, rebirth. Expectant mothers must always exit a house head-first, for the tunnel is the image of the birth canal, and every exit the enactment of birth. Although the structure of houses has recently changed to federally-funded, rectangular frame houses, these behaviors persist. The house is no longer structurally a microcosm, but the rituals survive.

Modern societies conceptualize and organize time in lines, boxes on calendars, appointment books and travel schedules. Chronological time moves irreversibly forward, flowing like a river toward the sea. The present moment is unique, unrepeatable and fleeting, moving into the past before one can grasp it. Historical time is also, however, a sign of impermanence and mortality. Because it cannot be halted nor reversed, chronological time is merciless and deadly, an enemy which people need to "kill" before it kills them. The harshest punishment modern culture can dole out to criminals is to sentence them to "serve time."

Traditional societies conceptualize time in a radically different way. While building a house according to the eternal and divinely-instituted plan, a human being imitates a changeless and timeless action, and thus participates in the reality of "those days." Human actions mimicking atemporal prototypes participate in the constitutive and significant events of the beginning, escaping historical/chronological time, or rather, abolishing it. The hours spent building a house are not work time as opposed to leisure time, but meaningful, sacred time, in contrast to meaningless, profane time. By applying this pattern to simple everyday behaviors, traditional peoples avoid the tyranny of linear time and fill it with a cycle or eternal remembrance and eternal return to the time of origins. The sacred stories contain the divinely instituted and fully-human ways for doing the most ordinary tasks. There is *the* way to dress, wash, eat, exit the house, prepare the meals, sit, sew, hunt, fish, carve, chop, butcher, rest, pick, gather, travel and sleep, according to the age and sex of the performer and the seasons of the year. Of course, there are also innumerable actions which have no paradigm in the mythological corpus, but this means these actions have no significance and are assigned to temporal oblivion.

In his *Cosmos and History*, Mircea Eliade described the function of myth and the "primitive" ontological conception in this way:

> ...an object or an act becomes real only insofar as it imitates or repeats an archetype. Thus reality is acquired solely through repetition or participation; everything which lacks an exemplary model is "meaningless," i.e., it lacks reality. Men would thus have a tendency to become archetypal and paradigmatic...the man of a traditional culture ceases to be himself and is satisfied with imitating and repeating the gestures of another. In other words, he sees himself as real, i.e., as "truly himself," only and precisely insofar as he ceases to do so...

> ...an act (or object) acquires a certain reality through the repetition of certain paradigmatic gestures, and acquires it through that alone, there is an implicit abolition of profane time, of duration, of history, and he who reproduces the exemplary gesture thus finds himself transported into the mythical epoch in which the revelation took place.

The abolition of profane time and the individual's projection into mythical time do not occur, of course, except at essential periods—those that is, when the individual is truly himself: on the occasion of rituals or of important acts (alimentation, generation, ceremonies, hunting, fishing, war, work). The rest of his life is passed in profane time, which is without meaning: in the state of "becoming."[9]

It is not true that traditional cultures think of time as moving constantly in repetitious circles, for time does move forward linearly. But chronological time is understood as profane and meaningless. Time becomes meaningful and sacred because from the "primitive" perspective, it can be reversed or momentarily abolished through imitation of the deeds of the spirits or ancestors as described in the myth. By reenacting the eternally significant actions of "the Beginning," each generation is also united to and placed in solidarity with its ancestors. The elders of every tribe always give in response to the question "Why do you do this in this way?" the same answer: "*This is the way we have always done it.*" The weight of cultural tradition maintains continuity and stability in pre-modern societies without stifling artistic creativity. In any case, faithfulness to the eternal models bestows meaning on activities and chores that in the modern world have assumed the character of drudgery.

Taking out the garbage is hardly anyone's favorite household job, but in traditional Alaskan hunting societies the proper disposal of the unusable parts of an animal constitutes a ritual action. Bones of water mammals such as muskrat and beaver must be returned respectfully to the water. Good table manners require that all the meat be removed from even the tiniest crack or cranny, from sinew and joint. The bones must not be stepped on or thrown to the dogs, or the animal's spirit will be offended and the entire species may withhold itself from that family or village. While putting the larger bones of a game animal through the river ice, the traditional person invokes the *Inua* of the creature, saying "Come back."

The Shaman

Traditional Alaskans believed that an elite minority within each tribe have recaptured some of the abilities most humans lost at the time of origins.

9   Mircea Eliade, *Cosmos and History* (Sheed and Ward, New York, NY, 1989) p.34-35.

They speak with animals, communicate with the spirits, and know first-hand the mythological creatures and characters about which the sacred stories speak. In Yup'ik, these are the *angalkut*, in Koyukon the *diyinyod*, in Tlingit the *ix.t*, the shamans. These powers come to a shaman through instruction and initiatory rites, or less frequently by direct election in the form of life-threatening accidents. One becomes a shaman by leaving one's body and making the journey to the spirit world. Originally access to the realm of the spirits was possible via a rope, ladder or tree which connected the various levels of reality, but this access was disrupted by human foolishness or evil. Human beings are no longer able to visit the spirits at will, as was once true. People can still make the trip, but now, for most mortals, there is no return.

The power of the shaman arises from his or her knowledge of the route to the spirit world which they visit when the need arises to persuade or manipulate the spirits to alter their behavior, and thus restore or disrupt the balance and harmony of the world, depending on the shaman's purpose. A shaman is always one who died and returned to life, thus gaining experience which bestows the spiritual ability to help or harm others.

> Aside from curing (or causing) sickness, shamans used spirit power to manipulate the environment for their own or someone else's benefit. Before caribou hunting, for example, they made medicine to bring animals to the hunters, to foretell their chances of success, or to show them where to find game. Spirit helpers assisted them by communicating with a protective spirit of the caribou.[10]

That shamans actually cured sickness and prophesied accurately has been too well documented to dismiss the phenomenon as simple superstition. Shamans effectively treated disease and manipulated nature often enough to convince traditional societies that their powers were genuine. More important was the fact that the shaman's success affirmed the mythological structure, the interconnectedness of the pre-modern world view which reflected the ultimate reality of the world. The myths were true, the ceremonies efficacious, the structures of the cosmos accurately described, for in the final analysis, it all "worked." Shamanism was the visible confirmation of the holistic world view of traditional Native Alaskan society.

10 Nelson, *Make Prayers to the Raven, op. cit.*, p. 30

Shamanism did not disappear with the arrival of the first missionaries or explorers, but persisted into the early decades of the twentieth century. Some elders explain that in the final years of their era, shamans used their powers more to harm than to help others, thus hastening the end of their profession by their malicious curses and spells. Others claim that during the First World War, shamans attempted to direct their powers to the battlefields in a coordinated effort to protect Allied troops. This diffused their powers to such an extent that they were never able to recollect them. In any event, traditional Alaskan shamanism is no longer practiced anywhere in the state. Other aspects of the integrated pre-modern world view, however, survive to the present day.

The late twentieth century debate over subsistence has proven unresolvable because western institutions have never succeeded in defining its basic terms. Certainly the right to hunt, fish and gather directly on the land involves political, legal, social and economic questions, but Native Alaskans cannot accept such a restrictive definition of their way of life. To live meaningfully according to the traditional paradigms for authentic human behavior requires men to hunt, trap, and snare, the women to skin, tan, cook and sew, all in harmonious relationship with each other, the spirit world, the animals, plants and the earth itself. Life in rural Alaska elicits and demands an essentially spiritual relationship to the land itself. It is only from this context that an authentically Alaskan Christian theology can arise, and in the popular mind has already evolved. A primary goal of this book is to articulate a Christian version of the traditional Alaskan world view as it seems to be developing on America's "last frontier."

A Native Alaskan View of Subsistence

In July 1983, Canadian jurist Thomas R. Berger was appointed by the Inuit Circumpolar Conference to review the impact of the *Alaska Native Claims Settlement Act* (ANCSA) of 1971. This federal legislation recognized Native title to millions of acres of land traditionally used for subsistence activities in rural Alaska, and paid millions of dollars to thirteen regional corporations for the rest of Alaska. ANCSA was, in effect, a second purchase of the territory, for the 1867 treaty of sale transferred sovereignty rather than real estate from Russia to the United

States government. The terms of the sale specifically guaranteed the property rights of "civilized tribes," while leaving the others to whatever regulations the Congress would later enact. For over a century, all Alaskan land was treated as federal property, but when multinational oil interests attempted to secure right of way for the Trans-Alaska Pipeline, Native groups protested, and the Secretary of the Interior imposed a "freeze" on all land transactions in the state until the Native Claims issue was resolved. The state government, which was entitled to receive millions of acres under the terms of the 1958 Statehood Act, was also directly affected by the land freeze and actively participated in the resolution of the land claims issue.

The terms of the Settlement Act provided for the formation of profit-making corporations and the awarding of one hundred shares of stock in these corporations to federally-certified Native Alaskans. Native share-holders and village corporations were entitled to select so many acres of land to which they received legal title, and the corporations were awarded millions of dollars in cash payments in return for the lands the government had already appropriated or would acquire.

Twenty years after the passage of ANCSA, all corporation lands and profits were to become taxable. This provision in effect requires Natives to develop their land, to make it "profit-making" or risk losing it. While Native groups fought for legal title to their traditional lands in order to maintain their subsistence lifestyle, the Settlement Act requires that they develop it in order to retain title. Furthermore, the original act permitted individual shareholders to sell or transfer their stock to non-Natives, allowing multinational corporations to buy controlling interest in any region they choose. What was given with one hand in 1971 could foreseeably be taken back with the other. Fear of losing their land prompted the ICC to hire Justice Berger as a sympathetic consultant to examine the impact of ANCSA and to make recommendations to the Native People of Alaska. The report of the Alaska Native Review Commission which he headed was issued in July 1985.

In his preface, Justice Berger discussed the task assigned to him by the Inuit Circumpolar Conference and co-sponsored by the World Council of Indigenous Peoples.

Some persons are skeptical of the Natives' claim to a special attachment to their land. They are worried by the fact that the Native peoples believe in self-determination and a just settlement of their land claims rather than letting themselves be quietly assimilated. At the other extreme, there are persons who romanticize the Natives, trying to discover in them qualities lost by urban residents, and are dismayed when Natives do not conform to an idealized image.

It has not been easy for the people of village Alaska to be heard. For many years, they have been caught up in the cultural uncertainties of assimilationist policies. Yet I am convinced that in the villages of Alaska I have hears the authentic voice of the Native peoples. I have tried to capture it in this book.

...Native peoples everywhere insist that their own culture is still the vital force in their lives; the one fixed point in a changing world is their identity as Natives.[11]

Self-identity in traditional cultures is essentially spiritual, and its survival demands a theological articulation and defense. Since Eastern Orthodoxy became "indigenized" among many Native Alaskan peoples, the secularization of rural Alaska poses a direct threat to the Church, since by becoming "incarnate" in the traditional cultures of Alaska, the church has linked her destiny with them. The problems and crises of village Alaska require the Church's response.

The Berger Commission report discusses the Alaskan struggle in global terms in a chapter entitled "The Fourth World":

With the independence of so many Third World nations, the condition and claims of indigenous peoples who are locked into nations they can never hope to rule must now be considered. They constitute a Fourth World, and it extends from Alaska to Tierra del Fuego; it encompasses the Ainu of Japan, the Aborigines of Australia, the Maori of New Zealand, the Sami of Scandinavia, and the tribal peoples of the Soviet Union, China, India and Southeast Asia.

Attempts by the indigenous peoples of the Fourth World to achieve self-determination face greater odds than most nations of the Third World have had to meet. Indigenous peoples of the Fourth World are usually minority populations within their own nations. Once the only inhabitants of their homelands, they have been overwhelmed by settler populations. They have survived long campaigns to persuade them to assimilate and persistent demands to subscribe to mass values...Nations that have acknowledged individual rights have often opposed the recognition of indigenous peoples' rights because they imply territorial rights and a sovereignty in competition with that of the nation...Some nations oppose recognition of indigenous rights ostensibly out of concern over the possibility of secession and a need for greater industrial development...Native claims and the idea of Native governments are not, as some believe, based on

11 Thomas R. Berger, *Village Journey*, (Hill and Wang, New York, NY, 1985).

any kind of apartheid...The Native peoples of Alaska want their own lands and their own forms of government, and they also want access to the social, economic, and political institutions of the dominant society. Only if they are denied access to them could any suggestion of apartheid be made...

In its own way, the reemergence of the Fourth World is as great a challenge to the West today as the reemergence of the Third World was during the period of decolonialization, when so many Third World nations achieved independence. The relationship the indigenous peoples of the Fourth World seek, once achieved, cannot be carried on at arms length; they must live side by side with and interact within the dominant society.[12]

If governments continue in their efforts to force Native societies into molds that we have cast, I believe they will continue to fail. No tidy bureaucratic plan of action for Native people can have any chance of success unless it takes into account the determination of the Native peoples to remain themselves. Their determination to retain their own cultures and their own lands does not mean that they wish to return to the past; it means they refuse to let their future be dictated by others. Because Native peoples have accepted a dominant society's technology does not mean they should learn in school no language except that of the dominant society, and be governed by no other institutions but those of the dominant society. The right of Native peoples to have their own distinct place in the contemporary life of the larger nation must be affirmed. At the same time, they must have full access to the social, economic, and political institutions of the dominant society...

The indigenous peoples of the world are raising profound questions that cannot be answered by technical science, material progress, or representative democracy. All of these questions must be answered in Alaska. The problems are now manifest; the means of resolving them are ready at hand. All that is needed is will, good will.[13]

It is certainly true that, from a traditional religious perspective, both western secularism and Soviet communism are hostile to spirituality, since neither considers religion necessary or essential. The Communist East persecuted religion, while the West relegated it to the realm of the individual. Private belief and public policy are so distinct that religious faith becomes irrelevant in national life.

Secularism has Christian roots. Its historic origins have been analyzed perhaps most brilliantly by Father Alexander Schmemann.[14] To what

12 Berger, *ibid.*, p. 177-8.
13 *Ibid.*, p. 178.
14 Schmemann, Alexander, "Sacrament and Symbol," in *For the Life of the World* (St Vladimir's Seminary Press, Crestwood, NY, 1973) p. 135-151.

extent are the spiritual experiences and affirmations of Alaska's Native peoples not only compatible with or acceptable to Orthodox Christian theology and world view, but not eternally significant as an American "incarnation" of certain truths? Or, to rephrase the question, what does the Alaskan Orthodox experience have to contribute to Eastern Orthodox theology in the modern world?

Quite obviously, Native Alaskan Orthodoxy challenges the Church in America and Christians everywhere to reconsider and explore the theological meaning of the created universe and the cosmic dimensions of the Gospel, not only as an interesting and relatively unexplored field for theological speculation, but as the critical—life and death—issue confronting the indigenous peoples of a last frontier.

The Alaskan Orthodox Mission Today

The Orthodox Church is intimately involved in the current debate on the survival of the traditional Alaskan lifestyle, for in becoming "incarnate" in the native culture during the first century of her mission there, her destiny and that of the indigenous people of the region have merged. The Orthodox mission in Alaska is a Native institution. The overwhelming majority of clergy and faithful are Native Alaskans. During the decades immediately following the Russian Revolution and Civil War, when not only Alaska but the church in the New World in general was suddenly left without financial support or administrative guidance, the survival and growth of the Orthodox Church in Alaska depended almost exclusively on local commitment and initiative. Without any well-funded, centralized administration, without any coordinated plan for maintenance or expansion, the Church not only continued but increased. Regional conferences and lay preachers worked with Native clergy to propagate the Faith. New translations of liturgical and biblical texts were transmitted orally from village to village. Brotherhoods and sisterhoods repaired and renovated parish facilities. This dedication and commitment derives directly from those aspects of Eastern Christianity with which traditional peoples could immediately identify: the cosmic dimension of Orthodoxy.

It is this essentially cosmic spirituality, biblically based, patristically affirmed, and liturgically celebrated in the Orthodox tradition that is being obscured among Orthodox believers descended from Old World immigrants to the New World, and being undermined by the secularizing influences of public institutions among Native Alaskan Christians. Assimilation into the "American mainstream" requires abandoning the essentially spiritual world view with which Orthodoxy itself is identified.

The Church's expression and maintenance of solidarity with Native Alaskans can assume many forms. Most essential, perhaps, is a theological articulation that affirms the doctrinal and spiritual foundations for this common vision, commitment and purpose. The secularizing institutions and influences that have already conquered most of the planet threaten to overthrow the essentially spiritual world views of traditional peoples in the Third and Fourth Worlds. In this collision of cultures, the unschooled and politically powerless masses suffer tremendous casualties. The government, as the agency for "enlightenment," imposes a new "scientific" world view based on philosophical materialism and naturalism. Secular societies assume that reality as explained by chemists, physicists, geneticists, geologists and meteorologists is the sum total of all that exists. Those who posit the belief or recognize the possibility of another, spiritual reality in conjunction with the visible world are regarded as backward, ignorant or superstitious. The real division, from this point of view, among human beings today is between the masses of traditional but politically powerless believers and a powerful elite ruling class of secular political leaders, economic managers and intellectual experts. This tension divides each nation on earth, giving rise to various reactionary and often violent fundamentalist political movements on every continent. The Alaskan situation is part of an international struggle, and its resolution has global significance.

At a time when thoughtful, spiritually thirsty people are searching for a religious philosophy that will integrate their sensitivity to environmental issues with a tradition of liturgical and private prayer and a value system consistent with divine revelation, the Orthodox experience in rural Alaska offers a Christian alternative to oriental mysticism or various neo-pagan, "new age" ideologies. While providing the historical and theological contexts for the development of indigenous Alaskan Christianity, Part I of this book addresses this theme as well.

For Alaskans, however, the issues are far less theoretical, as Justice

Berger concluded:

> I have seen the effects of assimilationist policies in the villages. Among some Alaska Natives, there is a feeling of deep, bitter resignation, a sense of irretrievable loss that has weakened the hold of some on their very lives. This sense of loss, of intolerable grievance, has a bearing on the rates of alcoholism, violence, and suicide in rural Alaska. Notwithstanding an undoubted rise in living standards during the past decade, these rates have increased. No one can be certain of the causes of social pathology or of its cures, but it seems reasonable to suppose that if the Native peoples can regain a sense of self-worth, a measure of control over their communities, and an opportunity to make a living off the land, they will have a firm basis for a renewed collective and personal sense of well-being.[15]

"A renewed collective and personal sense of well-being" is not only the product of additional political power or economic security, but grounded in an authentic spirituality. The formulation of a theology that is both consistent with the faith and tradition of the ancient, undivided, catholic Church and also meaningful and enriching for Native Alaskan Christians constitutes a critical task of the Orthodox mission. Rooted in biblical, patristic, and liturgical traditions of the Church, such a theology may have important implications for Christians beyond the Alaskan context in which it is originally formulated. Some reflections on this theme are offered in the concluding chapters.

The introduction of Orthodox Christianity into Moravia, and later Kievan Rus', its spread across Siberia and the Bering Straits to Alaska in the course of the next thousand years, and the history of the Orthodox Church in Russian America, as well as its survival and growth in the difficult years following the transfer of Alaska to American rule, constitute the bulk of this volume. The Alaskan story, as presented here, is itself, however, a myth, containing many a paradigm with relevance to situations and personalities far removed from the Arctic. The heroic example of Alaskan Christians will inspire many who never knew them personally, who were never blessed to walk with them in the forests or on the tundra of what the world calls Alaska—"the Great Land."

---

15 Berger, *Village Journey, op. cit.* p 187.

PART I

The Historical Background of the Alaskan Orthodox Mission

1

Parallels Between the 9th Century Mission of Saints Cyril and Methodius to Moravia and the Alaskan Mission

While it is unclear exactly when Byzantine influences first penetrated Central Europe, it is well known that the first missionaries to Moravia were most certainly Latin-rite Christians from Bavaria. Whether these were Celtic monks or Frankish Benedictines is not important here, but that political relations between the Slavic princes and their German neighbors deteriorated. The attempt to expel western Christian missionaries and replace them with Byzantine clergy was linked to other international political considerations. If Father Francis Dvornik is correct,[1] it was the threat of a Frankish/Bulgar alliance against the Moravian ruler that prompted him to seek closer ties with Constantinople. The exact date for the founding of an Orthodox mission to the Slavs can therefore be set precisely. In 862 Prince Rastislav sent a delegation to Emperor Michael III with this message:

> Our people has renounced paganism and is observing the Christian law, but we do not have a teacher to explain to us the true Christian faith in our own language in order that other nations even seeing this, may imitate us. Send us therefore, Master, such a bishop and teacher, because from you emanates always, to all sides, the good law.[2]

In a later account, *The Life of Methodios,* the author quoted the embassy as delivering this message:

> Thanks to the Grace of God, we are well. And many Christian teachers have come to us from Italy and from Greece and from Germany, teaching us in different ways. We Slavs are a simple people, and we have nobody who would lead us to the truth and interpret its meaning. Thus listen, Master, and send us such a man who will teach us all law.[3]

1   Dvornik, Francis, *Byzantine Missions Among the Slavs,* (Rutgers University Press, New Brunswick, NJ, 1970), p. 102
2   *Ibid.,* p. 73.
3   *Ibid.,* p. 74.

Christian influences had arrived, but the people required learned preachers, familiar with their language, to explain the faith and strengthen their understanding and commitment. This is precisely the situation that arose in Alaska nine hundred years later, where Christianity was introduced by frontiersmen and merchants. The request for missionaries, addressed to Empress Catherine II, appealed for teachers to explain further the tenets of the faith. When, thirty years later, a resident pastor was recruited for the Aleutian Islands, his task was not so much to baptize or convert but to chrismate and confirm the indigenous people of the region by learning their language and deepening their understanding of the Gospel. Catherine, like her Byzantine forbear, dispatched missionaries to the field immediately.

The two Thessalonian brothers, later canonized as Saints Cyril and Methodius, had probably learned to speak Slavic in their hometown years earlier. Both had prepared for their Moravian mission by serving the Church and Empire in various other capacities. Constantine (who assumed the name Cyril only much later, when he took monastic vows) was a professor of philosophy in the capital, while Methodius was abbot of a monastery in Greece when they were assigned the task of evangelizing the Slavs. Within Byzantium, churchmen had already attempted to translate liturgical and Biblical texts into Slavonic using the Greek alphabet, probably in the expectation that the Slavic newcomers would be absorbed into the dominant culture. Far beyond the borders of the empire, however, the continued use of Greek letters to represent Slavic sounds made much less practical or political sense. Since the mission had been invited to Moravia specifically to explain Christianity to the Slavs in their own language, the need to develop a uniquely Slavic orthography became critical. The mission's first task, therefore, was to devise an alphabet for Slavonic, the common tongue from which the various modern Slavic languages later gradually diverged and evolved.

The writing system which Constantine invented (according to some ancient sources, by divine inspiration) was likely the style today known as "Glagolitic." It does not resemble any alphabet known to the Thessalonians of that time, but was a deliberate attempt to give the Slavs an alphabet as unique to their culture as the Latin, Greek, Armenian, Hebrew or Arabic scripts were to each of these nationalities. The modern

"Cyrillic" alphabet, devised by disciples of the first missionaries and based primarily on the Greek model, with only a few uniquely Slavic characters, appeared a century later in Bulgaria. In Alaska, early missionaries followed this second course, basing their writing of Alaskan languages on Cyrillic letters, while devising a few unique Aleut characters.

Once they arrived in Moravia, Constantine and Methodius faced the active opposition of the resident Frankish clergy. While the Byzantine mission had been invited to the country by its ruler, Rastislav himself was still, at least nominally, a vassal of Louis the German, Prince of Bavaria, who the next year invaded Moravia and reasserted his authority. The enthusiastic reception of the Slavonic liturgy threatened the Latin clergy, who insisted that Christian scriptures and worship could only be translated into three "sacred" languages, Latin, Greek and Hebrew. Pope Nicholas I was himself uneasy about the expanding influence of the German episcopate in Central Europe, and invited the brothers to Rome in 867.[4] Constantine and Methodius journeyed to visit the Pope to secure his backing for the continued use of Slavonic in their missionary work. In Venice, a lively debate on the propriety of using a barbarian language for the worship of the True God ensued. Centuries earlier, St John Chrysostom had delighted in the multinational celebrations in Constantinople, rejoicing that "the teaching of the fishermen and tentmakers shines in the language of barbarians more brightly than the sun."[5] The legitimacy of multi-lingual worship had been a long-standing tradition in the East, but seemed a novel and even dangerous innovation in the West.

While the proponents of universal monolingualism on one hand and the champions of tolerant multilingualism on the other disputed the social and cultural benefits and dangers of each position, it should be noted that the eastern and western Mediterranean had historically been divided on this issue centuries before the birth of Rastislav. Generally speaking, the ancient Middle East had been polyglot, perhaps as much as a matter of practicality as of principle. When the Babylonians or Persians conquered the Phoenicians or Egyptians, they incorporated into their realms entire nations who already possessed their own literatures and

4 Obolensky, Dimitri, *The Byzantine Commonwealth*, (SVS Press, Crestwood, NY, 1982), p. 191.
5 PG 63, col. 501; quoted in Obolensky, *op. cit*. p. 201.

sacred scriptures. There was no question of abolishing or assimilating these as a necessary political or cultural measure. When Alexander the Great conquered northern India, he annexed to his empire a culture far more ancient and more sophisticated than his own. Although the ruling class might be expected to master the imperial language, the average citizen's cultural and religious life was not directly affected by his nation's conquest.

By contrast, when the Roman Republic extended its rule into barbarian territory, it simply imposed Latin language and Roman institutions on tribes which had known little of literacy or written law prior to Roman rule. The historical experience, if not the philosophical principle, that all citizens should speak (and if formally schooled, read and write) the imperial language developed almost unconsciously in the West. The eastern—Babylonian, Greek, Byzantine, Ottoman, Arab and Russian— empires, generally speaking, have been multilingual and multicultural entities, whose very stability has been seriously threatened whenever the majority attempted to suppress or assimilate minority cultures (as, for example, Finland, the Baltic States and the Ukraine under the last two tsars). The western empires—Roman, Spanish, French, English and American—have tended to expect monolingualism or have attempted to establish a prestige dialect or language, knowledge of which was not only useful but required for full citizenship.

The collision in ninth-century Moravia between these two attitudes or approaches to cultural and linguistic pluralism recurred in nineteenth-century Alaska. Orthodox Alaskans, literate in their native language and Russian, were deprived of the American citizenship the Treaty of 1867 had promised them, and were persecuted for their refusal to conform to the monolingual (English only) policies established by the Rev. Dr. Sheldon Jackson, the Presbyterian missionary appointed by the federal government to establish public schools in the new territory. With other American Protestant leaders, Jackson insisted that the Natives of Alaska needed to adopt the language, dress and manners of their new masters. With the full authority of the United States government, and in historical continuity with the negative western Mediterranean attitude toward cultural diversity, Jackson labored for three decades to suppress both Native Alaskan languages and the Orthodox Church, which professed the more tolerant, positive eastern Mediterranean approach to cultural pluralism.

During the relatively brief periods during which local languages were permitted to serve as the expression of a national literature in Central Europe and Alaska, a remarkable cultural synthesis of Christian and indigenous elements evolved. The process by which nomadic tribes became literate, cultured Christian nations as members of what Obolensky has called the "Byzantine Commonwealth," was repeated in Alaska, with similar results. As a political and cultural unit, the Byzantine Empire disappeared five hundred years ago, but as one Orthodox historian has noted, it "died and went to heaven."[6] The cultural foundation of the empire survives in the communion of self-governing (autocephalous) Orthodox Churches which share a common doctrinal, liturgical, and sacramental tradition derived primarily from the Byzantine Church, but each possessing its own independent administration, its own cultural heritage, its own indigenous style in iconography, music, and architecture, as the legitimate expression of its unique character. In most of the Christian East, this synthesis is identical with the greatest artistic achievements of the nation. All this is true for Alaska as well, where the development of Aleut culture followed exactly the same pattern.

More historical parallels can be listed. The Apostles to the Slavs were both monks, as were the original Alaskan missionaries recruited from Valaam and Konevitsa monasteries in Finland. Like St Cyril, who was tonsured only after having completed much of his missionary work, St Innocent Veniaminov entered monasticism only after serving many years in Alaska. The German clergy opposed and persecuted St Methodius, while the administration of the Russian American Company created nearly intolerable conditions for the original missionaries at Kodiak. The changing political fortunes of the Moravian kingdom made a sustained Byzantine missionary presence in the region impossible, just as the transfer of Alaska to American rule adversely affected the progress of the Orthodox mission there.

In both Moravia and Alaska, the monolingual western approach to culture enjoyed far greater political support and eventually triumphed. In both cases, the proponents of the multi-lingual, multi-cultural eastern

6 Schmemann, Alexander, classroom lecture, St Vladimir's Seminary, Crestwood, NY, spring 1973.

attitude became, in the course of many years, marginalized, even disenfranchised, minorities. Both suffered tremendously during the Second World War: hundreds of Aleuts were captured by Japanese invaders and taken as prisoners of war to Japan, or else forcibly removed from their villages and exiled to filthy American interment camps, where nearly one fourth of them died. Many Slavs were imprisoned, enslaved and murdered by the Nazis. In the case of Czechoslovakia, the Orthodox bishop was executed and the entire Church suppressed after the assassination of SS henchman Heydrich. Fortunately, since World War II (and especially in the last two decades), both Churches have enjoyed a period of stability, administrative independence, internal peace and growth.

Personal holiness has also proven to be an essential characteristic of any effective Christian witness, and the example of humility, poverty, devotion, commitment and spiritual maturity was an indispensable dimension of both the Moravian and Alaskan missions. The ideal of the Christ-like life would have appeared as an unrealizable theory were it not that the missionary saints exhibited such personal sanctity as to make the message credible. The challenge of salvation, conceived as an infinite process of growth-in-love of God and neighbor, was revealed as an attractive and realistic orientation, a beautiful way of living. Perhaps as important as explaining or translating, the example of the missionary's own life convinced doubters and converted them to an authentic Christian life. Such was the influence of St Herman's ascetic labors on the spirituality of the Kodiak Aleuts, not only during his lifetime, but for two centuries after.

In addition to sanctifying and endorsing the people's personality, the mission of an indigenous, self-governing church extends to the created universe, the entire cosmos. Christianity radically reorients or transforms human consciousness of and relationship with God and with neighbor; it also alters one's experience of and interaction with nature. The inclusion of all three dimensions—relation to God, relation to other human persons, and relation to the created universe—in the sacraments and rites of the Church derive from patristic theology, particularly the writings of St Maximus the Confessor. Maximus wrote that the Logos of God is continually willing to become incarnate,[7] going so far as to say that the Word has become embodied not just once but three times—in the creation of the

7   Thunberg, Lars, *Man and the Cosmos*, (SVS Press, Crestwood, NY, 1985), p. 75.

world, in the Holy Scriptures, and finally and most perfectly as a human being. The universe was created by the Word of God, Who said, "Let there be..." (Genesis 1). The cosmos is God's self-expression, and reveals His glory, for in the Word, "all things hold together and subsist," and "all things were made through Him and for Him."[8] The Bible is a second, more clearly focused expression of the Word's presence in the world. The Holy Trinity reveals itself more directly in the sacred texts, but this does not preclude God from manifesting Himself in and through nature. In fact, one presupposes the other, as the twentieth-century Serbian martyr and theologian, Bishop Nicolai Velimirovich, so beautifully expressed it.

> Theology means the word of God. Theology is therefore all or nothing. The whole of nature and of super-nature and subternature is all theology...If the whole of nature is not theology, then theology is nothing or nature is nothing. If the whole of nature does not speak about God, who will believe Isaiah or St Paul...If the whole of the world around is a wilderness, what can the voice of one prophet crying about God in that wilderness accomplish? If the whole universe does not speak of God, who can without contempt hear the words of one man?...The publicans and pharisees sought a sign and it was not given them. But our generation seeks...a miracle to believe. "Show us God," say many of our contemporaries, "and we will believe." But how? Do not these people who despise miracles and do not believe in them demand a greater miracle?...We must say to them: *Show us what is not God!*[9]

Orthodox *dogmatics* defines the new trinitarian relationship which the faithful, in Christ, through the Holy Spirit, enter with God as Father. Orthodox *ethics* delineates the new relationship which believers, united in the sacramental and liturgical fellowship of the Church, share with one another and all humankind. By combining the divine and human with the cosmic, the eternal and historical with the natural, and thus by uniting the world, the Church and the Kingdom of God, Orthodox *worship* actualizes the reality of the Kingdom which is to come, makes it accessible and actively present, so that for the believer the Word of God is revealed and communicated to His Mystical Body, the Church, on all three levels.

The mysteries of baptism and the eucharist demonstrate this. In both rites, the natural (water, bread, wine) is juxtaposed with the singing of biblical texts, liturgical poetry and the charismatic preaching of the Word in such a way that the cosmic and historical are imbued with an eternal

8 Colossians 1:17
9 From *Concern,* [no date or number].

significance. This is true in the writing of every icon, the building of every Orthodox church, the celebration of every sacrament. By taking natural elements of this world and linking them with the historical and eternally significant biblical words and deeds, proclaimed and accomplished once and for all by Christ, the Church manifests and actualizes eternity in the midst of time. In baptism, water is seen as the source of life, the primal element from which all creation was made, and also a sign of chaos and death. It is then revealed to be the manifestation of God's love and power, of Christ's saving action, and of the Holy Spirit's sanctification. At the eucharist, wheat and grapes which require the light and warmth of the sun, the nourishment of the earth, the moisture of the elements and the care of gardeners—in short, contributions from both the whole creation and from human beings—are offered "on behalf of all and for all," in remembrance of Christ. Through the invocation of the Holy Spirit, both the community and the gifts become the Body and Blood of the Word. Here and now, the faithful eat and drink at His table in His Kingdom. The life of the Church is realized eschatology.

The mission of the Church, from one perspective, can be described as introducing the themes of Christ's crucifixion, death, burial, resurrection and glorious Second Coming into the consciousness of a community, so that the tension between all that has come to pass and all that will be fulfilled on the Last Day animates and inspires, directs and critiques, judges and vindicates the actions and words of its members. Christian liturgy is the manifestation and celebration of this tension through art, architecture, music and ritual. The sacraments are its visible signs.

For the Church, Christ, whose Kingdom the faithful await, has already "filled all things with Himself," for "all things were made by Him and without Him was nothing made that was made."[10] The joyfully anticipated Kingdom which is "to come" is present, a future reality which the Church already remembers. This cosmic dimension of the Orthodox Christian faith is not the experience of a few mystics, but the common experience of the faithful. And this radically new vision of reality, this eschatological experience of God, humanity and the created universe, played an especially important role in the foundation and development of Orthodoxy among the Native peoples of Siberia and Alaska.

10 John 1:3

By the time the Slavs were baptized, Orthodox Christianity had already defined its doctrines, established its structures, and developed its liturgy. What remained for the Moravians, Bulgars, Serbs and Russians, as for any converts, was to receive this sacred heritage in humility and joy, and to deepen their understanding of it. Each nation did so, however, according to certain aspects of its history and culture which inevitably and uniquely influenced its reception of the Gospel. In this respect, while all Orthodox Christians affirm the same dogmatic faith, accept the same ecclesiastical system, and celebrate the same rites and ceremonies, it is also possible to speak of "Russian" or "Greek" or "Japanese" Orthodoxy. Since it was from Orthodox Russians that Native Alaskans first learned of Jesus Christ, it is necessary to devote a chapter to features of Eastern Christianity common to the entire Orthodox communion, and the next chapter to specific characteristics of Russian Christianity which influenced the evolution of Aleut culture. The circumstances that brought Russians and Siberians to the New World and the impact of their arrival on the indigenous tribes are the subjects of the final chapter of this section.

2

A Survey of Orthodox Church History, Dogmatics, Patristic and Liturgical Theology

There are no eyewitness accounts of the Sugpiaq response to the arrival, in August 1784, of the ship *Three Saints*, at the bay that now bears that name on the southeastern shore of Kodiak Island, with about 130 frontiersmen aboard. From what is known about the Kodiak people and their beliefs, however, the landing of these settlers could have only represented an unwelcome intrusion, almost a sacrilege. To have non-Sugpiaq permanently dwelling on this hallowed ground was unimaginable, and the only possible course of action would have been to drive them out.

The *Three Saints* was named by Siberian entrepreneurs seeking profits and perhaps wives in the New World. The leader of the enterprise, Gregory Shelikov, hoped to establish an outpost in America as a base for trade in sea otter pelts, which in turn he planned to export to China, via Irkutsk, in central Siberia. This was not the first Russian vessel to visit these waters. For decades, various sea captains, some with honorable and others with not so honorable methods, had competed with each other in the lucrative fur trade. Shelikov sought to end this competition by gaining a monopoly for his company from Empress Catherine the Great, once he had proven himself a successful colonist.[1]

It is necessary to understand how it happened that Russian and Siberian frontiersmen ventured to Alaska at all, to discern the intangible forces that drove the empire eastward toward the Pacific and beyond. But before that, it is essential to become familiar with the worldview of this empire, for Eastern Orthodoxy became one of the most important elements of Aleut society in the decades that followed. Aleut culture is incomprehensible without understanding some of the cardinal features of Orthodox theology and the traditional missiological approach employed by Orthodox missionaries in their attempts to evangelize shamanistic Siberian

1 Shelikov, Gregory, *A Voyage to America*, (Limestone Press, Kingston, Ont., 1981), p. 20.

tribes. The cultural and religious evolution of the Aleut identity needs to be viewed in this historical and theological context.

Orthodox Christianity

When the Christian faith first appeared, it faced the three-fold challenge of religious persecution by the Jews, social persecution by the Roman empire, and intellectual aloofness from the Greeks. It circumvented the first by attracting Gentile converts at a very early stage, and the second by winning government toleration and eventually favor by the fourth century. Five more centuries, however, were needed to overcome and transform the classical mind, the intellectual culture of the Greco-Roman world whose philosophical presuppositions differed radically from the Christian Gospel. The Cross was, as St Paul wrote, "a scandal to the Jews and a folly to the Greeks." It is necessary, therefore, to explore briefly not only the content of the Christian message, but also the way in which the Church bridged the linguistic and cultural gap between its faith and the worldview of the empire.

The Apostolic and Pre-Nicean Period

The communication of the Christian "good news" to the world beyond Palestine began seven weeks after Christ's Resurrection and ten days after His Ascension. On the day of Pentecost, the Holy Spirit descended on the assembled apostles and granted them the "gift of tongues," the ability to speak many languages. As St Luke records in the second chapter of Acts, the many ethnic minorities in Jerusalem that day heard "the wonderful works of God preached in their own languages."[2] This established a firm principle for early Christian mission: the Gospel would be presented to each nation in its own language. Later abandoned in the West, this approach remains a cardinal principle of eastern Christian evangelism, celebrated each year in the kontakion of Pentecost:

When the Most High confused the tongues He divided the nations.
But when He distributed the tongues of fire He called all to unity.
Therefore with one accord we glorify the most Holy Spirit.

This hymn, which recalls the biblical account of the origin of human languages at Babel (Genesis 11) and contrasts it with Pentecost, is sung in all eastern Christian churches on this feast every year. The positive

2   Acts 2:11.

attitude toward linguistic diversity within a framework of doctrinal unity is a familiar concept to any pious Orthodox Christian.

During the first three centuries of its existence, the Church endured many local and several widespread persecutions, during which numerous believers were arrested and executed. Some of these early martyrs wrote defensive treatises, attempting to explain the Christian faith to authorities who had been misinformed about it. St Justin, a second-century martyr and one of the first Greek intellectuals to join the Church wrote:

> We worship the Father of Righteousness and moderation and other virtues, the God who is without a trace of evil...We are not atheists, for we worship the Creator of the universe...We worship God alone, but in all other things we gladly obey...kings and rulers of the earth, praying that power will be combined with wisdom and prudence.
>
> On the day which is called Sunday, all...gather together in one place, and the memoirs of the apostles and the writings of the prophets are read...Then the reader concludes and the president verbally instructs and exhorts us to the imitation of these excellent things, then we all rise together and offer up prayers...bread is brought and wine and water; and the president...offers up prayers...and the people give their assent by saying "Amen."
>
> This food is called Eucharist with us...We do not receive these gifts as ordinary food or drink. But as Jesus Christ our Savior was made flesh through the word of God, and took flesh for our salvation; in the same way the food over which thanksgiving is made...is, we are taught, the flesh and blood of Jesus who was made flesh.
>
> There is a distribution and a partaking by everyone of the Eucharist and it is brought to those absent by the deacons.
>
> But Sunday is the day on which we hold our common assembly because...Jesus Christ our Savior, on the same day, rose from the dead.[3]

St Justin the Martyr tried to reconcile the empire and Church by demonstrating that Christians posed no threat to civil order. Nevertheless, the fact that the Church and the Hellenistic world were irreconcilably estranged was also a major theme of early Christian writing, as the second century "Letter of Diognetus" testifies:

> While they [Christians] dwell in the cities of the Greeks and Barbarians as the lot of each is cast, the structure of their own polity is peculiar and paradoxical...Every foreign land is a fatherland to them, and every fatherland is a foreign land...[4]

3   Bettenson, *Early Christian Fathers* (Oxford Paperbacks, London, UK, 1969), p. 62 (= *Apologia* I, 65-67).
4   Quasten, Johannes, *Patrology*, Vol. 1, (Spectrum, Utrecht-Antwerp, 1966), p. 250.

But as Father Georges Florovsky noted, this theme of spiritual estrangement "was coupled with an acute sense of responsibility." Christians were confined in the world, "kept" there as in prison; but they also "kept the world together" just as the soul holds the body together. Moreover, this was precisely the task allotted to Christians by God "which it is unlawful to decline."[5] It was this tension between the worldviews of the early Church and the contemporary Hellenistic culture that compelled Christian thinkers to articulate their experience in terms intelligible to the Greeks, using Greek language and its philosophical categories to describe and define the Christian faith. This was, of course, true from the very beginning, since the Christian revelation declares that God sent forth His Son at the "fullness of time."[6] As Father Schmemann summarized,

> The world that was the "historical flesh" of the Church met Christianity with hostility and persecution, yet it ultimately proved capable of heeding the Christian teaching and to some extent of responding to it. Nor can it be merely chance that the sacred words of the Gospels were written in Greek, or that the theology of the Church, the human answer to divine revelation, was clothed in Hellenic categories of thought. The Gospel cannot be thoroughly understood if separated from its Jewish, Old Testament sources; it is also inseparable from the world in which the Good News was first destined to be proclaimed.[7]

The Church has, since its founding, been conceived of as the "Mystical Body of Christ," in and through which believers are incorporated into unity with God and become "partakers of Divine Nature,"[8] by growth, with God's help (or grace) "to the fullness of the measure of the stature of Christ."[9] As a corporate and historical organism, the Church has had, since Pentecost, a divinely-instituted structure composed of *episcopoi* (bishops), presbyters (priests) and deacons, each with a particular function or ministry within the larger body.

Another ancient martyr, Bishop Ignatius of Antioch, also composed a series of letters to local Christian communities through which he passed on his way to trial and death at Rome. He repeatedly pleads for unity, centered on the local bishop, saying,

5   Diognetus 5,6.
6   Galatians 4:4.
7   Schmemann, Alexander, *The Historical Road of Eastern Orthodoxy*, (St Vladimir's Seminary Press, NY, 1977), p. 23.
8   2 Peter 1:4.
9   Ephesians 4:13.

Let no one do anything that is to do with the Church without the bishop's approval...Where the bishop is present, there let the congregation gather, just as where Jesus Christ is, there is the Catholic Church...Take care then, to partake of one eucharist; for one is the flesh of our Lord Jesus Christ, and one the cup to unite us with His Blood, and one altar, just as there is one bishop, assisted by the presbyters and deacons.[10]

Yet another ancient document, the *Didache*, exhorted:

Baptize as follows: after explaining all of these points, baptize in the Name of the Father and the Son and the Holy Spirit, in running water. Let no one eat and drink of your eucharist except those who are baptized in the Name of the Lord. On the Lord's day, assemble in common to break bread and give thanks (eucharist) but first confess your sins so that your sacrifice may be pure.[11]

While each local congregation gathered around its bishop for the celebration of the Eucharist constituted the Body of Christ in that place, no single community could claim to be "more" the Church than another; in this sacramental sense, the universality and fullness of the faith demanded cooperation and unity on a regional and global scale. Each bishop was not only elected by his own flock, but approved and ordained for his ministry by the bishops of neighboring cities or provinces, after being carefully examined and instructed in the tradition. When internal questions or disagreements threatened to disrupt this unity, councils of bishops gathered to discuss, debate and pray over these matters, asking the Holy Spirit to guide them to an agreement. This follows the pattern established in the New Testament, when, as in Acts 15, the apostles settled a dispute on church doctrine by arriving at a unanimous consensus and declaring that their decision "seemed good to the Holy Spirit and to us." During the centuries of hostility and persecution, the Church maintained its unity and governed itself by this network of local bishops, who, in council with their presbyters, administered their local communities and met together in regional synods to deal with matters of wider interest or concern. It was in this way, during the first century and a half of church development, that the list of accepted books which now constitute the New Testament was compiled. Certain ancient manuscripts were excluded, others added, by the unanimous consensus of Christians, that is, the "mind of the Church," which existed for a century without a univer-

10   Quasten, *op. cit.*, p 66.
11   Quoted in Thomas Hopko, *The Orthodox Faith*, Vol. 3, *Worship*, (Dept. of Religious Education, Orthodox Church in America, Syosset, NY, 1981) p. 123-125.

sally recognized written expression of her faith, known as the New Testament.[12]

During the apostolic age, it was not necessary, of course, to rely on written documents as sources of Christian teaching, for the eyewitnesses to the eternally significant events of "those days" remained in this world. As the disciples were martyred, the need to transcribe their message arose, in order to preserve its original authenticity and authority. Since the written Gospel could be produced only in manuscript form, it required decades for these writings to circulate and become accepted as the accurate expression of the apostolic preaching. Even then, there seemed to be no pressing reason to define a complete list of genuine Christian scripture until certain oriental religious sects began reinterpreting and redefining the Christian message by introducing pseudo-gospels or by radically editing the genuine New Testament.

The Hellenic culture into which Christianity entered after Pentecost was dominated by neo-platonism, a worldview that fundamentally opposed spiritual and material reality. For the Greco-Roman world, the spirit, the soul, was essentially good, but the physical, the body, was the source of temptation, delusion and evil. Ever since Plato had written the "Phaedon" four centuries earlier, classical society had assumed that death was the liberation of the good soul from the physical, and therefore evil, prison, the body. Like traditional societies, Greek civilization believed that the eternal existed outside time and space, beyond history. Therefore, when the Emperor Constantine decreed toleration "for Christians and all others to follow whatever religion they wished"[13] in 313, the Church could claim victory in only two of its three challenges. Christians outnumbered the scattered Jewish population and could no longer be troubled with hostility from that quarter. They had won toleration from the empire. But the struggle to transform the Hellenistic mind and soul to Christian Greek culture, would continue for another five hundred years.

The Age of the Ecumenical Councils

Because of the fundamental opposition between the spiritual and material, the soul and body, the eternal and the temporal in the Hellenic

12 Schmemann, *Historical Road, op.cit.*, p. 43.
13 Schmemann, *Historical Road, op. cit.*, p. 67.

worldview, the ancient Church faced several challenges which, in one way or another, undermined the essential Christian doctrine that Jesus Christ is both fully God and completely human. This assertion was viewed as "folly" to the Greeks, and, while claiming to be nominally Christian, the Greek intelligentsia attempted to explain Christianity in ways that kept the old dichotomies of matter and spirit intact. Arianism, the first attempt that threatened to divide the Church on an international level, originated in Egypt and spread rapidly through the Church, winning even the allegiance of several emperors. Arius taught that Jesus of Nazareth was a unique person, but not divine. Rather, He was a special created being sent by God to reunite humanity with God, an intermediary between the totally transcendent Father and His creatures. According to Arius, there was a time "when the Son was not."

This dispute, centered on Christ's divinity, may seem irrelevant or esoteric to many today, but to Christians it is a critical point. If the purpose of Christ's coming is to reunite God with a humanity separated from Him by rebellion and disobedience, and if this union is to be accomplished by being connected to Jesus Christ in the sacramental life of the Church, then to reject Christ's divinity is to render salvation, as participation in the divine nature, impossible. Defining Christ as a mediating creature, however, satisfied the neoplatonist tendencies of Greek culture, and thus appealed to the masses of new converts and the majority of church leaders. To accept Arianism would have been to admit defeat on the third level, to allow the Gospel to succumb to classical philosophical assumptions.

> Arianism was a rationalization of Christianity. Here, living religious experience was no longer fertilizing thought, forcing it to see and understand what it had not previously understood. On the contrary, here faith was dried out by logical analysis and distorted into an abstract construction. Arianism was in tune with the times in its strict monotheism and desire to prune out everything irrational and incomprehensible. It was more accessible to the average mind seeking a "rational" faith than were the biblical images and expressions of Church tradition.[14]

Fortunately, precisely at this time, several brilliant theologians appeared to defend the faith. St Athanasius was at one time the only Orthodox (non-Arian) bishop in the eastern Mediterranean. However,

14 *Ibid.,* p. 75.

his fourth-century treatise, *On the Incarnation,* eventually persuaded succeeding generations of the validity of the Orthodox position. The Cappadocian Fathers, St Basil and St Gregory the Theologian and St Gregory of Nyssa, as well as the Antiochene bishop, St John Chrysostom, discredited Arianism. This struggle required half a century and was resolved only after two general councils had been convened, at Nicea in 325 and in Constantinople in 381.[15]

The Christian doctrines of the Incarnation and the Holy Trinity are often misunderstood today, but to the ancient Church, their articulations were crucial and essential steps in the intellectual process of defining and proclaiming the faith. Christians believe that God has revealed Himself as three divine Persons, Father, Son and Holy Spirit, and that humanity was created in the "image and likeness of God."[16] Only by knowing God can human beings discover their own identity. In logical, mathematical terms, God cannot be Three and One simultaneously, but the Fathers of the undivided Church attempted not so much to explain God as to eliminate exaggerations or misconceptions about the Trinity.

The Father, Son and Holy Spirit are all equally God. Each Person possesses all the attributes of divinity: almighty, all-wise, all-perfect, all-merciful, all-loving, eternal, uncreated, etc. Yet the Church insists that the God of the New Testament is one, not three, for the three divine Persons so totally and perfectly love one another that there can never be any division or separation among them. Each human person embodies "human nature" which each shares with other *homo sapiens,* but human persons are divided, each against all others. Only with difficulty can even two people agree to cooperate for a limited time on specific projects. God is a perfect unity of three divine Persons, and this is the image in which humanity was originally created. The Holy Trinity, the Orthodox liturgy proclaims, is "one in essence and undivided." Humankind is also "one in essence," but because of sin, it is also divided, one person against others, all people separated from God. The Son and the Holy Spirit, in humility and love, always fulfill the will of the Father. God has invited human persons to enter, to join in this divine unity, a free and loving community

15 The ship, *Three Saints,* which brought the first colonists to Kodiak in 1784, and Alaska's first parish community, now located at the village of Old Harbor, was named for Saints Basil the Great, Gregory the Theologian and John Chrysostom.

16 Genesis 1:27

of persons. The saints, literally in Greek, the "holy ones," are those human persons who have accepted this invitation and fulfilled their eternal human destiny by conforming their lives to God's purpose and plan, not only by imitating Christ, but with the Son and the Spirit empowering and inspiring them in the total life of the Church. The Scriptures, rites, sacraments, prayers, feasts, fasts, doctrines, canons, and traditions of the Church are the means for attaining this goal, for becoming "gods by grace," in St Athanasius' bold expression.

In the Orthodox Church, salvation is understood as a process by which each person freely chooses to orient his/her life toward Godlikeness, without compulsion, in humility, joy and love fulfilling the Father's will. No one is "saved" or justified as an isolated individual. Each person is transformed in community, in and through loving, eternal relationships to others. The process of salvation begins at baptism and continues forever. In this world, "divinization," known traditionally as *theosis*, proceeds by means of the cross—with difficulty, temptation, struggle, pain, and finally death. In eternity, the process continues as each person, purified of all sinful characteristics, suspicions, anxieties, passions and fears draws infinitely closer to God and all others. The process begins with faith and continues in hope, but its content, means, and goal is love.

Seven times in the history of the ancient undivided Church the struggle between classical dualism and the Gospel reached such crisis proportions that the imperial government summoned "world-wide" (ecumenical) councils to resolve the matter. Each distortion of the Christian faith sprang from the same philosophical assumption that the divine and human were opposite, irreconcilable realms. After the intellectual defeat of Arianism, which denied Christ's divinity, various attempts were made to compromise Christ's full humanity.

The most important of these first appeared in the empire's capital, Constantinople, when Nestorius, the local bishop, refused to apply the traditional title "Theotokos" (literally "God-bearer") to the Virgin Mary. Nestorius insisted that Mary gave birth only to a human, not a divine Son. The ensuing crisis was complicated by the lack of clear, suitable terminology for either side to articulate its position precisely. Moreover, the leader of the anti-Nestorian party, Cyril of Alexandria, was not very tactful or patient with his opponents and antagonized many—even the emperor.

The third ecumenical council was a tragic affair, but eventually the "mind" of the Church accepted its decisions as having adequately articulated the apostolic faith: Jesus Christ, while being both God and Man, is one Person. The radical distinction between His divine and human natures implied by Nestorius is a distortion of the Gospel. The Virgin Mary gave birth to a divine-human Person who was God before eternity and became flesh "at the fullness of time." In harmony with the traditional teaching about the incarnation, therefore, the Virgin is correctly addressed as "Theotokos." Every Orthodox chapel contains icons of the Virgin holding the infant Christ in her arms as a visible confirmation of the ancient doctrine proclaimed at Ephesus in 431.

The question then arose, if Christ is one divine-human person, what principle or characteristic unifies Him. This is an important issue, for if human beings are called to imitate Christ and grow increasingly like Him, they must know what He is "like." One explanation, rejected at the fourth ecumenical council at Chalcedon in 451, was that Christ's divine nature dominated his humanity. If this is so, the Church reasoned, human beings, lacking a divine nature, can never succeed in imitating Him, for his sinless life was due to an inimitable domination of his human nature by his divine nature. Again, much of the terminology generated at Chalcedon was not precise enough to assure mutual understanding. Nonetheless, the notion that Jesus was fully God but only appeared to be a man was in essence rejected there in 451.

The main issue at the Fifth Ecumenical Council was the relationship between God and the created universe. The writings of earlier theologians were drawn upon to guide the deliberations. Of particular importance were the ideas of St Gregory of Nyssa, St Basil's younger brother.

St Gregory of Nyssa

St Gregory, Bishop of Nyssa in Asia Minor in the late fourth century, brilliant articulated the relationship between Creator and creation by using the term *diastema*, which may be roughly translated "gap" or "distance," but with the essential distinction that the gap or distance is from one side only. As Bishop Paulos Gregorios of India writes,

> To apply the term *diastema* to this gap between Creator and creation is...slightly misleading, for it is not the distance between two points—one at the boundary

of creation and the other at the boundary of God. For God is infinite, has no
boundary. The creation is finite and has a boundary. The creation cannot exist
but in God, but God is not spatial, and therefore *diastema* between the Creator
and creation cannot be conceived in spatial terms. It is a *diastema* between the
Boundless [undiastatic] Creator and the diastatic or extended creation...The
diastema between the Creator and the Creation in Gregory is a one-way gap. All
creation is immediately present to Him in all its extension of space and time. All
time and all space has come to be "at once" and are together in their entirety
always present to God or "in God."[17]

In his commentary on Ecclesiastes, St Gregory writes,

...in discoursing about God, whenever the enquiry turns to the *ousia* (essence),
that is a "time for silence," but whenever it concerns any of the operations of the
Good, the knowledge of which comes down even to us, then it is time to speak,
to use words, to speak of the powers, declare the marvels, to narrate the works,
but in the matters that go beyond, it is not permitted to the creature to go outside
its own limits, but it should be content if it can know itself. For, in my opinion,
even the creation itself I have not known, for I have not comprehended the *ousia*
of the soul, what the nature of the body is, whence the existence, how generation
takes place by mutual interaction, how that which is not can come to be, how
that which is can pass to non-being, how contradictories are fitted together in
harmony in our universe. If then I do not even know the creation, how shall I
discourse on That which lies beyond the creation itself? When we come to that,
it is "time for silence." For these matters, silence is definitely superior. It is "time
to speak" then how our lives can be led to virtue in Jesus Christ our Lord...[18]

This respect for God's transcendence is the context for one of St
Gregory's most basic theological propositions, that the *ousia* (essence) of
anything cannot be deduced from its *energia* (energies/activities). That is,
one cannot know the essence of any reality simply by studying its behavior, for the essence of the reality will always be *more*. In human terms, one
may know another person by his words and actions, but ultimately can
never fully comprehend the totality of a human being, not even one's own
self. God's *ousia*, being infinitely "other" than ours, is totally transcendent
and therefore totally unknowable. In relation to Him, we can only know
His *energia*. *That* God exists can be known, but *who* God is can never be
known. This is true, St Gregory maintains, not only for God, but for

---

17 Gregorios, Paulos, *Cosmic Man* (Sophia Publications, New Delhi, India, 1980), p. 95. St
    Gregory points out in his Commentary on the Psalms, "Through these [passages] we learn that
    to God nothing is in the future or in the past but all things are immediately present" (Part II,
    Chapter 13).

18 *On Ecclesiastes*, PG 45: 729A-732 D, from Gregorius, *Cosmic Man*, p. 92.

many created phenomena, such as time, space and the human mind.

God does not impart his infinite, divine essence to His creation, nor does His *ousia* sustain all that exists. The world came into being and continues to be, not through God's inner being, but by His will, power and wisdom, that is, by His *energia*, His free creative *act*. Nevertheless, to be in the *energia* of God does mean, in some way, to be "in God." Only the Father, the Son and the Holy Spirit share the divine essence. All else exists from the common will, power and wisdom of the Holy Trinity, its unified *action*. Contrary to later medieval Latin theology, there is no "supernatural" quantity which is distinct from the cosmos and which links souls to God—*All is Grace*. To be in communion with God through His *energies*, His will, His power and wisdom, is the *natural* condition of the world. The world is not divided between "natural" and "supernatural" but between created and uncreated natures. The former depend entirely on the latter for their existence. In fact, any being that is not "in God" is in "non-existence," for all things subsist in Him. Sin is not so much a violation of a divine command as a rejection of communion with God, with existence itself. This is why sin is always destructive—"mortal"—not as an external punishment for wrong doing, but as a "natural" consequence of separation from true Being, from life.

As Bishop Gregorios notes,

> By immanence of will, Gregory means that while the cosmos does not affect the Creator in any way, the cosmos itself derives its *arche* (origin), *telos* (goal/end) and *dynamis* (power, energy) to move from *arche* to *telos* from the will of God...the whole creation is present to God as an expression of His will, and...He is present in it not by His *ousia* but by His creative will. God's *ousia* is free from the creation, but His will, dynamic, free, and creative, is the ground of the creation.[19]

And he continues,

> To be self-governing, self-regulating, self-authoritative, self-propelling, to be not the effect of outside causes but a new cause which creates effects outside itself for the good—that is the essence of both freedom and transcendence—not spatial separation or temporal potentiality. This is the quality that God has given to man as his most precious gift, the greatest value that makes man "lord of the earth"...The creation is not free from God in the sense that it can exist without Him. It is only free in the sense that certain free beings in it have been given the

19 Gregorios, *ibid.*, p 141.

freedom to accept or refuse the existence given to them. They can choose to refuse; this would be a choice of non-being, a choice of evil, for the existence given to them is a good existence, but not compulsorily good.[20]

Thus, for St Gregory, to do freely what is good is to act according to the divine prototype. A human person, if he/she is in the image of God, acts virtuously, not out of compulsion, not in obedience to some power outside himself, but because this is the authentic and *natural* condition of a human being.

The cause of sin, and therefore of death, lies paradoxically in the absolute God-given freedom with which the Creator endowed man. According to St Gregory, freedom is precisely that human characteristic which renders human persons "like God":

> He who made man for participation in his own good and built into his nature the potentialities for all good things so that by each of these possibilities he might be impelled to the corresponding good, would never have deprived him of that most excellent and most honored of all goods, I mean the grace of having no master and having one's authority in oneself. For if some kind of necessity overruled human life, the image would have been partially falsified in this respect, being estranged from its archetype by this dissimilarity.[21]

Sin has disastrous consequences for humankind, for by it human nature is separated from God. From "the light [it] sank down towards sin and was no longer in its right form, having been alienated from the true life itself" (Psalm 1:8). Adam was originally created to be the unifying link between God and the cosmos. When humanity rejected this role, the entire created universe immediately suffered the consequences. The tragedy of sin, of the disruption of the original and natural relationship which human persons were intended to enjoy with the Creator, produces an inner contradiction in human beings as they are now constituted. Seeking immediate gratification of various urges and cravings instead of everlasting joy, the earthly instead of the heavenly, the animal instead of the god-like, all represent a total misdirection of human energy and a rejection of the high calling to which human persons are summoned. The opposite of pleasure, wrote St Gregory, is not pain but blessedness. Temptation is not an urge to seek what is evil or even a lesser good, but "to be placed on the middle ground between pleasure and joy."[22]

20 *Ibid.*, p 148.
21 St Gregory of Nyssa, *Catechetical Orations* 5.
22 Gregorius, *Cosmic Man, op. cit.*, p. 151.

Humanity is not called to become changeless, for this is impossible for created beings. Rather it is called to change its direction from nothingness to true being. The Christian is not commanded to suppress natural desires for the good, but to understand what the genuine good is and actively pursue it. It is not sinful to have a high regard for oneself, since each person is fashioned in the image and likeness of God. Each human being is conscious of and greatly appreciates his or her own uniqueness. What is sinful, however, is that while recognizing one's own privileged position and exercising one's own God-like freedom one denies the same uniqueness and freedom to others. Jesus Christ is Perfect Man because He manifests the "natural" condition of humanity and realizes its eternal purpose, affirming the total uniqueness, freedom and value of each human person. He thus reunites not only humanity, but all creation to God. In the sacraments, "the Lord enters into an alliance with the doers of good and at the same time...it is not necessary for people considering human efforts to think that the entire crown rests upon their struggles, but it is necessary for them to refer their hopes and their goals to the will of God."[23]

> When man separates himself from evil, attaches himself to God, lives a life of holiness and service and dedicates himself unremittingly to prayer and virtue, then the Spirit abides in man and man becomes the presence of God in creation—which is what it means to be the image of God.[24]

Human and cosmic transformation are intimately connected, then, in the thought of St Gregory of Nyssa. God the Father remains totally transcendent and the *ousia* of the Holy Trinity remains beyond the grasp of the human mind and unaffected by the creation, but the creation exists in God, and through the free cooperation of human persons, it is restored to its proper relationship with the Creator. This restoration and transfiguration does not ultimately depend on human effort, for God is the *arche*, *dynamis* and *telos* of everything that exists outside Himself. Human persons may freely choose to cooperate in God's plan and live in "natural" harmony with the Creator, becoming His presence in the creation. Or, they may reject their vocation, choose pleasure over joy, nothingness over being. In Christ, the ultimate fulfillment of God's plan has come, for in Jesus, God's presence has become immanent in creation.[25]

23 St Gregory of Nyssa, *De Instituto Christiano* 8:1, trans. V.W. Callahan, p. 47.
24 Gregorios, *Cosmic Man, op cit.*, p. 217.
25 *Ibid.*, p. 149.

Three centuries after St Gregory, St Maximus the Confessor resumed work on a theological articulation of the Christian vision of the cosmos, basing much of his theology on the thought of his fourth-century predecessor.

Origen

During the sixth century, the writings of Origen, an influential third-century Egyptian theologian, figured prominently in a major controversy. Origen had been one of the first Christian thinkers to attempt a synthesis of neoplatonic philosophy and Christianity. In the process, he accepted many classical assumptions about the created universe, such as the essentially evil nature of the material world. According to Origen, everything that exists pre-existed from all eternity, as a purely spiritual reality. This perfect world was non-material and in a perfect, static harmony with the Creator. When the eternal intellects began to move by exercising their free will, they separated themselves from God and acquired varying degrees of material existence. Rebellion against God therefore brought the material world into being.

In rejecting Origen's claim that the physical universe exists only because of sin, the Church affirmed its traditional belief in the basic goodness of the cosmos, and in its creation by God "out of nothing," by an act of divine will. In turn, this raised questions about the proper Christian attitude toward the natural world, thus providing the context for the work of one of Byzantium's greatest theologians, St Maximus the Confessor.

St Maximus the Confessor

The immediate crisis that provoked the response of the monk Maximus arose when the emperor and many leading seventh-century theologians attempted to reconcile Egyptian and Arab churches which had broken with the universal Church during earlier controversies, by proposing a new explanation of the unity of Christ's Person. They reasoned that while Christ had two natures, one human, one divine, and was really God-Man, He possessed but one will, which was divine. This teaching, known to historians of Christian theology as "monotheletism" (Greek *mono*, "one," *thelema*, "will"), was championed by the government but opposed by various synods, especially in North Africa, and by Pope Martin of Rome, who was arrested, tortured, and exiled during the dispute. In order to articulate the Orthodox position on this subject, Maximus developed, despite persecution, an unsystematized but nonetheless cohesive theology that corrected the errors of Origen and further refined the Christian vision of creation and humanity. Eventually the emperor forbade any further discussion of the issue, but after his death, the Sixth Ecumenical Council declared monotheletism and its supporters, including an earlier Pope, Honorius, to be heretical.

In Origen's writings, the created world is understood as pre-existing eternally in spiritual form. It assumed its present physical existence only when each intellect used its free will to rebel, to move away from God. If there had been no rebellion, no sin, the material universe would never have come into being. For Maximus, the eternal plan for the creation of the world existed from all eternity in God, but the "blueprint" for each creature in the "mind" of God constitutes its potential existence, not its actual existence. Each being begins to exist at the moment God summons it from non-existence into being, according to His plan. In Maximus' understanding of creation, then, there are no pre-existing or eternal forms or ideas, as in Plato's or Origen's conception. This understanding has since formed the basis for traditional Orthodox teaching about creation and the creative process.

According to Origen, the ideal condition for everything that exists is motionlessness, a static peace or rest resulting from the communion with God which all things enjoyed before they misused their free will and moved away from Him. All movement, therefore, is necessarily a product of evil, of rebellion, and must someday cease. Before the world began, according to Origen, everything existed in perfect, spiritual, static, harmony. Maximus reverses this process by stating that it is God Himself who puts all things into motion, and creates everything according to His eternal plan (*Logos*), in which each being carries within itself the plans (*logoi*) according to which it was made. In this sense it is true that, "the heavens declare the glory of God and the firmament makes known His handiwork" (Psalm 19). All the different individual forms (*logoi*) are contained within the Divine Plan (*Logos*), and it is this *Logos*, the Divine Word, who becomes Man and reconciles all things to God. All things move, but their proper movement (according to the Divine Plan) is movement toward, not away from God. Creation exists "by participation in God who alone exists in himself."[26]

With the scriptural authority of St Paul's epistle to the Colossians 1:16 to support him, Maximus writes:

> We believe the logos of the angels preceded their creation; that the logos of each essence and of each power which constitute the world above, the logos of men, the logos of all to which God gave being—and it is impossible to enumerate all things—is unspeakable and incomprehensible in its infinite transcendence, being greater than any creature...but this same logos is manifested and multiplied in a way suitable to the Good, in all the beings who come from Him according to the analogy of each, and He recapitulates all things in Himself...for all things participate in God by analogy, insofar as they come from God.[27]

As Father John Meyendorff continues,

> Any object receives its very existence from the logos that is in it and makes it participate in God. Separated from its logos, a creature is but non-being. This participation of beings in God allows Maximus to distinguish in Scripture the "letter" and the "spirit"; in creation, the "logos" from the "appearance"; and in man, "sensation" from "intellect," for God is to be found in the spirit of Scripture, in the logos of creation, and in the mind of man.[28]

This does not mean that Maximus is a pantheist, for he maintains that the divine *Logos* is above all created essence, being infinitely "more" or "above" or "beyond" the total of all the *logoi* in creation. Each creature fulfills itself only insofar as it conforms to the divine logos it bears. Human beings receive as part of their common human logos a spiritual nature, which includes four divine characteristics: existence, eternal-existence, goodness and wisdom. Of these, two constitute the "image" and two the "likeness" of God in which humanity was first created in the Beginning.

> First, in the image of his being, by the fact of existing; secondly, in the image of his ever-existing by the fact of being always, if not without beginning, at least without end; as being good from Him who is Good; as being wise, resembling in this way by grace Him who is wise and good by nature. In this way, every reasonable nature is the *image* of God; but in His likeness are only those who are good and wise.[29]

God not only creates, but assigns to every creature a goal which implies

26 Meyendorff, John, *Christ in Eastern Christian Thought*, (St Vladimir's Seminary Press, Crestwood, NY, 1971), p. 134.
27 *Ambigua*, PG 91:1080AB.
28 *Christ in Eastern Christian Thought*, *op. cit.*, p. 135.
29 PG, 91:1024BC.

movement toward Him.[30]

But every person created in God's image is also free, for God is free, so that as part of humanity's composition, each person has a "natural" will, which in a perfect world would lead all toward their "natural" goal, toward God. By abusing this freedom and rejecting its "natural goal," however, humanity has rejected its proper nature, and acquired an irrational personal will. Because of man's refusal to fulfill the goal given to him by the Creator, the entire cosmos disintegrates. Unnatural divisions stem from this catastrophe: the created is separated from the Uncreated; the tangible and the intelligible, earth and heaven, male and female. It is man's task to overcome these unnatural dualities, but his own spiritual resources are, after the fall, insufficient.

> Originally man was called to overcome the sexual opposition by impassibility, and to unite through holiness paradise and the universe, thus making one single and new earth. He was then to unite earth and heaven by virtue, in order to make one single, tangible creation, to unify the tangible and intelligible worlds by acquiring angelic knowledge, so that creation might no longer be divided between those who know and those who do not know God. Finally man was to reunite by *agape* (love) the created and the uncreated, so that in his love for creation, God might become all in all.[31]

Sin prevents human persons from realizing their "natural" goals, not only in relation to God, but to all creation. Adam's rebellion had disastrous consequences for the entire cosmos.

Christ comes to "recapitulate" all things in Himself, for he is the Divine *Logos* "by whom and in whom all things were originally created, to provide a new orientation and integration to the whole creation by assuming it after it had abandoned the movement assigned it by God."[32] He fulfills for man what no one had ever done, but which all had been expected to accomplish from all eternity. It was God's intention, says Maximus, that the "whole man should become God, deified by the Grace of God-become-Man, becoming entirely man, soul and body by nature, and becoming whole God, soul and body, by grace."[33] This requires a double movement, from God to man and from man to God, and thus two wills or energies meeting each other. It is for this reason that Max-

30 *Christ in Eastern Christian Thought, op. cit.,* p. 137.
31 *Ibid.*
32 *Ambigua,* PG 91:1308D.
33 *Ibid.,* 1088C.

imus so adamantly opposed the monotheletism of his times, for only if Christ possesses both a human and a divine will could He have reconciled and fulfilled them both.

This theology in effect laid the foundations for the positive view which Orthodox missions generally have had of traditional societies in central and eastern Europe in the ninth and tenth centuries, and across central Asia and into eastern Siberia and Alaska over the next eight hundred years. Orthodox evangelists felt no obligation to attack all the pre-contact religious beliefs of shamanistic tribes, for they could perceive in them some of the positive appreciation of the cosmos that is central to St Maximus' theology. They could affirm that the spiritual realities these societies worshipped were indeed "*logoi*," related to the Divine *Logos*, whose personal existence these societies had simply never imagined. The missionary could announce the revelation of God in Christ as truly "Good News," without completely denigrating the religious beliefs or pagan practices the tribe had traditionally maintained. Maximus' positive view of humanity as potentially divine, with every individual person moving toward unity-in-love according to the divine plan, yet each distinct and unique, and created to be eternally so, brought a greater appreciation for cultural and personal diversity to the Eastern Church.

Iconoclasm

In the century following the Monothelite controversy, the imperial government attempted once more to impose its theology on the Church by decreeing that all icons (religious images), in homes and church buildings alike, were to be confiscated and destroyed as idols. The ensuing iconoclastic controversies, therefore, were the last, ultimately unsuccessful attempt of the Byzantine emperors to influence Church doctrine as it had often influenced church administration throughout the post-Constantinian period. In its intellectual struggle with the empire, however, the Church emerged victorious.

Once again, the debate over the use and veneration of icons required the Church to define its attitude toward the material world. This time, however, the issue was not the person of Christ, but a related problem: should images of the God-Man be permitted in Christian liturgy? The iconoclastic emperors insisted that all material images were idolatrous and forbidden by the Mosaic law. Their opponents, mostly monastic theologians living beyond the boundaries of the empire where they could preach and write in relative security and peace, countered by pointing out that while the Old Testament God never assumed visible form and could not be depicted, He had now become flesh. Consequently, it was not only proper but essential that His icons adorn the churches and dwellings of believers. To forbid icons of the Savior, they argued, was tantamount to denying His humanity. They insisted that Christ not only assumed flesh temporarily, but also ascended in glory as transfigured man, having fully retained his human nature. His post-resurrectional appearances to the apostles demonstrated this, since, although his body exhibited remarkable properties, it was nevertheless tangible to Thomas and the others in the upper room (John 20). All icons testify to this reality.

By basing their argument on the theology of the Cappadocians as well as on that of St Maximus, the defenders of icon veneration could also insist that Christians who had undergone the process of *theosis* should also be depicted, since they were real persons who had achieved the goal common to all believers. This is why traditional eastern Christian art does not attempt to depict sacred persons in "natural" or "realistic" forms, but rather in their transfigured state. Since salvation or deification is understood in the East as an eternal process in which each individual is called to overcome his or her self-love and redirect it outward, toward God and neighbor, relationships between persons assume an eternal value. The Christian is required to develop a loving relationship with all others, beginning with members of the Mystical Body of Christ, both living and departed. The veneration of the saints of the past is an integral part of this process, for the Christian will dwell not only with Christ but with His entire company of holy ones for all eternity. One begins developing those essential relationships of love at baptism, but because love never ends, neither does the process. This interpenetration of spiritual and physical realities is basic to the Orthodox Christian worldview. The incarnation of the Word inaugurated an age of "holy materialism."

Since the basic materials employed in the writing of an icon include animal, vegetal and mineral matter, each icon re-forms the created universe in order to proclaim the wonderful works of God in the universal language of beauty and art. This parallels the proclamation of the Gospel in spoken and written language through preaching and reading Holy Scripture. Icons re-present—make present again—the eternally significant events and persons of sacred history. They are, as one Russian theologian has called them, "theology in color."[34]

So central to the Orthodox faith is the veneration of icons that the day designated to celebrate the restoration of icons each year is called the *Sunday of Orthodoxy*. The Eastern Church never reduced the sources of her inspiration to the written word, for it knows that God reveals Himself in art, music, poetry and ritual. Orthodoxy has always appreciated the divine presence in the created universe, which it considers God's "self-portrait." While the Orthodox never claim to have explained the central mysteries of their faith, but have sought only to safeguard their experience from exaggerations or distortions, they have always been equally anxious to affirm that God manifests Himself in a vast variety of ways. Indeed, the only word Orthodox theology appears to reject is the restrictive modifier "only."

The Liturgical Synthesis

Only after all these theological disputes had been resolved did the Byzantine Church become actively engaged in foreign missions, first among the Bulgars and Moravians, later among the Serbs, Romanians, and Russians. The doctrinal positions of the seven ecumenical councils were not restricted to the theological manuals of specialists, but celebrated in the liturgical texts sung throughout the year. Every Sunday, the Orthodox worshipper participates in a rich liturgy in which the fundamental principles of the faith are poetically and musically presented. For example, one such hymn, attributed to the sixth-century Emperor Justinian, is included before the introit at every Divine Liturgy:

> Only Begotten Son and Immortal Word of God
> Who for our salvation did will to be incarnate
> of the Holy Theotokos and Ever-Virgin Mary
> And without change did become Man
> and was crucified, O Christ our God,
> trampling down Death by death

34 Trubetskoy, Eugene, *Icons: Theology in Color* (SVS Press, Crestwood, NY, 1973).

Who are One of the Holy Trinity, glorified with the Father and the Holy Spirit:
Save us!

In these few lines, which are familiar to every Orthodox Christian, are the essential dogmas of the faith—the incarnation and resurrection of Christ, and the confession of God as Trinity. Public worship in the Eastern Church is a liturgical catechism. The Scriptures are not only read and preached but incorporated as hymns and into hymns. They are celebrated.

Many of the most beautiful hymns are poetic commentaries on the crucial events of "those days," as, for example, this hymn from Good Friday:

Today is hung upon the Tree He who suspended the land in the midst of the waters.
A crown of thorns crowns Him who is the King of Angels.
He is wrapped in the purple of mockery, who wrapped the Heavens with clouds.
He receives buffeting who freed Adam in the Jordan.
He is transfixed with nails who is the Son of the Virgin.
We venerate Thy Passion, O Christ!
We venerate Thy Passion, O Christ!
We venerate Thy Passion, O Christ!
Show us also Thy Glorious Resurrection.

The entire universe is understood as participating in the eternally significant saving events. At Christmas, for example, the two main hymns underscore the participation of the star which guided the Magi:

Thy Nativity, O Christ our God, has shone on the world as the Light of Wisdom,
For by it those who worshipped the stars were taught by a star
To adore Thee, the Sun of Righteousness, and to know Thee
The Orient from on High: O Lord, Glory to Thee.

Today the Virgin gives birth to the Transcendent One,
and the Earth offers a cave to the Unapproachable One.
Angels with shepherds glorify Him;
The Magi journey with the star,
Since for our sake the Eternal God is born as a Little Child.

Perhaps even more dramatic are the hymns and prayers at Epiphany, when the Orthodox Church celebrates the baptism of Jesus Christ and the revelation of the Trinity:

When Thou, O Lord, wast baptized in the Jordan,
The worship of the Trinity was made manifest,
For the voice of the Father bore witness to Thee, calling Thee His Beloved Son,
And the Spirit, in the form of a Dove,

Confirmed the truthfulness of His Word.
O Christ, our God who hast revealed Thyself
And hast enlightened the world, Glory to Thee!

Twice during the Epiphany season, the Great Blessing of Water is performed, on the first day inside the church, and, weather permitting, on the second day outdoors, at the seashore or by a lake or stream. Nothing more graphically demonstrates the Orthodox understanding of the cosmos than this annual celebration, including these prayers which reiterate the Orthodox Church's positive appreciation of the created universe and which themselves constitute the fulfillment of the prophecy contained in the fifty-fifth chapter of Isaiah:

Today the nature of waters is sanctified and the Jordan bursts forth and turns back the flood of its streams, seeing the Master wash Himself...

...Thou hast clothed Thyself in our weak and poor substance and has condescended to the stature of a servant, Thou who art King of all, and yet didst deign to be baptized in the Jordan at the hands of a servant, that, having sanctified the nature of water, O sinless One, Thou mightest lead us to a new birth through water and the spirit and restore us again to our first freedom. Celebrating the memory of this divine mystery, we pray Thee, O Lord, sprinkle on us, Thine unworthy servants, according to Thy divine promise, cleansing water, the gift of Thy Compassion, and may the supplications of us sinners over this water be well pleasing to Thy goodness...

...Thou by Thine own will, from nothingness has brought all things into being, and by Thy might dost Thou uphold all Creation, and by Thy providence Thou dost direct the world...All reason-endowed powers tremble before Thee: The sun sings to Thee, the moon glorifies Thee, the stars intercede with Thee, the light obeys Thee. The deeps shudder before Thee, the water springs serve Thee. Thou hast spread out the heavens like a curtain. Thou hast established the earth upon the waters. Thou hast set about the sea barriers of sand. Thou has poured forth the air for breathing. The angelic powers minister to Thee. The many-eyed Cherubim and the six-winged Seraphim, as they stand about and fly, cover their faces in awe before Thine Unapproachable Glory. For Thou, the God Uncontainable, without beginning and ineffable, didst come down to earth, taking the form of a servant and being made in the likeness of man. For Thou couldst not endure, O Master, to see the human race oppressed by the Devil, but Thou didst come and didst save us...Thou didst sanctify the streams of the Jordan, and didst send down from heaven Thy Holy Spirit, and didst crush the heads of dragons who lurked there.

Therefore, O King who lovest all people, do Thou be present even now through the descent of the Holy Spirit and sanctify this water. (*Repeat three times*)

And give it the grace of redemption, the blessing of the Jordan. Make it a fountain of incorruption, a gift of sanctification, a remission of sins, a protection against disease, a destruction of evil spirits, inaccessible to hostile powers, filled with angelic might.

And may it be for all those who draw of it and partake of it unto cleansing of their souls and bodies, unto the healing of their passions, unto the sanctification of their homes, and unto every expedient purpose. For Thou art our God who through water and the Spirit hast renewed our nature, grown old through sin. Thou art our God, who with water didst drown sin in the days of Noah. Thou art our God who by the sea, through Moses, didst set free from slavery to Pharaoh the Hebrew race. Thou art our God who didst cleave the rock in the wilderness, so that water gushed forth and streams overflowed, and didst satisfy Thy thirsty people. Thou art our God who by water and fire through Elijah didst bring Israel back from the error of Baal.

Do Thou Thyself, O Master, sanctify even now this water by Thy Holy Spirit. (*3 times*)

Grant to all who touch it, anoint themselves with it and partake of it, sanctification, blessing, cleansing and health...

That Thine all-holy Name may be glorified, together with the Father and the Holy Spirit now and ever and unto ages of ages. Amen.

A striking feature of these texts is the constant juxtaposition of the temporal and eternal, the spiritual and material, the transcendent and the historical realms. They are characterized by a fascination with the paradoxical and inexplicable nature of the good news of Christ. Because this vision is not restricted to theological specialists, but is the common liturgical and sacramental experience of the entire Church, the cosmic dimensions it includes have become, over the centuries, an intrinsic part of the traditional Orthodox Christian worldview, shared by even the most humble and even illiterate believer.

3

Russian Orthodoxy

History records that St Cyril, later the "Apostle to the Slavs," evangelized tribes on the north shore of the Black Sea before accepting his more famous assignment as missionary to Moravia. A copy of the Gospel and Psalter which St Cyril had prepared in Macedonia had already reached this remote area, to which a bishop was eventually assigned. Thus, over a century before the popular date of the "baptism of the Russian people," the millennium of which was marked in 1988, there were already hundreds of Orthodox Christians within the Kievan kingdom.

St Olga, the grandmother of St Prince Vladimir who forcibly introduced Christianity during his reign, was herself baptized at Constantinople and sought to influence her grandsons likewise, but due to the opposition of her son Sviatoslav, she could not convert them. Sviatoslav was himself a committed pagan who persecuted the Church after Olga's death. Once Sviatoslav had died on the battlefield and Olga's two older sons had perished in the ensuing civil war, Vladimir, the youngest grandson, became Prince of Kiev at the age of seventeen.[1]

After reunifying the realm, Vladimir erected pagan altars and offered human sacrifices in thanksgiving for his victories. When a certain John the Vareg, a Viking, refused to surrender his son for such a sacrifice, a riot erupted in which both John and his son were crushed by their collapsing house. When he later accepted baptism, Vladimir built the Church of the Assumption on this site and made it the cathedral for Kiev, endowing it with ten percent of his income. The martyrdom of the first Russian Christians, therefore, also predates the official founding of the Orthodox Church in Russia.

As prince and commander-in-chief, Vladimir could force his troops and vassals into the waters to be baptized, but it remained for dedicated

1 "The Conversion of Russia," Sr Thais, *Orthodox Alaska*, Vol. 4, no. 3 (Kodiak, AK), p 22.

Christians to transform the nation into a Christian people, to convert them truly to Christ. This work was done primarily through the evangelistic efforts and example of monks, who from the time of Vladimir exercised tremendous influence in the cultural and intellectual, as well as the spiritual, life of the Russian people. Beginning with the Pechersk community on the outskirts of Kiev, St Anthony and his successor, St Theodosius, imported from Constantinople not only the Studite rule of common life, but the ancient spiritual, doctrinal and liturgical tradition of the Orthodox East.

Monastic centers represented Christian oases on the frontiers of "civilization" and introduced nomadic tribes to the Christian Faith, not so much by preaching or teaching but by their effective witness as examples of Christian piety, philanthropy and love. Centuries later, Saami ("Lapp") tribes would accept Orthodoxy after Tryphon of Kola and Pechenga had labored among them for a half century. Valaam and Konevitsa Monasteries along the Finnish border served as centers of Orthodox Christian spirituality for centuries, and the Solovki Monastery in the White Sea sent missionaries to the mainland to evangelize the region. It is necessary here to devote some pages to a brief survey of the uniquely Russian character Orthodoxy assumed as it became incarnate among the Eastern Slavs.

The Popular Religious Faith of Russia

By the time Vladimir invited Byzantine missionaries to Kiev to teach and baptize his people in 988, the Eastern Church had articulated its doctrine and developed its liturgy as outlined in the preceding chapter. It remained for the Slavic people, therefore, to accept and deepen their apprehension of this faith, and to develop expressions of it according to their own cultural genius. The Bible, the writings of the Fathers, and the entire treasury of liturgical texts were translated into Old Slavonic, and an indigenous clergy were trained in the performance of the various rites. The translation of the word "Orthodox" as "Pravoslavnii" testifies to the centrality of worship as the essential expression of the Faith: *pravo* means "correct" or "true," *slava* means "worship," or literally, "glory." It is not insignificant that one of the most popular legends about the initial encounter with Orthodoxy describes a delegation from Kiev attending services at Hagia Sophia in Constantinople and reporting to their prince:

We knew not whether we were in heaven or on earth, for we cannot forget that beauty: only this we know: that God dwells there among men.[2]

This emphasis on beauty remains a characteristic feature of Russian piety, and, in fact, the rich decor of eastern churches exists precisely to evoke the *presence* of the image of the Kingdom which is to come. The church building is itself an icon of the Kingdom, for the Church community is perceived ideally as the presence of that reality, the yeast within the dough, interpenetrating and "percolating" through the existing world. An Orthodox temple is built according to a definite floor plan along two perpendicular axes. Along the north-south axis, on the eastern side of the building, stands the iconostasis, or icon screen. This has three doorways, one on the north, another on the south, and the third in the center, where the east-west axis intersects. These central or "holy doors" through which the eucharistic gifts pass, lead directly to the "throne" or altar table directly behind the screen.

The icons on the iconostasis are arranged in a traditional pattern, with the icon of the Theotokos, the Virgin and Child Jesus, to the left of the holy doors, and the icon of Christ Pantocrator, the Almighty Judge, to the right. This is a visual proclamation of the creed: almost 2,000 years ago, God became man of the Virgin; at an indeterminate moment in the future, He will return. In the meantime, between His first and second comings, He is present in history through His Mystical Body, the Church, and most especially in the sacraments, of which the eucharist is central. During the eucharistic liturgy, the celebrants enter and exit the sanctuary through the holy doors four times, twice with the gospel book, twice with the gifts of bread and wine, the symbols of Christ as Word (Logos) and as the Bread of Life, and the believers commune with Him in both preaching and sacrament.

Along the east-west axis, the building is divided into three sections. The vestibule represents the world, the nave, where the baptized believers stand as the "royal priesthood," and the sanctuary, beyond the iconostasis, where the Lord Himself rests on the throne. The seven-branched candelabra, the incense, and the vestments are similar to those which were mandated by the Lord in Exodus, and the icons of the saints of more

2   *Russian Primary Chronicle*, (quoted in Timothy Ware, *The Orthodox Church*, Pelican Books, New York, NY, 1976, p. 269).

recent generations represent an attempt to reflect St John's vision of heavenly worship in the Book of Revelation. All the basic structures of Orthodox worship are based on those of the Jerusalem Temple and the synagogue.

It is in the context of worship that Orthodox believers receive their religious education. They not only memorize entire passages of the Old and New Testaments, which constitute most of the hymns, but also learn church doctrine as these are expressed in liturgical texts. Believers contribute music, painting, architecture, poetry, tapestry, wood carving and metal work to their churches, making them, by consequence, repositories of the finest national art. This is true of Alaskan churches as well.

The presence of the holy is not, in the Orthodox perspective, limited to the church building, but made visible and tangible in beauty everywhere. Every home has its "beautiful corner" where the family icons hang, and before which the faithful pray. Pierre Pascal writes:

> The Russian peasant greets the icons on rising. When he leaves his house in the morning, he signs himself three times, looking first toward the church or chapel, then towards the east, then the three other points on the compass, to give thanks to the Creator. He takes no food without making the sign of the cross...He multiplies...such exterior manifestations...to the point of giving the impression that these are mechanical exercises without interior reality. However, it would be a mistake to think this: while they may not necessarily express authentic devotion, they do correspond to an habitual disposition.[3]

All sources testify that this was the type of popular religious practice introduced into Alaska before the first permanent settlement was established there at Three Saints Bay in 1784. Reports mention frontiersmen remaining with their Native wives and building small chapels in the Aleutians. Many such pioneers baptized their children and taught them the Christian faith. The lack of rigid distinctions between the sacred and secular in Orthodox tradition made this possible.

> ...Pastors are so very close to their flocks [because] the "distance" necessary for respect is lacking, as also is any superiority of an intellectual or moral sort...Russian popular religion is about as un-clericalist as it could be, not in any way tied to the clergy. It would not cross a peasant's mind to abandon the church because he thought the priest unworthy. The inadequacy of the clergy will never put his faith at risk. Similarly, this religion is as little as possible tied to the church. It

3   Pierre Pascal, *The Religion of the Russian People* (SVS Press, Crestwood, NY, 1976), p. 19.

can be practiced, if circumstances dictate, in the humblest oratory or simply at home. It is to the house that the priest comes to give a blessing, to baptize, or conduct one of those private services known as *molieben*—whether as a thanksgiving or a supplication, or out of simple devotion. When there is neither church nor priest, the head of the family can conduct a simplified form of worship at home.[4]

These characteristics of popular Russian religion survive today in Alaska, and for many of the same reasons. Perhaps even more important to the early phase of the conversion of the Alaskan Native peoples was the survival among Russians of a cosmic dimension to the Christian faith which was theologically affirmed by the sixth and seventh ecumenical councils:

> The peasant, together with Genesis and St Paul, believes that the whole creation, which the earth represents, is affected by man's sin and called to renewal with him. His religion has hardly any conception of individual fall and individual salvation; it is more collective, cosmic, never forgetful—as the West has tended to be—of the great visions of the Apocalypse. It is on that level that it exists. It is powerfully aware of a mystical communion between man and nature, both alike works of a good God. Nature is always pure. Man, when he sins, separates himself from it and sees no more than what can be seen from the outside. But the pure man perceives its beauty, its oneness with God and his own oneness with it...If nature puts him in contact with God, it is not through any confusion with God, but because nature is His creation.[5]

The ancient Church affirmed and the Orthodox continue to celebrate this positive spiritual vision of the created universe, as the examples cited in the previous chapter indicate. Here it is important to mention an essential point of divergence between eastern and western Christianity: the definition of "symbol." Since the late Middle Ages, this term has been radically reinterpreted in the West in a way that has contributed to a tragic misunderstanding of the Gospel, and the subsequent division of the Western Church into hundreds of competing and conflicting denominations.

The Greek word "*symbolon*" means "to hold together." To the ancient Church, this meant that a symbol, while not fully encompassing the reality it "symbolizes," nevertheless participates in and communicates that reality. A symbol, in other words, does not "represent" an absent "thing"

4   *Ibid.*, p. 20-21.
5   *Ibid.*, p. 10-11.

or stand in place of it, as a mere substitute or reminder. It is what it symbolizes, without totally manifesting or revealing it. It was in this sense that the ancient fathers wrote that the entire cosmos is the "symbol" of God.

Father Alexander Schmemann explains this as follows:

> In the early tradition, the relationship between the sign in the symbol (A) and that which it signifies (B) is neither a merely semantic one (A *means* B), nor causal, (A *is the cause of* B), nor representative (A *represents* B). We called this relationship an *epiphany*. A *IS* B means that the whole of A expresses, communicates, reveals, manifests the "reality" of B, (although not necessarily the whole of it) without, however, losing its own ontological reality, without being dissolved into another "*res*" (thing).[6]

It was precisely this relationship between A and B, between the sign and the signified, that was changed in medieval Latin theology.

> The symbol may still be a means of knowledge, but as all knowledge, it is knowledge *about*, and not knowledge *of.* It can be a revelation about the "*res*" but not the epiphany of the "*res*" itself. A can mean B or represent it, or even in certain cases be the "cause" of its presence; but A is no longer viewed as the very means of "participation" *in* B.[7]

Knowledge and participation became two different realities, two different orders. Within this framework, the created universe lost all "religious" value in the West. Yet in the East, it was precisely the maintenance of this original vision within the liturgical life of the Orthodox Church that made the gap between the pre-contact worldview of the Unangan, Sugpiaq, and Yup'ik peoples and the Christian worldview a relatively narrow one.

The Monastic Tradition

One of the most important elements of the Russian Orthodox worldview which contributed to the evolution of Aleut culture and identity was the monastic tradition which had its roots in antiquity. The lack of a separate ascetic institution in the apostolic era seems to have been due to the ancient church's self-understanding as distinct, a radically new society preparing for the imminent return of the Lord. The Jewish religious tradition, from which the Christian faith sprang, however, had already

6   Alexander Schmemann, *For the Life of the World* (SVS Press, Crestwood, NY, 1973), p. 141.
7   *Ibid.*, p. 142.

developed a wilderness spirituality which viewed the desert as Satan's domain, a place where no one could live, and therefore as the symbol of death. Since no one can survive in the desert without divine assistance, to dwell there means to confront Satan on his home ground. This gave significance to the desert lives of Elijah in the Old Testament and John the Baptist in the New. Christ himself led the way for later ascetics by fasting forty days in the wilderness. While it was not necessary for the persecuted apostolic church to retire to the desert, because it viewed the entire world as a spiritual desert, the baptism of the emperor and with him of the empire spurred the growth of a maximalist reaction, early monasticism.

> Monasticism renewed the prophetic ministry of ancient Israel in the Church. It bore witness against a bourgeois and worldly Church that easily welcomed the Greco-Roman masses and accepted the bounties of the "most pious emperors." Throughout the history of the Orthodox East, the Church was saved from absorption into the Empire by the hermits of the desert, the stylites standing year after year on their pillars, the great monastic communities that, like the monastery of Stoudion in Constantinople, preached the monastic ideal at the very heart of the city, commanding the reverence of the emperors and the Christian people. The essence of their testimony was that of the New Testament, not of the Old, insofar as the latter identified the chosen people with the nation and the state. Against the theocratic claims of the Christian Empire the monks affirmed that the Kingdom of God is a Kingdom of the world to come; it is not a sociological or political phenomenon in human history; it is the very Presence of God. And the monks were the authoritative spokesmen for the Eastern Church. The Church adopted their liturgy, their spiritual way, their type of holiness. In the sixth century it even decreed that the episcopate (bishops) be recruited exclusively from among the monks...[8]

The importance of monasticism and monastic spirituality in forming the worldview of the Eastern Orthodox Church can, therefore, hardly be overestimated. Based as it is on the Gospel injunction to become "perfect as your Heavenly Father is Perfect," and to "put on the whole armor of God" in order to "fight the good fight" and to "grow to the fullness of the measure of the stature of Christ,"[9] Christian asceticism—prayer, fasting, charitable deeds, and the like—is required of all Christians. The Orthodox Church teaches that each person is born to fulfill a God-given

8 John Meyendorff, *St Gregory Palamas and Orthodox Spirituality* (SVS Press, Crestwood, NY, 1974), p. 17-18.
9 Matthew 4:48; Ephesians 6:13-17; 4:7-13.

function, a purpose for which each human being is created. Some are called to be teachers, others healers, others buyers or sellers, and some, the monastics, to pray. All have a function within society and within the Christian community, but the monastics serve everyone, offering perpetual supplications on behalf of all and for all. Every Orthodox liturgical service is offered in the same spirit, in fact, so that all the faithful participate in this offering of universal supplication some of the time. But the monastics seek to live a life of prayer, to *become* prayer. Their struggle and goal is common to all Christians. They wage "unseen warfare" most intensely, renouncing the pleasures of this life, not because these are themselves evil, but because ascetics are called to deny themselves, to take up their cross and follow Christ in order to demonstrate that Christian perfection is, even in this world, attainable.

The basic outline of this spiritual struggle is contained in the New Testament.[10] The practical details have been supplied by the experience of the hundreds of Christians who have withstood temptation, and left a record of their experience so that others could benefit from it. Each passion and its remedy has been described and catalogued, so that the pitfalls along the path of salvation might be avoided by future generations. The goal of this struggle is to become a "new creature," a person restored to God-likeness. As St Isaac the Syrian writes:

> This is the mark of those who have reached perfection. If each day he should pass through flames ten times for the love of others he is not satisfied. As Moses said to God (Exodus 32:31), "If you do not forgive them their sins, erase me from the book you have written." And as the Blessed Paul said, "I prayed that I would be condemned for the sake of my brothers" (Romans 9:3). And again (Colossians 1:24), "I now rejoice in my suffering on behalf of you, the nations." And the rest of the Apostles, for the sake of their desire for the life of humanity, accepted death in a multitude of ways.

> And what is a merciful heart? The burning of the heart on account of all creation, on account of people and birds and animals and demons, and for every created being. Because of their remembrance, the eyes fill with tears. Great and intense mercy grasps the heart and wrings it out, for he who is merciful is not able to bear or hear or see any harm or the slightest sorrow which takes place in the created world. For these he offers prayers continually with tears for their protection and for their redemption. He does the same thing even for the snakes

10   Georges Florovsky, *Byzantine and Ascetic Spiritual Fathers* (*Collected Works*, Volume 10, Nordland Press, Belmont MA, 1987), pp. 17-59.

that crawl on the ground. All of this he does out of great mercy which moves his heart without measure, in the likeness of God.[11]

There is no escapism here, no denunciation of the world or hatred of society or of sinners, but only compassion, patience, and love. This is not love of the world for its own sake, however, but love of the world as God loves it. St Isaac concludes:

> Thus do all the saints achieve perfection. When they become perfect, they are consumed by the outpouring of love for God and for their fellow human beings. The saints themselves seek this sign of their union with God, that is that they have a passionate desire to be merciful to their neighbor.[12]

Prayer is the essential component of this spiritual struggle, the "sword" in the warfare every Christian must wage. In the Orthodox spiritual tradition, one particular prayer has become, over the centuries, the preferred method for achieving the self-control, patience, perseverance, faith, humility, purity and serenity demanded of the pray-er: the Jesus Prayer: "Lord Jesus Christ, Son of God, have mercy on me, a sinner." Longer prayers are too easily disturbed, the worshipper too easily distracted. This short invocation of the name of Jesus is considered a sufficient means of attaining spiritual virtue together with the liturgical and sacramental life of the Church.

Since its appearance in the fourth century, Christian monasticism has been organized into communities, some of which survive to this day. When Orthodox Christianity came to Russia, monasteries appeared immediately, since the missionaries who came to teach the Slavs were, for the most part, monks. After the Tatar invasions of the thirteenth century, monastic communities sprang up in the northern forests, in a frozen arctic wilderness very different from the burning sands of Egypt. And yet, the phenomenon was the same: believers dedicating their lives to prayer for all humanity and for the whole cosmos, "invading" Satan's domain, bringing life and the Gospel, the Word of life, to a region in which no one had previously been able to live. Consequently, Russia, Central Asia and Siberia were settled first not by adventurers or frontiersmen, but by monks who journeyed to remote corners of Eurasia to continue the struggle against the evil one, in the world and within themselves. The

11 Christophoros Stavropoulos, *Partakers of Divine Nature* (Light and Life Publishing, Minneapolis, MN, 1976), p. 88.
12 *Ibid.*, p. 89

most prominent of these monasteries, in Kiev (the Pecherskaia Lavra or Monastery of the Caves) and near Moscow (Holy Trinity Monastery, founded by St Sergius of Radonezh) have been national shrines and cultural centers since their founding, playing a vital role in the creation of the Russian national identity, and inspiring generations of Orthodox faithful. Many Russian monks travelled to the centers of Byzantine monasticism, especially Mount Athos, where the first community had been founded in 957, to learn the ancient spiritual tradition directly and disseminate it among their own people.

Valaam, the community from which the first Alaskan mission came, was founded on Lake Ladoga in ancient times, perhaps even before the conversion of St Vladimir. Saints Sergius and Herman, its founders, were Greek monks whose biographies were lost when the Swedes first destroyed the monastery in the twelfth century. Immediately rebuilt, it was burned by the Swedes during the Great Northern War in the reign of Peter the Great. Despite these calamities, Valaam regularly attracted many novices because of its reputation as a very traditional community. Although not specifically founded to do missionary work, Valaam, together with other northern monasteries such as the Solovki, Pechenga and Konevitsa, had a profound influence on the nomadic peoples of the region, all of whom accepted the Orthodox faith primarily because of the monastic witness these communities provided.

One of the last great theological debates in Byzantium before its fall to the Turks in 1453 concerned monastic piety and theology, when the question of what Christians ultimately experience when they claim to "know" God was debated. Can human beings in a state of purity actually participate in God's very Nature, as Almighty, Omnipotent, Omniscient? And if not, then is it not true that all human beings can attain knowledge about God, but never, at least in this world, *of* Him. St Gregory Palamas, the spokesman for the monastic tradition, maintained that God is unknown and unknowable in His divine nature, being so totally different from our human nature that our minds will never comprehend Him. He is, however, known and knowable in His "energies," that is, His actions. When monks speak of beholding God's glory, as Moses did on Mount Sinai, they do not experience a created or intermediary "disguise," but the brightness, the light which is God.

By analogy, no one knows himself "in essence," nor does any person *a,* really know another "deep down"—what he or she *really* is, for each person is a mystery, even to himself, and no one really knows or understands his own personality fully. Only God fully knows Himself. This essence, then, is what is unknowable, not only in God, but in one's self or in the neighbor, no matter how intimately one might be related to another person. Yet each person can still, in another sense, claim to "know" others, not in their inner being or essence, but by what they say *b* and do, by their actions, or as Palamas termed it, their "energies." In this sense too, monks insisted that human beings can indeed *know* God.

Westernization

With the Tatar conquest in the thirteenth century, and the fall of Constantinople to the Turks in the 15th, the Orthodox world was totally overrun by Moslems. As the Russians emerged from their belated Dark Ages during the next three centuries, they discovered that they had fallen technologically and culturally behind their western neighbors. The Renaissance, the rediscovery of classical Greek philosophy, had begun in Italy and spread northward, while Moscow had been occupied with pushing the Mongols back into Asia and reestablishing national independence. With this task well underway in the middle of the sixteenth century, Russia could turn her attention to reconstructing national, cultural and intellectual life so badly disrupted during the Tatar occupation. But the ancient sources of her own culture were themselves ruled by Turks, and a united Polish-Lithuanian kingdom had annexed large sections of the Ukraine while national attention had been necessarily focused on Kazan and Sarai.

Consequently, Greek and Russian intellectuals travelled west, to Rome, Padua, Venice, Wittenburg and Geneva, seeking a "modern education," and returned with a worldview totally disconnected from that of their own country. Those who studied in Roman Catholic universities tended to be influenced by the discipline and philosophical presuppositions of medieval Latin theology, just as those who attended German or Swiss colleges returned home with Protestant notions.

Within the Russian Church for the next century, all the issues raised

by the Reformation and Counter-Reformation were discussed and debated. In its external affairs, the Orthodox Church used Protestant arguments against the Roman Catholics and Roman Catholic arguments
against Protestants for the next three hundred years. (Only in the nineteenth century would Orthodox begin to rediscover their own authentic
tradition.) Kievan leaders argued that only the adoption of western forms
and language would place Russia on equal footing with its neighbors:

> We need Latin so that no one can call us "*glupaia Rus*" (stupid Russia). To study
> Greek is reasonable, if one studies it in Greece, not in Poland. Here, no one can
> succeed without Latin—in court, at meetings, or anywhere, for that matter.[13]

This is putting the issue on its most superficial, linguistic level. More
profoundly, the Russian culture and worldview were at stake. Latin became
the language of instruction in Russian Orthodox seminaries for the next
three centuries. In a sense, Russia became the first "third world" country,
forced to choose between her own authentic cultural tradition and that of
the West. After four centuries of such subordination, she further rejected
her own roots in favor of a totally alien ideology imposed upon her by a
ruthless cadre of dedicated, thoroughly westernized revolutionaries. Soviet
culture, at least temporarily, resolved the national identity crisis by rejecting
and brutally persecuting a thousand years of Christianity.

All this confusion in national priorities did not much affect the
rank-and-file membership of the Church. During the Polish occupation
of the Ukraine, several bishops defected to the Roman Catholic Church
under a special arrangement that at least initially allowed them to retain
all their Orthodox liturgical practices, and even permitted parish priests to
marry. This introduced into the Catholic Church, however, an administrative division that could not be easily resolved. Over the next several
centuries the "Uniats" (those former Orthodox in union with Rome) were
gradually latinized. For decades the Orthodox Church in western Russia
was declared nonexistent, and it was even a crime within Poland to profess
an Orthodox religious identity.

In the face of this persecution, the Orthodox laity were obliged to
defend the faith their own hierarchs had betrayed. They founded "brotherhoods," probably inspired by similar organizations in the Greek dias-

13 Georges Florovsky, *Ways of Russian Theology*, Vol. 1, (Nordland Press, Belmont, MA, 1979),
     p. 65

pora. These groups financed the printing of Orthodox educational material, operated schools, promoted international Orthodox unity, and continued the charitable activities of the local parish. It was during this time that many of the "Starring" customs and songs (see Part III, Chapter 9) evolved. While many of these folk customs were unknown in Moscow or Siberia, they helped maintain a separate Orthodox identity for centuries in those regions of western Ukraine occupied by Poland until the end of the First World War.

Poland hoped that the "Uniat" Church would be one means by which the Orthodox population could be assimilated into its empire. While it did not succeed, the Unia had a significant impact on the intellectual and theological development of Russia for the next three centuries. The bishops who defected to the Western Church were the forerunners of many of the Russian aristocracy and intelligentsia who believed that their nation had fallen behind during the years of Mongol rule, and that the task Russia needed to undertake was to catch up with the West by adopting, as quickly as possible, western standards. Whatever was western was modern, up-to-date, progressive; whatever was Russian, automatically needed to be abandoned as obsolete, irrelevant, backward. This attitude had little impact on the masses, but within a few decades it dominated the ruling classes. Long before Peter the Great imported German and Dutch experts to teach Russians western navigational science, Ivan the Terrible had brought Italian architects to Moscow to design the Kremlin.

Westernization, however, produced a backlash. When the printing press was introduced, the Church decided to publish liturgical books and Bibles, but could not determine an authoritative text. Patriarch Nikon brought Greeks to Russia to "correct" the manuscripts that had been in use for centuries, and the foreign scholars found many discrepancies between their supposedly original versions and the prayers the Slavs had been reading since the time of SS Cyril and Methodius. Nikon decreed that the service books should be corrected to conform to Greek usage, but many Orthodox Russians balked. So violent was the reaction to Nikon's reforms that thousands left the Church, separating themselves from the "Nikonians" in order to preserve what they considered to be the authentic Orthodox faith of their ancestors. No prelates joined the schism, forcing most of these groups to forego sacramental life in order to maintain practices of far less importance to any unbiased observer. But the schismatics saw the patriarch's actions as a betrayal of the true faith, a portent of the end of the world. Not only had the Turks taken Constantinople, the Arabs Jerusalem and the philosophers recaptured Rome, but even Moscow had now fallen into error. Millions fled to the wilderness, or were exiled to Siberia, and as recently as the end of the twentieth century, one such group found refuge on the Kenai Peninsula in Alaska. In the West, divisions often occur when a faction wants to strike out in a new direction and finds the "establishment" too conservative and inflexible to allow their innovations. In the East, schisms more often develop because the recognized leaders break with the past, becoming "innovators."

Peter the Great's "westernization" program, which required a long and costly war with Sweden for domination of the Baltic Sea and the construction of a new national capital on its shores, must be seen as the culmination of several centuries of intellectual westernization which began with a "pseudomorphosis" of the Orthodox mind. Seminaries taught a theology which was Latin in origin and outlook, unrelated to the liturgical and sacramental life of the believing community. Not until the nineteenth century would Russians begin to rediscover their own theological and cultural roots in translations from the Greek Fathers undertaken in the eighteenth century. Not surprisingly, this renaissance of Orthodox theology began in monasteries, when Paiisii Velichkovskii travelled to Mount Athos to discover and translate the classic works of Eastern Christian ascetic literature into modern Russian. This process was only beginning when the exploration of Alaska began.

4

Explorers, Exploiters and Entrepreneurs

In 1648, the Yakutsk seaman Simeon Dezhnev became the first Russian to explore the straits which separate Asia and America, but his discoveries were a closely guarded state secret, leaked to the West only in 1730. The pioneers were anxious to keep this information from their own government as well, for any trade conducted in North America did not have to be taxed as long as the state remained ignorant of the commerce. Only when a certain Tabbert, a prisoner of war from the Swedish campaigns smuggled a map out of Siberia did Europe learn of Dezhnev's voyage, and many remained skeptical for a long time. American scholars well into the twentieth century tended to dismiss reports of Russians in Alaska prior to 1700 as folklore rather than fact.

In 1719, at the end of the Great Northern War, Peter the Great commissioned Vitus Bering, a Danish-born Russian citizen and convert to Orthodoxy, to lead the "First Kamchatka Expedition" and personally wrote specific instructions for it. Modern scholars have questioned anew the tsar's real objectives. Some experts accept the traditional opinion that Peter wanted to know if Asia and America were, in fact, separated by water. Since he could have learned this from Dezhnev's reports, other authorities believe that the tsar wanted to stake a claim to a portion of America. In any case, after taking one and a half years to prepare for an expedition that lasted only two summer months, Bering was convinced that the two continents were not connected by any land bridge. In 1732, Ivan Fedorov was commissioned to map the Aleutians and collect tribute from the native tribes, but this venture was only partially successful. Twenty-two veterans of this voyage later joined Bering for his second expedition in 1741.

Since officially the results of Bering's first voyage were deemed inconclusive, he was sent again across the sea which bears his name on one of the largest, most expensive scientific expeditions ever undertaken by the

Imperial Government: over 150 participants at a cost of two million
rubles. Bering on the *St Petr*, and his lieutenant, Alexei Chirikov, aboard
the *St Pavel*, mapped some of the western Aleutians before heavy fog
separated the two vessels from each other and from land for six weeks. On
July 15, 1741, Chirikov sighted the western coast of Prince of Wales
Island, and the next day Bering sighted and named Mount Saint Elias.
Both are in the "Panhandle" area of Alaska, along the U.S.-Canadian
border. Chirikov sent armed men ashore to reconnoiter and fetch water,
but they disappeared, never to be seen again. The rest of the crew, many
suffering from scurvy, returned to Petropavlovsk in October 1741.
Bering's ship was tossed by severe storms as it sailed west, the men plagued
by illness, hunger and thirst. Nikita Shumagin, the first of Bering's crew
to die during the expedition, was buried on one of the "Shumagin"
islands, off the southern coast of the Alaska Peninsula. Tragically, Bering
himself never reached Petropavlovsk, but died on December 8, on the
island now named for him, where his ship had been wrecked a month
earlier. In June 1742, Chirikov sailed back in search of Bering. He even
landed on Bering Island, without, however, sighting any of Bering's crew,
and returned to Petropavlovsk on July 2. Meanwhile, the survivors of the
St Petr managed to build a new vessel from the debris of the old and sailed
to Kamchatka August 13, arriving at Petropavlovsk August 26. In thanksgiving for their deliverance, the crew donated two beautiful icons of SS
Peter and Paul, for whom their ships had been named, to the local church.

The expedition achieved its scientific goal of charting the coast of
northwestern North America. Of even greater significance was the cargo
of 1,500 sea otter pelts the crew managed to transport home from Alaska,
and sell for nearly 1,000 rubles each at the Chinese trading post near Lake
Baikal. With the Chinese paying such high prices, a "fur rush" ensued. A
few months after Bering's survivors returned, Emilian Basov and his
business partners, Andrei Serebrennikov and Nikifor Trapeznikov, had
outfitted a ship and recruited thirty frontiersmen for a foray to Bering
Island, only 115 miles off the Siberian coast. Beginning in 1743, Basov
made four trips to this base and realized a fortune. The stampede to
Alaska had begun. During the next fifty years, over 100 expeditions
succeeded in reaching the Aleutian Islands, Kodiak, or the Alaskan mainland, and earned over three million rubles in profit for their investors.

The Alaskan *promyshlenniki* were frontiersmen not unlike America's Daniel Boone or Buffalo Bill. They were experienced trappers and traders, with considerable navigational experience, since they had sailed the Arctic coast for decades. They left many of their initial discoveries unrecorded to prevent the government from interfering, investigating, or taxing their activities. A 1795 map of the western coastline of Alaska testifies to their many years of intense contact with the region.

Their vessels, held together with rope or thongs, were called "*shitik*" derived from the word "to sew." Sailing without maps or instruments, they had constantly to keep in sight of land. If a storm prevented this, they drifted, hoping that tides and favorable winds would eventually bring them to shore. Many who had sailed with Bering or Chirikov knew the course to the New World firsthand and guided their colleagues to Alaska. A typical voyage lasted about a year, but if disaster struck, hunger and even starvation and dehydration awaited. Some crews are known to have survived by eating their boots. One in five voyages never returned to Russia.[1]

Historians differ widely in their assessment of the *promyshlenniki* and their activities during the "Fur Rush" of 1741-1798. The sources of this confusion are many. The *promyshlenniki* themselves tended to exaggerate their accomplishments and inflate statistics relating to almost every venture they undertook, if it suited their purposes. Since it always seemed better to discover a heavily populated rather than an uninhabited island, the Aleutians were reported to sustain a very dense population, where seasonal camps were counted as being occupied throughout the year. No accurate count of the indigenous people can be reconstructed today based on these inflated reports. Trying to present themselves as patriotic heroes, frontiersmen boasted of fighting off hundreds or even thousands of hostile natives, where archaeological evidence indicates there were far fewer people living in the region. The earliest histories of this period were written to justify the suppression of individual commercial initiatives and the monopoly granted to the Russian American Company. Company spokesmen portrayed the *promyshlenniki* as lawless barbarians, and praised their company for having established law and order. Later American

1   Bishop Gregory (Afonsky), *A History of the Orthodox Church in Alaska* (St Herman's Seminary Press, Kodiak, 1974), p. 8.

historians relied on these distorted accounts, so that the earliest texts
about Alaska's past in English betrayed a definite anti-*promyshlennik*,
anti-Russian bias, which became even more pronounced during the Cold
War. Soviet writers, under ideological pressure, deprecated the accomplishments of the "bourgeois" or "capitalist" ventures of the imperial/co-
lonial era. Each writer, including some of the story's main protagonists,
has approached the subject of Russian Alaska from a particular perspective. Few have attempted to consider and evaluate all the archival evidence. It is beyond the scope of this study to reevaluate the role of the
promyshlenniki during the 57 years between Bering's second voyage and
the establishing of the Russian American Company. This is, nevertheless,
an important topic awaiting further exploration, and the question should
be considered an open one.

Over one hundred expeditions set sail for Alaska during this period,
and it is impossible to examine them all. The careers of a few central
figures, however, serve to illustrate those of many others.

The merchant and explorer Nikifor Trapeznikov financed ten voyages
to the Aleutian Islands and sailed on some of them himself. One of his
first investments was the *Evdokia,* a *sheetik* captained by silversmith
Mikhail Nevodchikov, who had come to Siberia to seek his fortune.
Unlike Emilian Basov, Nevodchikov did not steer for Bering Island to
wait out the winter, but headed directly for the Aleutians. Bypassing Attu,
he landed on the second island, where the local Unangan wanted to trade
a carved mace for a Russian gun. When the gun's owner refused, a scuffle
ensued in which one Unganan was wounded in the hand. Nedvodchikov
retreated to Attu, where the natives fled from the intruders. Friendly
relations were eventually established there, but another skirmish occurred
between a surveying crew and some Attuans. Fifteen more natives were
wounded. On the return trip, the *Evdokia* was wrecked on Karaga Island
and lost its entire cargo of furs. Thirty-two crewmen lost their lives on this
expedition, and the survivors were brought to trial on charges of cruelty
to the indigenous people. An Unangan, baptized Pavel (Paul), accompanied this unlucky crew to Siberia, and, once he had mastered the Russian
language, became an early informant on Unangan culture.

On the *Boris i Gleb* in 1749, Trapeznikov left for a four-year tour of
the region and returned with a cargo valued at 105,730 rubles, making his

the most profitable expedition of the decade. Under the command of Aleksei Druzhinin, this same vessel was wrecked on Bering Island in 1752, but again a new ship was built with the debris of the old. Many historians have contended that the *promyshlenniki* were inexperienced sailors and ship builders, but incidents such as this were not uncommon, and the record often indicates that they were capable of creating a new vessel from the wreckage of an old one. Druzhinin set sail again, only to be wrecked again on the same island. The following year, Andrei Serebrennikov and Maxim Lazarev, aboard the *Ieremiia*, set out to "discover new islands" and survey the Alaskan mainland. A storm blew them past many hitherto unknown islands, eventually wrecking them on tree-less Umnak, where they were attacked by dart-throwing, tattooed Un-angans. The next year they built the *Petr i Pavel* from what was left of their ship and sailed for Kamchatka, where they spent several months hunting walrus. In 1755, they finally returned home with 140 walrus tusks, valued at 65,000 rubles. Even disaster-plagued ventures could turn a profit.

Adrian Tolstykh, also financed by Trapeznikov, sailed to the Aleutians with 38 Russians and Kamchadals aboard the *Adrian i Natalia* in 1760. He spent three years establishing friendships at Atka, accumulating over 3,000 pelts, baptizing some of the local Unangan, and naming the central group of islands for himself as he departed. Like so many other return voyages, Tolstykh's was disastrous. His vessel was first severely damaged in a storm near Shemya, and later wrecked on Kamchatka. He survived to captain the *Petr* with 49 Russians, 12 Kamchadals and 2 Unangan aboard in 1765, when it sank. Tolstykh and 59 of his crew drowned.

In 1761, Trapeznikov cooperated with several other Irkutsk merchants in outfitting the *Zakharii i Elizaveta* under the command of Aleksei Druzhinin, the *Svyatyi Troitsy*, captained by Ivan Korovin, and a third vessel under an apprentice skipper surnamed Medvedev. Druzhinin sailed with a crew of 34 Russians and Kamchadals to the port of Petropavlovsk on the eastern shores of the Kamchatka Peninsula the first spring. The second year he continued as far as Unalaska, where he spent the winter. The following year he established a base on Inalak Island, where he erected a defensive stockade. As they were leaving a nearby Unangan village, Druzhinin was assaulted from behind and knocked unconscious. The Unangan killed him with bone knives and attacked his companions, one of whom, Gregory Shavyrin, defended himself successfully with an ax, and then fled to the stockade with Ivan Korovin. Surrounded by hostile Unangan there, the two broke out of their fortifications and escaped to a neighboring island where the rest of the crew had been hunting. They found all their colleagues dead, and worse, the *Zakharii i Elizaveta* burned. Six months later the starving men were rescued by the *Svyatyi Troitsy*, but there the exhausted Gregory Shavyrin died. Of the 175 *promyshlenniki* operating in that region that year, only eleven survived the massacre the Unangan had meticulously planned and executed.

Nikifor Trapeznikov should have died a wealthy man. After financing and participating in ten voyages to Alaska between 1743 and 1768, and earning astronomical profits in the fur trade, he was bankrupted by the loss of his ships and supplies during the Unangan uprising. Merchants who owed him money could not pay their debts to him. Hardly enough money remained in his estate to cover his funeral expenses.

The *promyshlenniki* did not restrict their activities to Alaska, the forests of Siberia or the Arctic Ocean, but also ranged down the Amur River into Chinese territory. At the end of the 17th century, five hundred pioneers fortified a site there in order to defend themselves from impending Chinese attack. They bravely withstood several assaults before being overwhelmed by a much larger force, and were taken prisoner. Among them was their chaplain, Father Maxim Leontiev, who carried with him the necessary articles to celebrate Orthodox services at the prison in Peking. There he labored until his death, fifteen years later, in 1698. In 1704, and again in 1707, replacement priests were sent, but neither remained in China for long.

In 1713, after thirty years in captivity, the prisoners and their children, who had known no other country, considered themselves citizens of China. They petitioned the Emperor, Kan Chi, to invite an Orthodox priest to serve them in Peking and to establish an Orthodox church there. The Emperor approved. When word reached Tsar Peter, he appointed Father Ilarion Leiaiskii to head a mission of two priests, a deacon and seven students to the post in Peking, where they arrived in April 1716. Kan Chi declared the clergy Mandarins and supported them with funds from the imperial treasury. Although Father Ilarion died just two years later, the emperor was favorably disposed to Orthodoxy and, for a time, his conversion seemed a likely possibility. When he allowed the Holy Synod to appoint a bishop for China, a former naval chaplain, Hieromonk Innocent Kutchinskii, was consecrated for this mission in March 1721. By the time Bishop Innocent reached the Chinese border, however, Kan Chi had died and the new emperor had revoked his visa. This provided the Orthodox Church the opportunity, however, to begin evangelizing the indigenous peoples of central Siberia. Bishop Innocent spent the rest of his life among the Buriat and Tungese, teaching, baptizing and founding schools for them throughout what would become the Diocese of Irkutsk. Innocent served as an exemplary missionary. He was an inspiration to the Valaam monks and later Alaskan clergy, many of whom were educated at the seminary in Irkutsk.

Solov'ev

Most historians have portrayed Ivan Maksimovich Solov'ev as the greatest monster of the *promyshlennik* period. He returned to the Fox Islands soon after the Unangan had massacred his comrades and vowed to avenge them. After landing at Unalaska, he set about his affairs as if nothing had happened, expecting an Unangan ambush. When the first attack was made, Solov'ev retaliated furiously. Eyewitness accounts published years later describe the slaughter of several hundred Unangan warriors who had barricaded themselves inside a fortified *barabara* (sod house). Solov'ev demolished this by detonating gunpowder-filled intestines. Ivan Lapin, who witnessed the scene that day, estimated that two hundred Unangan perished. Lt. Davydov, a fifteen-year-old juvenile delinquent who had been exiled from St Petersburg by the authorities, gathering tall tales from old time *promyshlenniki* forty years later at Kodiak, recorded ten times more casualties. This unsubstantiated and probably exaggerated figure, however, has often been cited by historians who have accepted Davydov's report without hesitation. It is important to remember that the Russians of this period had very primitive firearms. Their muskets were muzzle-loading single-shot antiques. They had no cannon. Their weapons of choice were pikes and swords. The numerically superior Unangan, on the other hand, also had muskets they had captured or had received in trade with friendly *promyshlenniki*, some of whom, it was reported, fought side by side with them. They could shoot many more arrows in the time that the Russians could fire musket balls. Certainly hundreds of Natives perished during the *promyshlennik* raids and in the inevitable skirmishes that occurred, but it seems unrealistic to attribute any substantial technological superiority to the Siberians. Solov'ev retaliated, brutally executing the Unangan he believed responsible for the deaths of his colleagues. By resisting him courageously, the Unangan won his respect. Solov'ev's journals clearly show his love for the Unangan and the Alaskan frontier. He spent years in the Aleutians, gathering furs and trading with natives, but in five months squandered and even gave away the fortune he had earned. Greed alone does not explain such behavior. And Solov'ev was not an exception. Many *promyshlenniki* remained permanently in the islands, took Unangan and Sugpiaq wives, raised—and baptized—their children. Some fought for, some against Solov'ev. In any case, Unalaska was renamed "Il'ul'uk,"—the Harbor of Good Accord—and a long-lasting peace prevailed in the Aleutians after Solov'ev's conquest.

During the fighting, Solov'ev destroyed the hunting equipment the Unangan needed to conduct their subsistence way of life, making them totally dependent on the *promyshlenniki* for their necessities. Unable to hunt, and without food for the winter, the Unangan were forced to submit. The Sugpiaq on Kodiak Island, however, maintained their independence from all intruders for another generation.

Glotov

Stepan Glotov is credited with discovering Kodiak Island in 1763, although the area was almost certainly visited by earlier *promyshlenniki* who were driven away by the local Sugpiaq. Aboard the *Adrian i Natalia* with an Unangan interpreter from Umnak, Glotov anchored off the Kodiak coast. His informant, however, was unable to communicate with the Kodiak natives, whose language is only remotely related to Unangan and much more closely related to the Yup'ik Eskimo of the mainland. Within days the Sugpiaq staged a surprise attack and forced Glotov to post sentries.

Some weeks later, several hundred Sugpiaq warriors massed for a well-coordinated attack. Dozens of Natives held huge wooden shields to protect the archers who rained arrows down on Glotov's crew. Gunfire eventually drove them back, but in less than a month they returned with seven moving shields screening thirty or forty spearmen each. They attacked in formation.[2]

Such resistance forced Glotov to keep his men aboard ship all winter, until in April, scurvy killed nine of them. He secured a temporary beachhead, maintaining some *promyshlenniki* on shore for most of the month. Although these men were able to establish trade relations with a few Sugpiaq, Glotov abandoned all attempts to subjugate the island and returned to Umnak in May. There he discovered the bodies of more *promyshlenniki*, killed in the Unangan uprising of that spring. Inhospitable as Umnak seemed, Glotov, still without any furs, believed he had no choice but to remain there. His landing party was attacked by Unangan, who then abandoned the island until the following spring, when they returned in force. It was only then that Glotov learned the full extent of the previous year's fighting and the considerable loss of Russian lives and ships. He promptly set sail for Siberia with a very small cargo, probably feeling fortunate to have survived the ordeal.

Shelikov

Gregory Ivanovich Shelikov certainly deserves to be considered one of early Alaska's most colorful characters. An exile from the Ukraine, he lived in Siberia for many years before investing in, and finally sailing on a voyage to America. He dreamed of building a Russian Empire on the Pacific, extending from California to Japan, from Kamchatka to Hawaii. Remarkably, he nearly succeeded.

Honesty was not one of Shelikov's virtues. He tended to inflate every claim, exaggerate every statistic, embroider every exploit. His book, *A Voyage to America, 1784-1786*, contains many fabrications. For all his mendacity, however, he comes through his own writings as an almost likeable, and certainly charming rogue.

Shelikov thought it was high time to end the free-booting *pro-*

2 Lt. Davydov's account (*Two Voyages to Russian America*, Limestone Press, Kingston, Ont. 1977, p. 188), seems ridiculous in light of this account, since he wrote fifty years later, "Of all the tribes known to us in northwestern America, the Koniags are the least suited to warfare...Lack of unity among the islanders has been a main factor in this." "Koniag" is the Unangan word for their traditional enemies, the Sugpiaq of the Kodiak area.

myshlennik trade and establish permanent bases on American soil, so that the resources of the country could be systematically developed and exploited. Other Irkutsk merchants agreed. If there were permanent detachments of men in the Aleutians, uprisings and ambushes would cease, crews and cargos could be protected, profits would soar. Together with his business partners, the Golikov family, Shelikov built three vessels, the *Tri Sviatitelei* (Three Saints or Hierarchs), the *Sviatii Simeon i Anna*, and the *Arkhangel Mikhail*, and set sail for America with 192 men, his wife and his two children aboard. Soon after leaving the Siberian coast, a storm scattered the ships. The *Arkhangel Mikhail* did not see the others again for another two years.

Stopping for supplies at Unalaska, Shelikov recruited ten Unangan laborers and two Sugpiaq-speaking interpreters, and continued on to *Qirtaq* ("*the* island," or Kodiak), which he reached on August 3, 1784. Shelikov captured a local hunter, gave him several presents, and released him, winning at least one local friend that day. Two days later, three *baidarkas* (boats made of skins) visited the ship, ostensibly seeking similar gifts, covertly reconnoitering the Russian strength.

Within a week, several hundred (or, according to Shelikov's account, several thousand) Sugpiaq gathered for battle. One eyewitness later estimated that there were about 400, but Shelikov claimed to have withstood the attack of 4,000. The battle, in any case, was brief. Unlike any of his predecessors, Shelikov had brought five cannon, which fired balls weighing approximately two pounds. The noise as well as the devastation these produced so terrified the Sugpiaq that many were killed in an ensuing stampede. Shelikov claimed to have taken a thousand prisoners, though again other eyewitness reports put the number at between two and three hundred. There is not standing room for a thousand people at Three Saints Bay, where Shelikov founded his settlement.

Decades later, a Native account of this battle was published:

The Russians had with them an old man from Unalaska named "Kashpak," who in his youth had been taken as a slave from Kodiak by the Fox-Aleuts (Unangan) and who now served as an interpreter for the Russians. They demanded hostages from our chiefs; we did not give any. The island of Sitkalidak had many settlements in those times, which, fearing retribution by the Russians because of their refusal, united into one settlement on the sea (east) side of the island to be able to oppose them. Twice Kashpak was sent there with the following offer:

"the chiefs should hand over their children as hostages, for the Russians wanted to raise them." Kashpak had many relatives among the inhabitants of the settlement...The second time he was warned that if he appeared again with such requests he would be treated as an enemy. After this, Kashpak betrayed the until then unknown portage across the island to the Russians. They went to the settlement and carried out a terrible bloodbath. Only a few men were able to flee to Aiktalik in baidarkas; 300 men were shot by the Russians. This happened in April. When our people visited the place in the summer, the stench of the corpses lying on the shore polluted the air so badly that no one could stay there, and since then, the island has been uninhabited.[3]

Shelikov concocted a different version of this battle in his memoirs. He identified the native traitor as an Unangan who had been held by the Sugpiaqs, rather than a Sugpiaq who had been enslaved by the Fox Island Unangan, and never gave him credit for revealing the portage. Rather, Shelikov wrote of his concern to avoid bloodshed:

I had already been warned about the aggressiveness of the Kodiak people, and how they had been able to repulse or annihilate all traders visiting them. However, my zeal for the interests of the Highest Throne encouraged me to overcome the fears instilled in me by my predecessors...the first duty was to pacify the savages in the interest of the government.[4]

He should have added: "and in my own best financial interests as well."

Whether by force, flattery or bribes, Shelikov did manage to secure Sugpiaq assistance, not only for building his settlement at Three Saints Bay, but for establishing other outposts on Afognak Island and the Kenai Peninsula. His claims of starting a school and converting many Sugpiaq to Christianity are substantiated by later investigators. In 1786, he returned home with 40 native "volunteers and prisoners" aboard the *Tri Sviatitelei*, and headed straight for Irkutsk as soon as he landed. Having secured the support of the Governor Yakobii of Siberia, he set off to present himself the reports of his heroic and self-sacrificial exploits and the governors favorable recommendations to the empress in St Petersburg. In the meantime, he hired a permanent manager for his Alaskan operations to replace a Greek officer, Delarov, who had assumed temporary command when Shelikov returned to Russia. Alexander Baranov, the new chief manager, left immediately for Kodiak to assume control of the enterprise during

3   Richard Pierce (editor/translator), Gregory Shelikov, *A Voyage to America*, (Limestone Press, Kingston, Ont, 1981), p 13.

4   *Ibid.*, p. 40.

Shelikov's absence. From the perspective of the company's investors, this was Shelikov's wisest act, but from that of the Native people, it was one of his cruelest.

Meanwhile, Shelikov lobbied for a complete monopoly of the Alaskan fur trade. By the end of 1787, the Shelikovs were in St Petersburg, petitioning the government for commercial rights, personal privileges and, of course, money. The empress shrewdly dispatched four ships to the North Pacific to inspect Shelikov's colony and verify his claims. War with Sweden unexpectedly forced three of these ships to remain in the Baltic, but one, the Billings expedition, visited Three Saints Bay in 1791-92.

Catherine the Great's own firm economic policy incorporated all the latest west European theories. Unregulated capitalism, "laissez-faire," was in fashion in France, the empress' favorite culture. Upon reviewing Shelikov's requests, her secretary exclaimed, "They want a monopoly over the entire Pacific Ocean!" Indeed, Shelikov was not one to be bashful. He asked for 20,000 rubles, a military installation or two, some serfs and clergy, a few extra ships, as well as complete control over the fur trade in the American colony. Since he claimed that he had risked his life and fortune to subjugate 50,000 new tax-paying subjects (this was a tremendous exaggeration) for no other reason than "love of our country and zeal for the public welfare," the Crown should honor him with awards, and even, perhaps, titles of nobility. For good measure, he asked for commercial rights to trade with China, Korea and maybe the Philippines.

The empress reacted quite negatively. "Such a loan," she wrote, "is like the proposition of the man who wanted to teach an elephant to speak during a thirty-year period. Asked why such a long time, he replied, 'Either the elephant will die, or I, or the one who loans the money to teach the elephant!'" Eventually she consented to bestow medals and ceremonial silver swords. Shelikov was lucky to get that much. No sooner had he returned to Irkutsk when reports from the Billings expedition arrived in the capital. Khrapovitskii, the empress' private secretary recorded, "...the description of Shelikov's barbarism on the American islands...has been presented to the Senate...and if there are more revelations, he will be in chains."[5] Fortunately for Shelikov, there were no more exposés. Even more fortunately, he was 7,000 miles away.

5   *Ibid.*, p. 22.

With the incorporation of the Russian American Company by Catherine's son, Paul I, in 1798, the *promyshlennik* period ended, and an age of centralized monopoly began. The original frontiersmen, most of them Siberian and Kamchadals, introduced Christianity to the Unangan – and Sugpiaq with whom they traded and lived. Earlier histories have blamed them for drastic declines in the Unangan population. Tensions ⁴. and conflicts certainly arose as intermarriage with local women became increasingly common. However, competing teams of poorly equipped entrepreneurs visiting the islands for a season or two and returning to Siberia could neither systematically plunder nor permanently enslave the *ß* indigenous people.

The *promyshlenniki* married Unangan and Sugpiaq wives, fathered hundreds of bilingual children, whom they baptized, and thus prepared the ground for the sowing of the seed, the Gospel message brought by *бе.* eight monks from Finland's Valaam. Gregory Shelikov, trying every possible means to gain imperial support for his ventures, had recruited them and provided their travel expenses. Rival groups of *promyshlenniki* welcomed them warmly. Alexander Baranov, the company manager, was much less enthusiastic.

PART II

The Alaskan Orthodox Mission

5

The Evangelization of Kodiak

The Setting

Kodiak is a very large island. Although dwarfed by the Alaskan mainland to the north and west, this emerald isle, geologically a continuation of the Kenai and Alaska Peninsulas, is larger than the states of Delaware and Rhode Island combined.[1] Like most of the Pacific coastline of Alaska, it is a land of deep fjords, narrow, rocky beaches, cascading waterfalls, and stormy seas, with a mild climate which suffers from an overdose of rain and wind. Norwegian seamen who have settled on Kodiak claim that its terrain reminds them of home.

The first settlers to paddle across the treacherous strait that separates the thirteen islands of the Kodiak archipelago from the mainland arrived some 6,000 years ago. Archaeologists believe that these brave seafaring colonists depended on seals, whales, sea lions and salmon to sustain themselves, and resorted to shellfish whenever the need (or urge) arose. Ocean Bay, on the eastern shore of Sitkalidak Island, was settled about 4,000 B.C. and represents one of the oldest cultures in southern Alaska.[2]

These ancient sea mammal hunters were among the well-to-do elite of Native American society, where wealth was (and is) traditionally measured in terms of food resources. The thriving wildlife of the land and ocean, the rich vegetation and flocks of water fowl made starvation practically unknown here. Families were free to roam throughout the large island, to establish seasonal camps wherever they found it convenient, and to return to larger, more permanent villages for festivals and communal subsistence activities, such as whale hunting. Ocean Bay, for example, has been a year-round settlement, a temporary camp and an abandoned site at various times since 1920.

1 Aleš Hrdlicka, *The Anthropology of Kodiak Island* (Wistar Institute, Philadelphia, PA, 1944), p. 5.
2 Donald Clark, *Ocean Bay* (Canadian National Museum of Man, Ottawa, Ont., 1979), p. iv.

The ancestors of the people of Three Saints Bay had long been residents of the Kodiak area and had travelled extensively throughout the region. Because annual rainfall varies considerably from one part of the island to another, certain subsistence activities could be more efficiently conducted at different locations. Thus, the southwestern corner of Kodiak, which receives 32 inches of precipitation annually was a better place to dry or smoke fish than Shearwater Bay, on the northeast side, where the average annual rainfall is 112 inches. Sea mammal hunting, with harpoons, arrows, spears and poisoned darts, required several kayaks for a successful expedition.[3] The Ocean Bay people, therefore, needed to organize themselves into centrally governed clans in order to exploit this resource. Some ethnographers believe that Kodiak culture was significantly influenced by the Tlingit Indians, who may have penetrated and even conquered Kodiak at some earlier time, for both societies were divided into ranks of aristocrats, commoners and slaves. Trading between Kodiak and both the Tlingits and "Tayaut" (Unangan) peoples to the east and west was conducted by small trading parties or merchant families who specialized in commerce. The possibility of attack from these neighbors, however, made a more hierarchical structure necessary, and determined the settlement pattern of Kodiak villages in more recent times. Sugpiaq communities were built on bluffs that provided a lookout in several directions, often with a stream of fresh water for cooking and bathing close by.[4]

The early style of making flaked stone tools at Ocean Bay was later replaced by a grinding technique by which stone hammers, adzes and lamps were manufactured.[5] Exactly what caused changes in material culture such as this is not yet clear. Some researchers believe that the original Kodiak people were assimilated by an invading or migrating Eskimo population from the north. In any case, the methods for making various tools changed during the last millennium, but the lifestyle of the people depended for thousands of years on sea mammals and fish. Sugpiaq culture reached its zenith about one thousand years ago. The rich natural resources allowed them enough leisure time to devote their talents and energies to producing ivory jewelry and decorating their most ordi-

3   Hrdlicka, *op. cit.*, p. 56-59.
4   *Ibid.*, p. 83.
5   *Ibid.*, p. 80.

nary household utensils. The early flaked stone implements of Ocean Bay were replaced by ground slate tools such as serrated knives, often with symmetrical barbed blades. They had diversified enough to begin trapping land mammals, especially foxes. Burial customs and religious rites became more elaborate, with aristocrats receiving preferential treatment. A village chief's slaves might be killed at his funeral, and soon after the burial, a memorial feast, at which his possessions were distributed to the guests, would be prepared by his surviving clan.[6]

The rugged terrain of the island itself did not invite the seafaring Sugpiaq to exploit the potential resources there. The lack of forests until very recent times forced the ancient hunters to adapt driftwood for building their large circular house frames which were then covered with sod.[7] Seal and whale oil lamps supplied both heat and light in these traditional "barabaras." Cooking was often done by boiling meat in containers into which hot rocks had been immersed.[8]

The primary role of the traditional Sugpiaq male was hunting and all activities related to the hunt. This included carving all the tools and household utensils, while the women gathered berries and shell fish, wove baskets and mats, tanned and sewed skins and supervised the pre-adolescent children.[9] Captured Indian or "Tayaut" slaves served as laborers until their relatives could rescue or ransom them.

As in all traditional cultures, teenagers were initiated into adulthood by a series of rites and ceremonies, after which both girls and boys were considered eligible for marriage. There does not seem to have been a special marriage ceremony, although the groom prepared a special steam bath for his bride as part of the procedure.[10] A boy's transition to manhood began with his first successful hunt, at which time special offerings and prayers would be offered to the spirits of that animal species. The meat of the first kill would be distributed to village elders to insure the good will of both. Feasting and gift giving might also accompany this distribution.[11]

6   *Ibid.,* p. 73.
7   *Ibid.,* p. 27.
8   *Ibid.,* p. 35.
9   *Ibid.,* p. 39.
10 *Ibid.,* p. 77. Also see Margaret Lantis, *Alaskan Eskimo Ceremonialism* (University of Washington, Seattle, WA, 1948), p. 8.
11 *Ibid.*

Girls were isolated in a separate hut under rigid restrictions at the time of their first menstruation, and "presented" as adult women at a special feast given by their parents afterwards.[12]

The Sugpiaq observed an annual Hunting Festival every December and conducted various secret rites related to specialized men's and women's societies, most notably the whale hunters' fraternity. In many of these practices, the Kodiak people closely resembled their Eskimo neighbors in Bristol Bay rather than their more distant cultural cousins, the Unangan, whom they called the "Tayaut," of the Aleutian Archipelago.

The Pre-Modern Worldview

For most modern people, the relative simplicity of Sugpiaq material culture infers a less sophisticated level of cultural and intellectual development as well. While one can admire the craftsmanship that was employed to create a particularly attractive lamp or knife blade, this technology ranks considerably below the achievements of the computer age. The modern mind is tempted to dismiss traditional cultures as "primitive" not only in the tools they created and used, but in their linguistic, psychological or philosophical development. This assumption proves to be invalid, however, when one examines the traditional culture's worldview.

Every literate society throughout history has assumed a superior attitude towards cultures which it encountered that had not yet created a written language. Illiteracy in the modern world is almost synonymous with ignorance, even stupidity. Without reading, one can make no personal economic progress in industrial societies. Since the eighteenth century, local and national governments have enacted compulsory education laws. Written language is more "real," more "concrete" and "permanent." The spoken word evaporates. Unwritten languages tend to be dismissed as not quite genuine, and "primitive" languages, it is often erroneously assumed, are so structurally limited that only the simplest forms of communication are possible in them.

The Sugpiaq, like traditional societies everywhere, did possess a very sophisticated language and a highly developed unwritten educational system. The methods and goals of this program, however, differed mark-

12 *Ibid.*, p. 80.

edly from those of modern literary cultures. Traditional or "pre-modern" societies were only secondarily concerned with teaching their youth various survival skills, and primarily interested in producing what each culture considered an "ideal" personality. In fact, the very name each traditional society had for itself indicates this. To be Tlingit or Unangan means literally to be a "human being." To be Yup'ik or Sugpiaq means, more emphatically, to be a "real person."

Every traditional society identifies itself as authentically human by specific and, it is believed, eternally fixed criteria. The Real People have their unique way of life. When the first people were created, they were given special instructions, special knowledge, which had to be transmitted to each succeeding generation. Only by living according to these standards could any individual attain genuine personhood, and only to the extent that the entire group strove toward this end could it succeed in its subsistence activities. Only Real People actually survive.

According to Sugpiaq (or Tlingit or Yup'ik) tradition, when the world was made, or at least when the first human beings appeared, each species was given its own language. Since then all languages have become less complex, have grammatically degenerated. In the Beginning, humans could comprehend the languages of the other creatures and communicate with them, but since the deterioration of language began very early, they can no longer understand what the animals say. The People once enjoyed access to the spirit world beyond, but most have forgotten how to reach that realm, and make the difficult journey only once, at death. Traditional cultures unanimously hold that their customs were legislated when the world began, and that since the world has been deteriorating, people can no longer do what their ancestors once did. Each generation, therefore, has a responsibility to explain these "facts of life" to the next, in order to minimize the loss of wisdom that both produces and results from this deterioration.

The crucial information is contained in the narrative form of the sacred stories of each tribe. The modern world popularly defines myth as an "ill-defined belief held uncritically by people, especially an interest group," However, its primary meaning is intended here: "a traditional story of ostensibly historical events that serves to unfold part of the worldview of a people, or explain a practice, belief, or natural phenomenon."[13]

13 *Webster's Ninth Collegiate Dictionary*, p. 785

The first report filed by the missionaries who arrived in 1794 describes in some detail the mythology of the Sugpiaq:

The world was made by a certain Kashshakhiliuk (wise man), i.e., to put it into more readily intelligible terms, there was an all-knowing, and at the same time personalized Principle, a Creator. There was neither day nor night. The Creator began to blow on a straw, and this is how the land eventually rose from the waters. Then, while he was still blowing, the sky opened, the sun appeared, and after dusk, the stars appeared and the moon rose... Finally animals and people came.

We are all born from one father and mother, and all are brothers and sisters of one another.

The place where the first people came from was warm; there were no winters or storms, but always gentle, healthy breezes. In the beginning, people lived in peace and knew no want. The first people were gifted with long life, and were strong and powerful. To begin with, people lived in friendship, knowing no envy, hatred or enmity—and also they wanted for nothing. But as the number of people increased, shortages and need began to appear, and need taught men to make weapons for hunting animals. Then disagreements arose, and enmity, and the weapons were turned on other people. Shortages and pressure from those who were stronger made people scatter further and further, and this is how all the different tribes arose.[14]

These brief passages from the 1797 report indicate that some of the universal motifs of traditional societies are part of the Sugpiaq mythology. Other sections of the report relate the Sugpiaq belief in two kinds of nearly omnipresent spirits, one which acts for, the other against human beings, but these seem to have been very little defined. Every village had a holy or forbidden place where villagers offered sacrifices, especially before a journey.

Early in this century, anthropologists recorded additional material about traditional Kodiak religion. The Sugpiaq believed that they were related to or descended from sled dogs, a tradition they shared with many Eskimo clans further north. They also believed that Kodiak Island was created by the son of the first people, and given to the Sugpiaq forever. This shows that the Kodiak people attributed to their remote ancestors powers and abilities that they no longer possessed.

Later ethnologists noted that Kodiak myths resembled those of the

14 Bearne, Colin (trans.), *The Russian Orthodox Mission to America* (Limestone Press, Kingston, Ont., 1978), p. 19.

Yup'ik Eskimo, on the north side of the Alaska Peninsula. Both shared beliefs about the creation of the earth, sea, and the emergence of the first people. But there are also characteristically Tlingit motifs in Kodiak mythology, such as the story of the bear woman, the creation of light, or rather its theft by Raven, the creation of streams, and the incorruptibility of a shaman's corpse. Uniquely Kodiak themes, such as warring mountains, sea monsters, earth pillars and one-eyed people, do not appreciably affect the fundamental unity of worldview among the indigenous peoples of southern Alaska.

Common themes in Alaskan mythology are the intelligence, and even superiority, of animals, and the possibility of human beings communicating with and even being transformed into other creatures. Indeed, several Kodiak legends conclude with the hero's remaining contentedly in animal form. Game can only be successfully hunted if the People have observed the proper etiquette, followed the proper procedures, showed the proper respect. The prey always knows that the hunting party is approaching, and can easily escape. Every catch, therefore, represents not so much the skill of the hunter as the self-sacrifice of the victim, which allows itself to be butchered in order to feed the otherwise helpless human beings. This appreciation of animals inspires the traditional art and ceremonies of hunting cultures everywhere, and provides the context within which many Alaskan myths and legends can be understood.

The Sugpiaq observed an annual winter festival with songs, dances and feasting at the beginning of the year. Again, this represents a universal phenomenon, celebrating an annual end and beginning, the death and rebirth of the cosmic cycle. Among the Kodiak people, these rites were directed by a master of ceremonies known as the "Kassaq." This person's function was to assure that the dances and songs were performed in their proper sequence. These were not mere entertainment, but a ritual reenactment of the creation of the world. Through symbols and gestures, the events of the Beginning were not only recalled but re-presented, that is, made present again. Time in the chronological sense was abolished. While the songs and dances were being performed, the time of day and the calendar date were of no consequence, for the community experienced the reality of "that time," the all-important events of "those days." Traditional societies tried as much as possible to live outside chronological time, historical time, to escape to cosmic time, and thus become contemporaneous with their origins, with the Beginning.

At first this may seem incomprehensible. Western European society conceives of time moving in a linear fashion, with no possibility of returning to the moment just passed. In the modern secular world, there is no way to turn back the clock. Traditional societies universally assumed the opposite: it is not only possible but absolutely necessary to reverse the flow of time, for only in repeating the actions, only in remembering and imitating the crucial deeds of "those days" can life be meaningful. One can become a real person only then, only in deliberate repetition of the all-important events of the Beginning.

As He made the world, the Creator followed a preconceived plan and established the permanent structures and laws that govern the universe. Knowing these basic structures is essential to survival. Hunters navigate home because they know they can recognize the fixed patterns in the skies or waters. Villagers erect their homes following the same divine blueprint, so that each house is a microcosm, a miniature universe. Not only does each dwelling reflect the structure of the world, but the process of building it follows the same sequence; for in erecting a house, human beings imitate the actions of the gods, and the time spent in constructing the building is not chronological, but cosmic time.

While secular cultures know nothing of this kind of time, it remains the temporal matrix for all religious experience. In the Christian faith, the most important collective action of the community is the celebration of the Eucharist. It matters not at all to what theology a believer subscribes, whether one considers the eating and drinking only a "memorial meal" or a miraculous transformation of the bread and wine into the Body and Blood of Christ. The point here is that whatever the apostles received in the upper room in Jerusalem about 33 A.D. is the same reality that the believer receives in church. The time of day and day of the week are of no importance while one is receiving the sacrament. What matters is that the believer enters into the experience of the disciples and participates in the same mystical supper, despite the geographic distance and the centuries that separate the communicant from the event; for the event, being of eternal significance, is never "past" but always present, always accessible.

A young Sugpiaq would learn the unalterable structures and realities of the world through the sacred stories told and retold by elders who knew them best, and would experience the reality of the eternally significant events of the Beginning in the annual festal cycle. But the fullest validation of the traditional worldview came through the Angalkuq, the shaman.

The shaman was not necessarily more familiar than his neighbors with the traditional mythology or rites of the people. He may or may not have played an active part in the annual celebrations. It seems unlikely, in fact, that the Kassaq and Angalkuq were the same person in Kodiak society. In most cultures, the shamanistic function was neither hereditary nor transferable, although in Kodiak it might have been both. The shaman did not create the myths. Rather he experienced the realities about which the myths testified more intensely than other members of the community. The shaman knew the spirit and animal realms existentially because, according to traditional belief, he had been there. In every shamanistic initiation, it was believed, the soul of the novice left the body and journeyed to the realm of the dead, to the spirit world, where it became familiar with the "geography" and the languages of some of the spirits and animals. In other words, the shaman was a charismatic personality whose authority and power rested on an experience of the sacred inaccessible to others. Central to this experience was nothing less than a ritual death and resurrection.[15] The shaman's soul left his body and returned from "beyond," and could do so again when circumstances required it. Because of his familiarity with the spirit world, with demons, animal spirits, and the souls of the departed, the shaman was able to cure certain ailments, invoke blessings and curses, and prophesy the future.

Although the basic mythological themes of any pre-modern people are considered divinely inspired and changeless, each generation, in fact, adapts and incorporates new as well as disposes of some old material. In an oral culture, collective amnesia can be an effective method of dealing with certain inconsistencies in the mythological tradition. As new circumstances arise, the models change to meet new needs, but meaningful conduct is always central to the continuing educational effort. Traditional societies are, by definition, conservative, but this does not mean they are totally inflexible. Problems arise usually only after the stories assume a

15 Mircea Eliade, *Rites and Symbols of Initiation* (Harper & Row, New York, NY, 1968).

final, written form. Thus, in pre-modern cultures throughout the world, an elder can sincerely respond with authority to a question about a particular custom or practice with the same eternal reply: "This is the way we always do it."

We have called this type of behavior "mythological," but it might also be defined as "non-rational" or "poetic" because it is really a very integrative and intuitive approach to reality, tending to view everything as "whole," in interrelationship and interdependence with everything else. No separate social, political, economic, intellectual or religious spheres exist in a traditional culture. The myths contain the models for appropriate human behavior in all meaningful areas of human existence. This integrated, homogeneous worldview is common to traditional cultures everywhere, and is shared also by religious believers of every tradition. While exploration and exploitation severely disrupted traditional Kodiak and Aleutian society during the first decades of European contact, the Eastern Orthodox missions brought an understanding of Christianity to Alaska that facilitated a rapid synthesis of traditional and Christian beliefs, and produced an indigenous Orthodox Church within a few decades.

The Valaam Mission

Gregory Shelikov, eager to win approval and glory for his Alaskan enterprise, boasted to Metropolitan Gabriel of St Petersburg that since 1784 "quite a few" Kodiak natives had accepted baptism and that Sugpiaq children were being instructed in the Christian faith at the school his company had founded at Three Saints Bay. He begged for a priest to be assigned there, and promised that the chapel he claimed had already been erected would be furnished with all the necessary articles, and supported at company expense.[16] He estimated that of the students now enrolled at his school, twenty of the best could be recruited to attend the seminary in Irkutsk and return to spread the Orthodox faith "in their own language." Considering that, according to Shelikov, there were already so many converts, it seems surprising he requested only one priest. Probably one was all that he was willing to subsidize.

The Metropolitan believed Shelikov's glowing reports, and not only

16 Bishop Gregory (Afonsky), *A History of the Orthodox Church in Alaska,* p. 19.

responded favorably to his petition, but, realizing the enormous task confronting this blossoming mission, recruited ten monks, four of them priests, for Alaska. Hieromonk Joasaph, a graduate of the Tver theological seminary, was appointed head of this mission and elevated to the rank of archimandrite, equivalent to that of an abbot. Metropolitan Gabriel seems to have known Father Joasaph well, for he recommended him with the following words:

> Joasaph was a monk who put not his treasure in worldly possessions, and gave himself to this God-loving work solely for the pleasure of the spiritual (ascetic) effort of spreading the Christian faith and the Holy Gospel...[17]

The other missionaries came mostly from poor families and lacked formal theological training. They were united in their dedication to the church and their desire to live completely Christian lives. None of them would have dreamed that their monastic vocation would take them to what, for them, must have seemed like the ends of the world. Some, indeed, were totally unprepared for the experience.

Hieromonk Makarii, a former serf who had been living at Konevitsa monastery for over twenty years, was forty-three years old when he volunteered for the Alaskan mission. Hieromonk Afanasii, also a former serf, had been living at Valaam for five years. Hieromonk Iuvenalii, originally from a middle class family in the Ural mountains, had resigned his commission as a military officer in 1791 to join the monastic brotherhood at Valaam. Hierodeacon Nektarii, like Father Iuvenalii, had been at Valaam only two years, and had been ordained just a few months before the mission left for Alaska. The monk Herman, probably from a Moscow suburb, had become a novice as a teenager at the Holy Trinity-St Sergius Skete, near the Finnish border, but had transferred to Valaam when he was 21.

The Valaam Mission was the first overseas mission of the Russian Orthodox Church, and as such, its departure was marked with public festivities. The empress herself donated funds for the support of the monks, who arrived in Irkutsk three months later. Their route took them through Kazan, Samara, Cheliabinsk, Tobolsk, Tomsk, and Krasnoiarsk, and enabled them in this way to review personally the missionary expansion of Christianity across Central Asia and Siberia.[18] From Irkutsk,

---

17 *Ibid.*, p. 20.
18 *Orthodox Alaska*, Vol. 4, no. 6, p. 3.

where Gregory Shelikov, several more monks and two novices joined them, they travelled to Iakutsk and finally to the port of Okhotsk. From there, Shelikov wrote to his manager, Alexander Baranov, "I present you with some guests. These guests are the Archmandrite Joasaph and the brothers chosen by the will of the empress to spread the word of God in America. I know that you will feel as great a satisfaction as I..." Shelikov might indeed have been sincere in this expression of fulfillment, since he spared no expense in assisting the monks on their journey to the sea. However, when he claimed that "we have supplied the holy fathers with everything they need for the next three years, if they are frugal,"[19] he was lying. No such supplies existed.

Baranov

Alexander Andreevich Baranov had arrived inauspiciously in Alaska. Departing Unalaska with fifty-three passengers on board, and Baranov in command, the *Tri Sviatitelei* sank in high seas. The new manager was forced to winter at Unalaska, and travelled to Three Saints Bay by *baidara*, a large skin boat, with fifteen of his crew the following spring. In 1788, seventeen days of severe tremors were climaxed by a terrifying earthquake and two tsunamis, which damaged some of the buildings and completely swept away several native barabaras. Understandably, Baranov decided soon after his arrival to relocate the settlement, first to Chiniak and finally to St Paul Harbor, the present site of the city of Kodiak. The Sugpiaq called the new town "Sun'aq"—the Harbor. The original settlement became known as "Sun'alleq"—the original or "Old Harbor," as the village is known today.

Shelikov instructed his manager to build a model town,

> In a word,...order this first settlement in America to be built as a standard city. Any disfiguring of it with crooked, narrow, impassable lanes and by-paths must not be permitted, so that in the future, this first settlement may become the beautiful abode of a multitude of people, and the glory and fame of Russian art and taste may not be impaired.[20]

Such commands were easy for Shelikov to issue, but impossible for

19 Michael G. Kovach, *The Russian Orthodox Church in Russian America*, unpublished thesis, University of Pittsburgh (1957), p. 59.
20 Kovach, *ibid.*, p. 39.

Baranov to fulfill. Without supplies, his meager resources stretched beyond limit, it was all the "Wild Ram" (*Baran* means "ram" in Russian) could do to maintain order in the colony. The arrival of nearly 120 more mouths to feed and few provisions aboard the first ship to arrive in over a year could only have angered or depressed him more.

Baranov was not the only one dismayed on September 24, 1794, when the missionaries arrived. No church nor any supplies existed for the mission, contrary to Shelikov's promise. The village was nothing like the picturesque community he had described. Before long, moreover, the clergy realized that they and the company management were working at cross purposes. Sugpiaq and Unangan hunters were often forced at gun point to search for sea otters in treacherous seas. Women were violated, children abused. Baranov, with a wife in Siberia, kept a Native mistress and encouraged his men to do the same. Father Joasaph reported conditions to Shelikov with admirable self control and righteous indignation, confident that the owner would dismiss his manager and restore decency and order in the colony.

The conflict between the missionaries and the company administration has hardly received the attention it deserves in popular histories. Many modern historians have erroneously assumed that because the Orthodox Church was the established church of the Russian Empire, governed since Peter the Great's time by a synod appointed by the state, that the clergy constituted a privileged class of petty bureaucrats whose function in Kodiak was to "pacify" the Natives and assist the colonial regime in subduing a recalcitrant population, by convincing them that it was their Christian duty to obey their superiors.

All the existing documents from the first years of the Valaam mission's presence at Kodiak testify that the opposite occurred. An immediate clash took place between Baranov and the monks, primarily because of Shelikov's deceptions. The archimandrite blamed Baranov personally for many of the hardships and deprivations the colony faced. In May 1795, eight months after their arrival, Father Joasaph wrote (not without exaggeration) to Shelikov:

> Since my arrival at this harbor I have seen nothing done to carry out your good intentions. My own pleasure is that so many Americans are coming from everywhere to be baptized, but the Russians not only make no effort to encourage

them, but use every means to discourage them. The reason for this is that their depraved lives become evident if compared to the good conduct of the Americans [the Native Alaskans]. Only with difficulty did I persuade a few Russian hunters to get married. The rest of them do not even want to listen to me. Everyone openly keeps one or several girls, which greatly offends the Americans; you know how they treat their women; they are capable of bringing disaster to the Russians to obtain revenge.

[Baranov] incites all the hunters against you, writes calumnies, and persuades everyone to sign them. He dissents from you in everything. He claims that everything—ships and other property—belongs to the company and not to the investors.

Only five children attend school. Most of the older pupils stay at home without any supervision...and now you cannot see any difference between them and other Aleuts...I do not know where to teach my five students. Our hut is always crowded with people who come to talk, and is also used for services, as we have no church building. I received a few of the church books from the company, about twenty altogether, among them ten service books which were so rotten they cannot be used; I have not seen the rest yet.

...from daybreak we have to think about food. We have to walk about three miles to find clams and mussels. There are no clams in the harbor; there are some mussels, but not enough for the domestic servants. Besides, we have to bring the wood, to make clothing, and do our laundry.

If I had to describe all his acts in detail, it would fill a book. According to the instructions given me, I should have informed...the Metropolitan or the Holy Synod, but my love and respect for you keeps me from doing so...With the consent of the manager, the hunters take their children from their mother (if the father is Russian and wants to take it to Russia). Some of the children are only one or two years old. I do not approve of this...it will be calamitous for the children...I see the possibility for the proper raising of these children, provided we have a good chief manager; meanwhile, let them be raised here.

...Several men have told me that Baranov and his mutineers frequently say, "It would be good to kill the Archimandrite and [Hieromonk] Iuvenalii. The rest we can crush like flies." I should not believe all the rumors I hear, but from such a brute I can expect anything. He has already sent many people to the next world, so he would not be scrupulous about killing me.[21]

For his part, Baranov defended himself against these charges as if he knew exactly what accusations his critics were making against him. In fact, he probably did, since all mail had to travel aboard company ships

21 Michael J. Oleksa, *Alaskan Missionary Spirituality* (Paulist Press, Mahwah, NJ, 1987), p. 58-63.

subject to his jurisdiction. He claimed that "It is not true that we drink vodka all the time,...or at least if a hunter takes too much it is done in secrecy and I never hear of it." He admitted that "I have for a long time now been keeping a girl..." He concluded his dispatch of May 1795 with this astounding statement: "As for the clergy, I feel it my duty to see to their well-being and to obey their will..."[22]

The tragedy here lay in the fact that Father Joasaph was so completely taken in by Shelikov. He was in good company on this score, of course, for many of Russia's most distinguished civil servants had also been deceived. But Joasaph seems to have blamed Baranov personally for all that was corrupt in the colony, and refused to concede that exploitation, immorality or terror could ever serve the national interest. The increasing number and seriousness of the charges filed against the company convinced authorities to solicit the personal testimony of respected eyewitnesses. Archimandrite Joasaph, therefore, was summoned to Irkutsk in the spring of 1798. He appointed the lay monk Herman to administer the mission until his return, and expressed complete confidence in his ability to fulfill this responsibility, writing, "I consider it unnecessary to tell you about many things and you can deal best with matters according to circumstances."

Father Herman was instructed to continue operating the school, since Father Joasaph had argued that training indigenous clergy was absolutely necessary for the growth and stability of the Church. After the Holy Synod had requested that he send promising students to Siberia for seminary training, Joasaph suggested instead that qualified instructors be sent to Kodiak to establish a seminary there. Thus, the inspiration for educating Native leadership for the Orthodox mission in America originated with Father Joasaph.[23]

In Irkutsk, the Archimandrite was consecrated bishop of Kodiak. Accompanied by Hierodeacon Stepan, he began the return journey to Alaska. His moral and political influence would have far surpassed Baranov's, and the new bishop would have had the authority to reform the colony. Meeting Father Makarii, who had travelled separately to

22 Richard Pierce [trans.] *History of the Russian American Company,* Vol. 2, (Limestone Press, Kingston, Ont.), p. 68-75.
23 Kovach, *op.cit.,* p. 72.

Siberia to report to the authorities on conditions in the Aleutians, the three missionaries sailed aboard the Phoenix in 1798. However the ship with its hopeful passengers aboard was wrecked near Kodiak. There were no survivors.

As for Shelikov, he had suddenly and somewhat mysteriously died. Rumor in Irkutsk suggested that his "faithful companion" Natalia had poisoned him. Some speculate that she was a shrewd, calculating, ambitious woman, who wanted to grab control of the now stable and prosperous company. Shelikov had written no will, and perhaps a quarrel in which he had threatened to disinherit her triggered the murder. Others believe that Natalia was avenging the forced marriage of her fourteen-year-old daughter, Anna, to the sadistic Nikolai Rezanov. Gregory had engineered this union to consolidate his ties with this personal friend of the future Tsar Paul, making shares in his company a major part of Anna's dowry. In 1802, six years after the death of her 46-year old father, Anna died too, only 21 years old. In the meantime, Catherine the Great's son, the incompetent Paul, had made Rezanov as well as Natalia Shelikova and her descendents members of the nobility.

The Baptism of the Sugpiaq

Initially, despite the confrontation with Baranov, or perhaps partly because of it, the missionaries were well received by the Native population. Hieromonk Makarii circled the island while the others preached at the main settlement at St Paul harbor. They were assisted for many years by their Native interpreter, Osip Priannishnikov. Having crossed Siberia and gained firsthand knowledge of the monastic missions there, the Valaam monks set out to study the culture and religious beliefs of the Sugpiaq people, reporting their findings to their brothers back in Finland.

"The place where the first people came from was warm...the people lived in peace and knew no want. The first people were gifted with long life" and so forth. What do we find in these ideas? This is the Biblical paradise, the innocent and blessed condition of the first human beings. The longevity of the first people is the longevity of the Patriarchs of the Bible.

According to the Kodiak account of the Creation, there was a certain wise man, that is, a certain all-knowing personalized principle, a Creator...At the same time, they believe there was neither night nor day; and the Bible says the same. He [the Creator] began to blow on a straw...The Bible also relates a similar, gradual process, with the land appearing from the depths of primal chaos...He, the Creator of the world, is so immeasurably great and powerful by comparison to his creation, that for him, the act of breathing alone is enough to create the earth, for there was nothing there before...There are omissions and distortions, but the actual account of Creation has not been lost at all. In the Bible we read: And the Lord God formed man...and breathed into him the breath of life. God is not a name but an idea deep-seated in the nature of human beings, something which can not be explained, as Justin the Philosopher wrote [Apology 2, chapter 6].

The detailed moral laws about respect for one's parents and elders and the promise of long life, are they not the same as the fifth commandment of Moses? "We are all born of one father and one mother, and are all brothers and sisters." This is what the Scriptures tell us.[24]

Through their sympathetic study of the traditional religious beliefs of the Sugpiaq, and through their defense of the Native people and their opposition to Baranov's exploitation, the monks established a bond of solidarity with the Sugpiaq, and even became godparents to some. Nearly the entire Native population of the Kodiak region accepted baptism during the first two years of the mission, a total of nearly 7,000 converts. Bishop Joasaph's godson, the son of a local chief, was the central figure in a major confrontation with Baranov concerning the administration of an oath of allegiance to the new tsar.[25]

Hieromonk Iuvenalii travelled in 1796 to the mainland, where he baptized the first Chugach Sugpiaq and visited the Tanaina Indians on the shores of Cook Inlet before crossing the mountains to the east and coming to Lake Iliamna, after which he was never heard from again. Before he left Kodiak, Father Iuvenalii had established that he intended to search for the Russian settlement rumored to exist on the Bering Sea coast, north of the Alaska Peninsula. Rival groups from other companies as well as Russian American Company employees learned of his murder, but the site and circumstances were, at first, unclear. Fifty years after his disappearance, Father John Veniaminov collected an account of the hieromonk's death, but its details contradict all other reliable documentary evidence, and its origins are uncertain. A hundred years later, a Russian-born charlatan, Ivan Petrov, produced a "translation" of Father Iuvenalii's personal diary, which American historians uncritically accepted

24 Bearn, *op. cit.*, p. 22.
25 See Appendix I.

as genuine. These are the sources of the tradition that Iuvenalii was killed at Iliamna, but the unanimous testimony of the Native people of the region, together with reports filed by later explorers and missionaries all indicate that he died at the village of Quinhagak, at the mouth of the Kuskokwim River, on the shores of the Bering Sea—the destination he himself had determined before leaving Kodiak. The newly baptized people of Quinhagak described Father Iuvenalii's death in some detail to the Protestant missionary, John Kilbuck, who resided there for a decade at the end of the nineteenth century. Father Iuvenalii, as their version goes, stood up to preach in his "angyacuar" [literally, "little boat"] but was forbidden to speak by the local shaman, who ordered him killed in a "hail of arrows." Shamans on both sides of the Bering Straits customarily wore chains of metal or ivory as a sign of their status and magical powers. Immediately before his death, a later report added, he seemed to be waving his arm, as if he were "chasing away files." This indicates that the hieromonk was blessing his murders with the sign of the cross, a gesture they had never seen before. His Tanaina Indian guide, probably from Kenai or Tyonek, tried to escape by swimming away, and impressed his Eskimo assailants by his remarkable swimming ability. They were forced to chase him in their kayaks, but he too eventually perished. The shaman then removed Iuvenalii's brass pectoral cross from his body and tried to work some sort of rite, but was unsuccessful. Removing the cross, he noted that there was some other power represented here that prevented him from doing his own usual magic. Some years later, a Russian explorer was "adopted" near Quinhagak in a ceremony that closely resembled the Orthodox rite of chrismation/confirmation, and a Yup'ik Eskimo, wearing a priest's pectoral cross, visited the Russian trading post at Nushagak. Later Orthodox missionaries, Hieromonk Ilarion (1864), Father Zakharii Bel'kov (1879) and Father Vasilii Orlov (1885), when each visited the village, all recorded that Quinhagak was the site of Father Iuvenalii's martyrdom. He was canonized by the Orthodox diocese of Alaska in 1977.

Hieromonk Makarii was "very useful here, contrary to all expectations," according to Archimandrite Joasaph's 1795 report. "I had not thought that he would make the journey here, but he has travelled around half the island, baptizing and marrying, and on the ship bearing this letter, he has set off for Unalaska and the surrounding islands to baptize the Natives there."[26] Thirty years later, Father Veniaminov recorded that upon his arrival at Unalaska, all the people had been baptized either by Father Makarii or older relatives who had been originally baptized by him. Veniaminov added that while they were anxious to increase their understanding of the Christian life, they had been committed to it since the time they had been converted and initiated by Father Makarii:

> The Aleuts [Unangan] accepted baptism willingly and speedily; witness to this is borne by the fact that Makarii spent only one year in the Unalaska district, and that as he travelled about the isolated islands from place to place, he had no guard with him. The very Aleuts whom he baptized, fed and sheltered him, and all without seeking any reward, or anything in return...It could be objected that the Aleuts accepted the Faith out of fear of the Russians, or that they were bribed...Such methods will make people adopt a new faith, but cannot make them ardent and loyal adherents to it. Yet the Aleuts remain just as godly now as ever...The Aleuts remained Christians, or at least as soon as they were baptized, they not only completely abandoned their pagan beliefs and rituals and rites, but even songs which might in any way remind them of their former beliefs, so that I could not, however much I looked, find anything of the kind when I arrived here.[27]

Conditions in the archipelago were no better than at Kodiak, and Hieromonk Makarii was enticed by competing merchants to return to Russia to report to the authorities in St Petersburg about Baranov's barbarous treatment of the Americans. Although he was the most energetic of all the monks, and had claimed the Alaska Peninsula as part of his missionary responsibility, he was also the first to leave Alaska. Arriving at the capital city with several Aleut chiefs who had come to substantiate his accusations, Makarii was, nonetheless, reprimanded for leaving his post without authorization from his superiors. He was ordered to return to Unalaska, but drowned with the sinking of the Phoenix.

With the loss of the bishop, two priest-monks and the deacon, the Kodiak mission was reduced to Father Nektarii, Father Afanasy, Father Herman, and a young novice, Father Joasaph. Baranov devoted much of his energy to expanding the company's operations on the Alaskan mainland, and establishing a new headquarters at New Archangel (modern Sitka). He occupied the site in 1800, but in 1802 it was completely

26 Bearn, *op. cit.*, p. 42.
27 *Ibid.*, p. 46-47.

destroyed by the Tlingit Indians of the region. The few survivors of this fiasco were rescued by an English ship and taken to Kodiak, where Baranov was forced to pay ten thousand rubles' ransom for his unfortunate settlers. He subsequently became consumed with the determination to recapture Sitka and reestablish company rule in southeastern Alaska. He spent over a half million rubles to equip the Neva for battle. A thousand Sugpiaq and Unangan "marines" assaulted the beach as the Neva's artillery bombarded the Tlingit fort and its 800 defenders when Baranov returned in 1804. Baranov himself was wounded in the fight, but at least one Sugpiaq warrior distinguished himself under fire.

According to a modern Tlingit account, a Kodiak native was able to load and reload his musket with amazing speed, although he seemed to be partially disabled and walked with a pronounced limp. Apparently, his partially paralyzed fingers allowed him to grip extra measures of gunpowder tightly, so that he was able to fire his gun faster and more accurately than his comrades. The Tlingit remember him as "Kitaq," which in Sugpiaq means "Come on!" or "Hurry up!" This is probably not the man's name, but rather the encouragement his friends shouted at their slow-walking colleague.

Once Baranov relocated to Sitka, one would have expected conditions in Kodiak to improve, but this does not seem to have been the case. The Holy Synod appointed Hieromonk Gideon of St Alexander Nevsky Monastery near the capital to inspect the colony and reinvigorate the mission. Gideon arrived on the Neva and was warmly received by the monks and the company administration. As he was a man who had access to the tsar, even Baranov had to be polite. Gideon's reports constitute a principal source of information about conditions at Kodiak at the turn of the century.

Concerning the monks, he wrote:

They cultivated vegetable plots with their own hands...they had considerable yield of potatoes...a reasonable crop of turnips and radishes. From the potatoes they made flour, the turnips were chopped and fermented, sea water substituted for salt, and used instead of cabbage. The remaining produce they gave to the islanders.[28]

28 Many of Father Gideon's letters have been translated and published in Lydia Black, *The Round the World Voyage of Hieromonk Gideon* (Limestone Press, Kingston, Ont., 1989).

Father Gideon compiled the first dictionary of Sugpiaq and described the physical as well as cultural characteristics of the Kodiak Natives. Travelling in a three-man *baidarka*, he preached and inspected all the settlements, baptizing "503 souls...between the ages of one and ten, and 22 others who were about forty." He also married 38 couples. His translation of the Lord's Prayer was sung at the Sunday liturgy, and he increased the enrollment at the Kodiak school to eighty Russians, Natives and Creoles. The curriculum included reading, writing, arithmetic, geography, catechism, church and world history and Russian grammar. Outside the school, students learned to cultivate gardens. After the Battle of Sitka, some Tlingit prisoners were enrolled in classes at Father Gideon's school. Graduation ceremonies were attended by government and company officials, and Baranov awarded cash prizes to four exceptional Native students, no doubt to enhance his public image more than to encourage enlightenment.

With the emperor's backing, Gideon could remind company officials that the government was well aware that

...the attitude of the Russians living here has, up to now, been based on rules incompatible with humanity. Their depraved minds result from their having gone to America to grow rich and only then to return to fritter away in a few days what they have earned from many years of other people's sweat and toil. Are such people going to respect their neighbors? They have given up family life altogether, and have no good examples to follow. Therefore the poor Americans are, to the shame of the Russians, sacrificed to their immorality.[29]

When he left America in 1807, Hieromonk Gideon claimed to have done all that he could to establish agriculture and education, and to stabilize the population, the government's main concerns. He admonished Baranov to make proper use of the remaining clergy, whom he asked to "exert all their efforts to make this great undertaking successful; and that...the worthy Father Herman should, in accordance with the emperor's will, have special care for the region."

The company feared Hieromonk Gideon's inspection and dispatched "Count" Nicolai Rezanov on an inspection tour of his own. Not daring to defy a representative of the tsar, Rezanov wrote to Gideon,

I shall make it one of my first tasks to go into the actual condition of the religious mission here, and to alleviate the sufferings of those worthy men who have

29 *Ibid.*, Letter to Baranov, dated May 26, 1807, p. 107.

rejected all secular pleasures and seek...to enlighten and educate...I would humbly request your honor to inform me how much is needed annually for the upkeep of the clergy and the Church buildings, and to provide me with the pleasure of supplementing this from my own means as a sign of my undying respect...for your honor, and all worthy fathers.

These flowery words ring hollow from the pen of the same man who slandered Hieromonk Iuvenalii, calling him "that freak" whom he held responsible for the company's inability to trade successfully at Iliamna. The monks contended that the company's own reputation for brutality explained the reluctance of the Iliamna natives to abandon ties with rival firms. When Gideon submitted his supply list, Rezanov angrily rejected the entire requisition, though his own initial letter does admit that the clergy had been suffering.

Gideon, not without sarcasm, replied,

Noting with heartfelt gratitude Your Excellency's favorable disposition toward the annual support of the clergy, the Fathers have expressed to me their deep gratitude for your decision to alleviate their shortages...The following are desperately needed: flour for bread, wine, incense, candles and wood oil—needed most of all to repair the leaking roof.[30]

When Gideon's sojourn ended, he took three promising students with him back to Russia—Prokopii Lavrov, Paramon Chumovitskii and Aleksii Kotelnikov. After completing their education they would return to Alaska as leaders of their people.

Baranov assured Gideon that "over the years,..the Fathers...have never been refused anything...I shall give orders that in the future their needs shall be met whenever they occur and the company has a surplus." Once Gideon left, however, the situation remained unchanged. Rezanov reported to the company's board of directors that "these monks did not comprehend the interests of the state and the company." Neither, of course, did the company comprehend the goals and priorities of the monks.

From the "Life of Father Herman"

In America, Father Herman chose Spruce Island as his home, calling it "New Valaam." This island is separated by a strait, about a mile and a

30   Michael J. Oleksa, *Alaskan Missionary Spirituality* (Paulist Press, Mahwah, NJ. 1987), p. 305.

quarter wide, from Kodiak Island, and had a Native style *barabara* and a small wooden church built on it.

Spruce Island is not large and is almost entirely covered by forest. Through its middle, a small brook flows to the sea. Father Herman dug a cave in the ground with his own hands and lived there his first full summer. By winter a hut had been built for him near the cave, and he lived in it until his death. The cave later became his grave. The wooden chapel, and later a small house for use as a school and a guest house were built at a distance from his cell, and he planted a garden in front of it. Father Herman lived here for more than forty years.

Father Herman's Way of Life

Father Herman himself spaded the garden and planted potatoes, cabbage, and various vegetables in it. For winter, he preserved mushrooms by drying or salting them with ocean water. Local tradition testifies that the wicker basket that the elder used to carry seaweed from the shore to his garden for use as fertilizer was so large it was difficult for one person to carry alone. But to the astonishment of all, Father Herman carried this basket filled with seaweed for long distances without any help at all. His disciple, Gerasim Zyrianov, saw him by chance one winter carrying a large log which would normally be hauled by four men; he was barefooted. Thus worked the elder, using everything that he attained from his innumerable labors for the feeding and clothing of orphans, and for books for his students.

Father Herman's clothes were the same all year. He did not wear a shirt, but instead a smock of deerskin, which he did not take off or change for several years at a time, so that the fur on it was completely worn off, and the leather glossy. He also wore boots or shoes, his cassock, an old, faded, and patched *riasa* (outer cassock) and monastic *klobuk* (cylindrical head covering). He went everywhere in these clothes, at all times, in any weather, no matter how cold. In this, Father Herman followed the example of many eastern ascetic fathers, who showed great concern for the welfare of others, yet themselves wore the humblest possible clothes, to show their disregard for earthly riches and their great humility before God.

A small bench covered with worn deerskin served as Father Herman's bed. He used two bricks, which he hid from his visitor's view, for a pillow. He had no blanket, but covered himself with a board that lay on the stove, expressing the wish that it be used to cover his remains after his death. The board was as long as Father Herman was tall. "During my stay in his cell," wrote Constantine Larionov, "I, a sinner, sat on his 'blanket,' and I consider this the highlight of my life."[31]

On the occasions when Father Herman was the guest of company administrators, he sat up with them until midnight, talking of spiritual matters. However, he never spent the night with them, always returning to his hermitage, regardless of the weather. If, for some extraordinary reason, it was necessary for him to spend the night away from his cell, the bed that had been prepared for him would be found untouched in the morning, the elder not having slept at all. Likewise, he spent his nights in his hermitage in prayer; he never rested.

The elder ate very little. As a guest, he either scarcely tasted his food or remained without dinner. In his cell, dinner consisted of a very small portion of fish or some vegetables. Secretly around his body, which was emaciated by fasting, labors, vigils and fasting, he wore sixteen-pound chains. No one knew this during his life. They were discovered only after his death and are kept in the Kodiak church to this day. His disciple, Ignatii Aligiaga, concisely summarized, "Yes, Ap'a [Father] led a very hard life. No one can imitate it."

In 1866, Bishop Peter, writing from Sitka to Valaam Monastery, assessed the significance of Father Herman's life in this way:

> His most important works were his exercises in spiritual endeavor in his isolated cell where no one saw him, but outside his cell they heard him singing and celebrating services to God, according to the monastic rule.[32]

Father Herman supported this assessment himself. When he was asked how he managed to live alone in the forest, how he combatted loneliness, he answered, "I am not alone. God is here, as God is everywhere. The holy angels are there. With whom is it better to talk, with people or with angels? Certainly with angels!"[33]

When the imperial government had received enough complaints to

31 *Ibid.*, p. 79.
32 Bearne, *op. cit.*, p. 96.
33 *Ibid.*, p. 86.

justify another official inquiry into the conduct of the colonial administration, it sent Captain Vasilii Golovnin to Kodiak in 1818. His report
constitutes a major source of information on Father Herman's life and
character during the last two decades of his earthly life. Father Herman
was invited to dine with Golovnin aboard his frigate. Golovnin was an
intelligent, well educated gentleman, surrounded by twenty-five of the
best officers in the fleet when Father Herman, a simple, poorly schooled,
little old man in thread-bare clothing, met him. But Father Herman
began posing questions which confounded them all.

"What do you love most? What is dearest to you? What would make
you happy?" he asked them. One wanted money, another fame, another a
beautiful wife, another his own ship—and many other things. Father
Herman said, "Is it not true that of all your answers and desires, one thing
may be concluded: each of you gentlemen requires whatever he thinks is
best and loves most?

They all agreed. Then he said to them, "What, though, can be better,
higher than all else, more worthy of love and more splendid than our Lord
Jesus Christ himself, who created the world and adorned everything in it,
who gave life to everything, who keeps everything, feeds everything, loves
everything, who is Love Himself! Should you not love God above all
things, and wish for Him, to seek Him?" Everyone answered, "But of
course. Naturally!" They even answered, "Of course we love God!" At
this, Father Herman sighed and said, "And I, poor sinner, have been
trying these forty years to learn how to love God, and I cannot say I even
now love Him properly, for if we love someone, we think of them always,
we try to please them day and night, our heart and mind are full of the
object of our love." Then he asked, "So then, gentlemen, do you love
God? Do you turn to Him often? Do you remember Him always, pray
always to Him, and do His will, according to the Scriptures?" They had to
admit that they did not. "For our good, for our happiness," he concluded,
"let us vow that from this day, from this hour, from this very minute, we
should try to love God above all else and carry out His teachings."[34]

Golovnin's Findings

By the time Golovnin arrived at Kodiak, Baranov had finally retired

34 Oleksa, *op. cit.*, p 52.

and had been replaced by a new manager, Hagemeister. When he asked about the condition of the mission, Golovnin learned that the monks had had hardly enough to live on. Moreover, several attempts had been made to kill Father Herman. Baranov had written disparagingly about him back in 1800,

> We have a monk here...worse than Makarii...He is a greater talker and likes to write. Even though he keeps to his cell most of the time, not even attending services here out of fear of worldly temptations, he knows nevertheless everything we think and do, not only during the day, but also at night. By means of pious cajoling, he extracts the information he wants from students and from among the servants here, and sometimes even from our own men. His principal helper is our "Mr Interpreter" [Osip Priannishnikov] who is so zealous when it concerns our chastity.[35]

But, Father Herman, in turn, had very little positive to say about Baranov. The second part of Golovnin's report contains Father Herman's testimony about the years of the Baranov regime. The inspector stated:

> The main accusation against the company is that it exhausts the Aleuts by work. Besides the yearly program of hunting parties, they were sent on remote hunting expeditions, lasting several years, where they died of hunger and privations, while in the villages their families, left without a hunter, were underfed and died prematurely; in that respect, I wanted to know in what proportion the native population had increased or decreased under the company's administration. Company agents were also accused of taking away wives and daughters to make concubines of them. I asked the Elder Herman if the company watched over the piety and morals of its employees, if the feast days were celebrated, the services attended, if the newly baptized were brought to take the oath of allegiance to the tsar [and become citizens], etc. Lastly I asked the same Father Herman how justice was administered, how punishments were inflicted.

> In response, the superior of the mission, the monk Herman replied that the company has never given the necessary material to keep registers of births and deaths; that women are indeed suffering greatly from the unrestricted domination of local managers over the Natives and no measure has been taken to protect piety and ethics, and that there has never been any justice; the will of one man decides everything and inflicts punishments.[36]

This testimony was given in 1818. Father Herman had been in Alaska 24 years. The Baranov regime had lasted thirty. Rezanov had "inspected"

35 Pierce, *History of the Russian American Company*, Vol. 2, *op. cit.*, p. 121.
36 Golovin, "Report," in *Naval Review* (St Petersburg, 1822), tr. by Vsevolod Roshchau in *Orthodox Alaska*, vol. 2, no. 2-3 (Kodiak, 1970-71), p. 5.

the colony fifteen years earlier and sided completely with Baranov, neu-
tralizing Father Gideon's critical report. Golovnin's findings, based primarily on Father Herman's testimony, however, had a significant impact
on the government's attitude and company operations in the years ahead.

Simeon Yanovskii

Before actually meeting Father Herman, the newly-appointed governor of the colony, Simeon Yanovskii, had heard nothing good about him
from the company men in Sitka. Even back in St Petersburg he had heard
how Father Herman incited the Natives to rebellion. As if he was aware of
this, Father Herman took the initiative, writing to Yanovskii before he
visited Kodiak and describing the condition of the community to him.

> Although perhaps you know me only by rumors, you have thus opened to me
> the way of boldness; confident in your generosity, allow me to speak: This
> country has been entrusted to our nation like a new-born baby, still incapable
> of acquiring knowledge...It is in need not only of protection but support...There-
> fore, I appeal to you in the name of these people, myself being their humble
> servant and nurse, writing my appeal with tears of blood: be a father and patron
> for us...wipe the tears of defenseless orphans, refresh our hearts burning with the
> fever of suffering; let us know what consolation is.[37]

When Yanovskii came to Kodiak he called on Father Herman immediately, and visited him daily. Promising to bring justice and relief to
the Aleuts proved a huge undertaking. That winter an epidemic swept the
island. Yanovskii described the scene:

> The epidemic affected everyone, even tiny babies...The death rate was so high
> that after three days there was no one to dig the graves, and bodies lay around
> unburied...Only Father Herman was not ill. God in His invisible way protected
> his faithful servant. The elder visited the sick, comforting, praying, healing some
> and preparing others for death, as well as praying for those who had already fallen
> asleep.[38]

During the final decade of Father Herman's life, he had to endure the
hostility of the young parish priest assigned to Kodiak, Father Frumentii
Mordovskii. Convinced that within Father Herman's cell a fortune in
gold was hidden, Mordovskii persuaded the local company manager to
search New Valaam, and even chopped apart part of the floor with an axe
in his attempt to locate the buried treasure. Of course there was no gold,

37 Oleksa, *op. cit.*, p. 310.
38 Bearne, *op. cit.*, p. 84.

but Father Mordovskii never ceased to believe that Father Herman was living a depraved life in the forests of Spruce Island.

The elder spent most of his last years secluded at "Monk's Lagoon," caring for the children at the orphanage and school he operated with the help of two Creole disciples, Sophia Vlasov and Gerasim Zyrianov. The characteristic features of Father Herman's life and personality can be discerned from their memoirs, together with Golovnin's and Yanovskii's reports, and the short biography of the elder compiled by Constantine Larionov, another Kodiak Creole who helped gather material for his "Life" when Valaam monastery asked for it. From these documents emerges an image of a traditional Orthodox ascetic who spent his nights in prayer, his days in physical work and service, continually fasting, constantly joyful, welcoming every opportunity to be of assistance to others. On the Feast of Epiphany each year, Father Herman would await the descent of an angel who would sanctify his spring. He would give the water to any who became sick during the following year, and, with his prayers, they regained their health. The healing qualities of this spring, which continues to flow on Spruce Island today, are recognized by the entire population of Kodiak, and many modern Aleuts testify to the miraculous cures God has worked through this holy stream. During the 1819 epidemic, Father Herman not only comforted the sick and dying, but cured many as well. This healing function played an important role in convincing the Sugpiaq of the truth of the Christian message, that the Christian sacred stories, ceremonies, and the entire tradition expressed ultimate Reality. It was clear that when a person lived this Christian life sincerely and intensely, as Father Herman had, one could be restored to the original, "natural" human condition, and "work miracles." It was in this manner that Father Herman verified and authenticated Christianity to the Sugpiaq, thus fulfilling, to some extent, the prophetic function of their ancient shamans.

According to modern Kodiak tradition, the local shamans had predicted the arrival of the monks and advised the people to welcome them and heed their instruction, although they themselves did not do so. Thus, much to the surprise of the missionaries, the people received them warmly rather than fleeing as they usually did when an intruder approached. If this traditional story is accurate, it indicates that the old shamans played an important role in preparing their people for the coming of the Gospel.

Aleut Orthodoxy

The transition to Eastern Orthodoxy from the shamanistic religious tradition common to the Unangan, Yup'ik and Sugpiaq cultures required several generations. However, it caused little disruption to Native society, for a variety of reasons. The structures of pre-contact worldview and the Orthodox Christian vision paralleled and complemented each other in many significant ways. The monastic mission studied the earlier Native tradition in order to present Christianity in intelligible terms, emphasizing similarities while introducing the truly unique features of their faith, the incarnation and resurrection of Jesus Christ. Orthodox theology and the liturgical tradition of the Eastern Church provided the context for this approach, and the historical evolution of monasticism and the historical experience of Siberian as well as Finnish monastic missions supplied practical guidelines for the evangelization of the Americans. Father Gideon's early work in Sugpiaq, and later Father John Veniaminov's studies in Unangan and Tlingit, came from the tradition established a thousand years earlier by SS Cyril and Methodius, and continued by the Perm, Kazan, and Irkutsk missions in Russia. Thus, the missionaries acted in accordance with the basic presuppositions of their Church and national culture.

The following chart illustrates the transition from one belief system to the other:

Pre-contact Shamanism	Orthodox Christianity
Mythology/Sacred Stories	Bible
Imitation of ancestral or cosmic (eternally significant) acts	Imitation of Jesus Christ
"Taboos": System of regulations for proper human behavior	Moral/ethical laws and standards; the Ten Commandments
Initiation by ritual death and rebirth	Baptism and Chrismation as ritual burial and sanctification

Pre-contact Shamanism	Orthodox Christianity
Yua/Inua: the life force that animates and enlivens everything	*logoi*, the life-giving and God-oriented power which directs and motivates everything toward the Logos, who recapitulates them all in Himself.
Annual festivals to appease spirits and celebrate/represent the sacred stories	Annual cycle of feasts, celebrating and commemorating crucial events of the life of Christ: "salvation history"
Ceremonies: music, dance and art as symbolic representations of primordial characters and events	Worship cycle: vespers, liturgy, icons, singing, architecture and vestments symbolize the reality and presence of the Kingdom which is to come.
Kassaq (master of ceremonies)	Clergy, choir director
Shaman: one who experiences the reality to which the myths refer and can deal with that reality in order to heal and prophesy	Saint: one who lives the Christian life fully, becoming God-like through *theosis*, restored to full humanity

In the Kodiak Mission, all of these parallels were fulfilled by the deliberate missionary policy of the monks, and by the life of Father Herman, who was, due to the overwhelming popular veneration of him by the Native people, officially added to the list (canon) of saints of the Orthodox Church on August 9, 1970, and is known today throughout the world as "St Herman of Alaska."

His troparion (festal hymn) refers to him as "Teacher and Apostle of the True Faith, Intercessor and Defender of the Oppressed, Adornment of the Orthodox Church in America..." His relics are enshrined within Holy Resurrection Church at Kodiak, and thousands of Orthodox Christians from all parts of the world come annually to celebrate his memory, to visit New Valaam, and to ask for his intercessions before God.

6

The Legacy of St Innocent Veniaminov

John Veniaminov was probably the most remarkable Alaskan of his century, perhaps of all time. His life and accomplishments have been well documented in excellent biographies in Russian and English. In popular histories he has often been singled out as the one truly bright spot in the darkness of the Russian-American colony. One of the first twentieth century scholars to produce a series of articles on Veniaminov, Father Andrew P. Kashevarov, published his work in 1927. Himself an heir to the multi-lingual educational program inaugurated by Veniaminov, Father Kashevarov, literate in Russian, English, Unangan and Tlingit, founded the Alaska Territorial Historical Library and Museum while serving St Nicholas Church in Juneau, the capital city. He wrote:

> In 1823, an order from the Holy Synod at Moscow was received at Irkutsk in which it was required that a priest be sent to take charge of the Unalaska district. What information was at hand regarding Unlaska came from *promyshlenniki* returning with furs, and these men pictured it as a wild country, inhabited by savages. When the order was made public and volunteers were asked for, there was no response, for the idea of going to such a wild country deterred them all from accepting the offers held out by the ruling bishop of Irkutsk. Time was passing; the order remained unanswered and the situation was fast becoming unpleasant for the bishop, when one day Father Veniaminov offered his services.

> This offer, coming from a promising young priest, puzzled the bishop who did not like to lose a man who stood so highly in the service. Upon interrogation, Father Veniaminov explained that he had met a man from Unalaska who pictured the life there as less harsh than it was generally thought to be, and he said the man from Unalaska told him many affecting stories of the Aleuts, of their kind, sympathetic and likeable nature, and their eager desire to be instructed in Christianity.

> For some time the bishop withheld his approval, but seeing that the young priest was determined to go, he reluctantly gave his consent and appointed him missionary for the Unalaska district. At the time, Father Veniaminov's family consisted of his wife, his mother, one brother and a very young son...

> ...Father Veniaminov brought his family to Okhotsk, where they boarded a ship

for Sitka, and from Sitka sailed to Unalaska on another ship, in which they finally reached their destination after fourteen months of travel, on July 29, 1824.

Beginning the Great Work

At Unalaska, the family, for want of quarters and houses, settled in a native *barabara* (a traditional semi-subterranean hut). Father John found a very small and dilapidated church at this site, and saw that the Natives were kindly people, but very ignorant of Christian teachings. During the first year, his principal work was to prepare sufficient material for building the church and the dwelling house, and this is where his thorough knowledge of mechanical work proved quite useful. He instructed the Natives in manual work, taught them carpentry, blacksmithing, brick laying, and masonry, and in the meantime strenuously applied himself to the study of their language, beliefs, customs, and traditions. It is surprising how quickly he acquired the language, familiarized himself so thoroughly with the character, the mental state, and the abilities of these Natives. And only then did he begin to apply the Christian teachings to his people. He did not change them too radically or too suddenly, and that is where his wonderful talent as a teacher and a missionary shows itself.

After all the material was at hand, he began the actual building of the church; the cornerstone was laid on July 1, 1825, and history tells us that most of the work on the building was done with his own hands. The work of christianizing the people then progressed successfully. Again history tells us that he made use of Native ideas in propounding Biblical truths. He began to travel among the many islands of the Aleutian group, going from one island to another, preaching, studying the language and the customs. One must understand that he did not have ships, launches, or boats to travel in. He used the *bidarka* [kayak] in which he covered hundreds of miles along that treacherous and dangerous coast.

The Aleut Bible

About this time he began his monumental work of translating the Gospel of St Matthew into [Unangan] Aleut. His subsequent labor in that line was a partial translation of the Gospel of St Luke...and the inspiring pamphlet, "Indication of the Way into the Kingdom of Heaven."[1]

In this translation work, Veniaminov was assisted by the Aleut chief Ivan Pan'kov, whom Veniaminov insisted be credited with his contribution on the title page. Together, like SS Cyril and Methodius a thousand years before among the Slavs, they devised a unique alphabet for Unangan Aleut and collaborated in devising the first primers for teaching native language literacy to adults and children.

1   Oleksa (1987), *op. cit.*, p. 344-345; English translation of "Indication," p. 80-119.

Ivan Pan'kov was chief of Tigal'da and descended from the organizers of the ill-fated uprising two generations before Veniaminov's coming. Records indicate that when the priest arrived, the Pan'kovs contributed generously to a monetary gift the parish presented to Veniaminov to ease his family's adjustment to their new home. He was already well acquainted with Orthodoxy, preaching in his village on major holidays, but how he learned theology is not clear. Dr Lydia Black, a world-renowned specialist in Aleutian studies, has worked to uncover the biographical details of Pan'kov's life. "There is no doubt," Dr Black writes, "that some of the *promyshlenniki* established and maintained cordial relations with the Aleuts; still others settled among them...That some *promyshlenniki* aided the Aleuts in their own conflicts is mentioned by Veniaminov."[2]

Dimitri Pan'kov, a *promyshlenik* who made three voyages to the Aleutians, enjoyed the respect and trust of the Unangan. During the uprising in 1764, when other expeditions were attacked, their ships burned and crews killed in the area, Pan'kov returned safely home with the richest cargoes. He seems most probably to be allied to the Tilgalda chief, Ivan Pan'kov's father Gavriil [Gabriel], or another of Ivan's older relatives.

Black continues:

> It is well known that some *promyshlenniki* acted as missonaries, and many administered baptism...As a rule, the newly baptized Aleut was given a Christian [saint's] name and the surname of his Russian godfather. Further, apparently on the basis of ritual rank, economic partnerships were created...In Russian practice, godparents are responsible for the spiritual and educational needs of their godchildren. This obligation would extend to the children of an Aleut with whom such a ritual connection was formed. It is possible to postulate that Dimitri Pan'kov...was charged with the supervision of Ivan's schooling. Ivan, who at the time of Pan'kov's last recorded voyage in 1786 would have been eight years old, probably was taken to Russia. I see, then, a very small Aleut boy, possibly a hostage, perhaps a godson, taken on a Russian ship to one of the ports on the Pacific and possibly traveling to a Russian town. I see him sent to school, surely at his sponsor's expense, perhaps living in his sponsor's household, a literate and religious household. I see a young man returning to the islands to assume his position in the Aleut social order as a chief or chief-to-be, trying to to make sense out of his experience in two different and conflicting worlds. And I see a mature man seizing the opportunity, provided by his meeting with Veniaminov, to reconcile these worlds.[3]

2 Lydia T. Black, "Ivan Pan'kov: Architect of Aleut Literacy"(*Orthodox Alaska*, Vol. 7, No. 4, Kodiak, AK, 1978), p. 8.

3 *Ibid.*, p. 9.

When Veniaminov travelled, Ivan Pan'kov served as his guide, informant, and interpreter. He helped the priest to make contact with important witnesses to the devastation wrought by Solov'ev sixty years earlier. He checked Veniaminov's Unangan language work and proofread the catechism before its publication. Father John wrote of him:

> I call upon...Pan'kov, the best interpreter in the entire chain. He is a native-born Aleut, but knows Russian well, speaking it without any accent, and he is literate. He is forty-nine years of age, lives in a a settlement where only Aleuts reside; so there can be no doubt about his perfect knowledge of his own language. The catechism was translated with his help...[4]

While working on the translation of the Gospel of Matthew, Veniaminov stayed with the Pan'kov on Akun Island. They were so grateful to have completed this work that Veniaminov recorded they celebrated a Thanksgiving Service on October 6, 1829, to mark the occasion.

Pan'kov was not the only extraordinary Unangan Veniaminov encountered during his first years in the Aleutians. In November 1829, he reported to his bishop his remarkable encounter with an Unangan "shaman":

> In 1828, I made a *bidarka* journey to the island of Akun, for the purpose of ministering to the Natives there. On coming close to the beach, all the people of the village dressed in their best clothes were gathered on the shore, evidently for my reception. On getting out of the *bidarka*, I asked the meaning of this. They answered that they knew I was coming and came out to greet me and welcome me to their island. I asked why they were so "dressed up" and they said, "We knew that you had left Unalaska for this island and would be here today, and to show our joy, we came here to welcome you."

> "And who told you I would be here today, and how did you recognize me as Father Veniaminov?"

> "Our shaman, old man Smirennikov, told us that you had started from Unalaska and would be here today, that you will teach us about God and how to pray to him."

> Later I met old man Smirennikov. He was about sixty years of age. He was believed to be a shaman. The reason for this was that this man performed unexplainable manifestations. One of the most striking was this: One woman, the wife of Theodor Zharov, stepped on a Klipts trap (a wooden trap powered by twisted rawhide which catches its victim by a single tong pressing against a flat board), thereby very severely injuring her knee. The barbs on the lever of the

4   *Ibid.*, p. 15.

trap, about two inches long, struck her knee cap, causing a very painful and dangerous wound. Blood poisoning had set in and the woman was at death's door. In fact, there did not seem to be any hope for her recovery. The relatives of the women appealed to Smirennikov for help. He came to see the woman, and after looking at her for a short time he said, "She will be well in the morning."

To everyone's surprise, the next morning this woman arose from her sickbed, perfectly well, with no indication of the wound or soreness in her knee.

Another striking incident was his help in procuring food for the whole village. During the winter of 1825, the Natives of Akun village were entirely without food. Some of the more venturesome asked old man Smirennikov to give the people of Akun a whale, so that they would not die of starvation. He said, "I will ask for it." Shortly afterwards, he came with the information that if they would go to a certain beach on the island they would find the whale they had asked for. All went to the designated spot and found the whale on the beach.

This instance of his wonderful prophetic power was borne out by his knowledge of my movements at a distance so great that he could not possibly have known about me unless he possessed occult powers... Similar narratives, confirmed by many reputable witnesses, induced me to interrogate old man Smirennikov. My desire was to know how he could know certain events ahead of time and by what means he cured sickness. Thanking me for posing these questions, he told me the following:

"Shortly after I was baptized by Father Makarii, first one, then two men appeared to me. They were not visible to others, but I could see them and talk to them, and they spoke to me. They had white faces and were dressed in clothing similar to the paintings in the church (representing Archangel Gabriel)."

These spirits told the old man that they were sent by God to teach the people and to guard them from harm. During the course of thirty years, these spirits appeared to him almost daily. They instructed him in the tenets of the Christian religion and the mysteries of faith. It is unnecessary here to repeat all that he said on the subject, for what he said were really the teachings of Christ.

These spirits rendered him, and through him to other people on the island, help in sickness, distress and trouble. In this connection, the spirits always said that they would ask God and if He were willing to help, the help would be received. Once in so often, he would acquaint the people with events taking place in other remote regions. In this, the spirits invariably said that what they told him was not of their own power, but came from God.

I asked him, "How do they teach you to pray? Do they want you to bow yourself down to them and pray to them?" He answered, "They teach me to pray to God alone. To pray in spirit and with a pure heart. They often prayed with me for long periods."

I gave him the following instructions: "I can plainly see that the spirits who visit you are good spirits, and you must follow their teachings. To those who ask you for help you must say that they must ask God themselves; God is our Father and He will help those who put their trust in Him. I do not forbid you to render help to those who are ill, but in helping them, you must explain that it is not you who gives this help, but God by His mighty power."

Veniaminov then asked if he could meet these spirits, and Smirennikov said he would have to ask them. The next day he came to Father John and told him that the spirits were willing to see him and let him see them. Reconsidering, Veniaminov concluded that he only wanted to see them out of curiosity, and if he did see them, it might make him proud of this distinction. He decided instead to report the matter to his bishop and ask for his advice, producing the account reproduced here.[5] A year later he received an affirmative response from his bishop, but when Father John returned to Akun, he learned that Smirennikov had died.

Priest and Scientist

Father Kashevarov, a century later, described Veniaminov's pastoral and scientific work at Unalaska:

Having mastered the Aleut language, he compiled a Grammar of the Aleutian-Fox Language. Commenting on this work he says: "In compiling the grammar of a language like the Aleutian, at first I deemed it to be useless; I knew it was of no use to the Aleuts, for without this grammar they can express themselves correctly to each other; neither was it of any particular value to foreigners. But knowing with what..eagerness many scientists are collecting all sorts of information, and how important every little discovery is to them, I decided to compile a grammar...It cannot be possible that the Aleutian language had any other spoken tongue similar to it, but that the grammar could show some evidence of its origin."

Aside from his literary work, the indefatigable missionary, during his ten years in this district, studied the climatic conditions, the population and products of the Unalaska area. From these scientific studies we have an authentic work, *Notes on the Unalaska District*. In the matter of industries, he also has rendered unprecedented service.

Having thoroughly acquainted himself with the fauna of the islands..especially the fur seal...he offered as a result of his extensive investigations certain valuable suggestions to the fur company for more sensible and scientific modes for

5   Oleksa,(1987) *op. cit.*, p. 132-135.

harvesting these animals. The suggestions were accepted and applied, and not only saved the seal herd from depletion, but also from complete extermination, thereby enriching the company by thousands of rubles.

When he first arrived at Unalaska, Veniaminov lived in a *barabara,* but later he himself built a good wooden house. The furniture was also made by him, as well as the wall clock; his practical mind and mechanical ability made him capable of meeting all the varied problems of life on the frontier, and of performing all the tasks necessary for his comfort and that of his family in this pioneer situation. He spent his evenings in mechanical pursuits, making clocks, hand organs, musical instruments. He made the candles for his churches. He not only taught the boys' school, but compiled the school books for use in that and other similar institutions in Alaska.[6]

Veniaminov later became bishop of Alaska and ultimately Metropolitan of Moscow. He was canonized by the Russian Orthodox Church as "St Innocent, Enlightener of the Aleuts," fifty years after Father Kashevarov's articles appeared.

Early Education in Russian America

Gregory Shelikov reported that he had founded a school at Three Saints Bay as early as 1784, but its impact was limited to a few local hostages. Archimandrite Joasaph, however, continued to operate a small school during his brief stay on Kodiak, and later Father Gideon's school attracted several hundred students. Even before any permanent settlement had been established in Alaska, *promyshlenniki* had been taking Aleut children to Siberia, where many became literate in Russian and familiar with a trade. Count Nikolai Rezanov, regardless of how depraved his personal character may have been, had the decency to pose publicly as a cultured and enlightened aristocrat, and donated over a thousand books to the Sitka library in 1803. Six hundred of the volumes were in Russian, three hundred in French, one hundred thirty in German, English and Latin, and the remainder in Swedish, Dutch, Spanish and Italian. Father Herman ran his orphanage and school on Spruce Island for three decades.

In 1805, the company administration decreed that within twenty years, Natives and Creoles should be serving as navigators, seamen, master craftsmen, "and eventually administrators." The next year, Prokopii Mal'tsov was taken to St Petersburg to study ship design. He proved to be

6   *Ibid.,* p. 349.

an excellent student, and upon graduation from the Kronstadt naval academy he was sent home to Sitka aboard the *Neva*. The ship, with Baranov's replacement and seventy-six passengers sank near Mount Edgecombe on January 9, 1813. Only twenty-two survivors were rescued. Search teams found little cargo, but discovered an icon of the Archangel Michael standing upright on the beach. This original painting, typical of the westernized "Italian" style of that period, is enshrined today at St Michael's Cathedral in the old capital of Russian America.

Within ten years of the company's 1805 edict, two schools at Sitka were training two hundred Native and Creole students, and the first Creole navigators were sailing aboard company ships. In 1825, four Creole boys were studying medicine, anatomy and surgery in Europe.

Father Veniaminov conducted his Unangan literacy and religious education classes at Unalaska during his final years there, then in 1834 entrusted operation of that school to his successor while he, first as priest and later as Bishop Innocent, organized a much more elaborate school at Sitka. This "All-Colonial School" was intended to be a secondary boarding school, but its curriculum included much more of what would today be considered college-level work: mathematics, history, medicine, Latin, Russian grammar, Native languages, rhetoric, geography, penmanship, logic, physics, astronomy, navigational science and biblical studies. The entire educational effort was, as stipulated by the company charter, financed by the Russian American Company, but the actual staffing of the schools consisted of Orthodox clergy and volunteers, most of whom were Creole.

Iakov Netsvetov

The first priest to serve in the western Aleutians, Father Iakov Netsvetov, was himself a Creole, whose father, Igor, had been among the first Russian workers sent to St George Island, becoming manager there by 1818. Igor's Atkan wife raised three sons and a daughter, all of whom were given a good education, probably at their father's (rather than at company) expense. Iakov's brothers both served the company, one as a sea captain, the other as a shipbuilder. His sister married a well-educated Creole, Gregory Terent'ev, at Sitka. Their son Iakov later trained to be a church reader under Father Iakov's guidance at Atka. Distinguished as the careers of his siblings were, however, Archpriest Iakov's accomplishments surpassed them all.

Born at St George in 1804, Iakov Igorovich spent his early years being taught reading and writing at home and preparing for studies at the Irkutsk seminary, from which he graduated in 1826. In Siberia he married Anna, a young Russian girl, and was then ordained and sent to Atka, his mother's birthplace and the site of his father's retirement and 1837 burial. The newly-ordained pastor travelled to Sitka, where he was cooly received by the rather anti-clerical Governor Chistiakov. Believing that the Russian American Company's first obligation was to earn profits for its shareholders, the chief administrator resented being obliged to support the church. It seems he was also a racist, opposing and attempting to prohibit Russian-Native marriages, and this may explain his unenthusiastic reception of the first Creole priest.

Aboard the sloop *Baikal,* with his wife and father, Netsvetov sailed from New Archangel on May 19, 1828, and arrived at Atka three weeks later. He wrote in his journal that the village

consisted of seven houses, four of which are for office use and the remaining three for living quarters for the Russians, Creoles and Aleuts. The household establishments are (a) reserve stores of goods and furs...(b) a retail store for selling the goods and supplies at fixed prices, (c) the so-called food *barabara*...(d) a barn for the cattle and (e) other buildings necessary for the economy. Creoles and Aleuts are the original inhabitants of the Atka district. They were converted to the Greek-Russian Church at the same time as the Fox-Aleuts, i.e., in 1790... All local Aleuts were baptized by Russian laymen except those who had the opportunity to visit the places where priests were stationed. Thus, I found the original inhabitants already baptized..., it remained for me only to establish them in the faith and chrismate [confirm] them.[7]

Initially, Netsvetov had to set up a tent chapel, but began construction of a church building as soon as he had unpacked and settled into his quarters. This endeavor was doubly necessary because the legendary winds which sweep the archipelago often made it impossible to conduct services in the tent.

In the autumn of 1829, Netsvetov wrote in his journal:

I made my wish about making a trip to Amlia Island known to the manager of

7 Lydia Black, *The Journals of Iakov Netsvetov: the Atka Years* (Limestone Press, Kingston, Ont., 1980) p. 13.

the Atka office, and he issued me his written approval on September 21, and informed me about the cases needing my attention, particularly matrimonial matters...On September 26, at 8:00 a.m., I loaded my prayer tent and necessary church things on *baidarkas* and put out to sea in a three-oared *baidarka*, accompanied by the manager, Sizukh, in another three-oared *baidarka*. Besides, we had several *baidarkas* with baggage and assistants...

Amlia village is located on the southwest side of the island, on a small open bay...There were not many buildings as the Aleuts only recently began to settle here and had not yet built their houses. The chief lived in a small skin tent, and I stayed with him. The Aleuts lived in scattered skin tents and mud huts. The company structures were not yet built, except for a food *barabara* where all the food supplies were kept. Most of the inhabitants were Aleuts with a few Creoles among them. The total population is about 300. They are governed by a chief who looks after the order and well-being of his people and a timely provision of sufficient food supply for them. The chief must be active, sagacious and considerate. The administrator general of the colonies grants him full freedom in managing the Aleuts in their occupations on land or at sea.[8]

While at Amlia, Father Iakov performed ten weddings, thus legalizing prior bonds between couples and registering their children as legitimate. All this was necessary for social and economic reasons, especially since the children of mixed (Russian-Native) parentage had officially been citizens of the Empire since 1818. At that time, the government decreed that the company was responsible for the education of all fatherless Creole children, who were to be trained at company expense and serve as apprentices until the age of sixteen, then assigned to various occupations until age twenty, and paid a regular salary, plus food and clothing. The most talented were to be promoted, receive privileges and titles, and advance to the status of district managers. Registering the births of Creole children was an important clerical responsibility, therefore, and Igor Netsvetov had requested that his personal friend, Governor Murav'ev, certify Iakov as his legitimate son in writing when the family had visited Sitka in 1824, even though he was anxious for his sons to escape all obligations to the company.

Father Iakov's parish included Amchitka Island, where fifty "free" Aleuts, not employed by the company, traded their furs with a resident company agent, and Attu, where about 120 Aleuts, "all baptized" by 1830, were governed by their chief. Besides these scattered Aleutian

8   *Ibid.*, pp. 20-21.

communities, Father Netsvetov had to visit Bering Island, where 75 Russians, Creoles and a few Unangan hunted and trapped for the company, and the Kuril Islands, just north of Japan and hundreds of miles from Atka. It was always with great relief that he returned home after the long months of travelling on the open sea in a tiny *baidarka*.

In November of 1830, the chapel at Atka was consecrated. That year, Netsvetov recorded 32 births, 11 weddings, and 24 deaths, at Atka and Amlia, and 9 births, 200 chrismations, 30 marriages, and 6 deaths on Amchitka, Attu, Bering and Copper Islands. In early 1831, the new Governor, Baron von Wrangell, entrusted Father Iakov with the organization of the Atka school, and assigned John Galaktionov, a Creole medical student, to assist him. A rather disorganized attempt at starting a school at Atka had already been made in 1827, but by October 25, 1831, Netsvetov had constructed a two-room schoolhouse, which opened the following day with twenty Aleut and Creole boarding students. Netsvetov taught catechism, ethics and biblical studies twice a week, while Galaktionov served as reading instructor.

In 1833, Netsvetov began construction of a new house for his family, into which they moved in late October. No sooner was this complete when work began on a chapel at Amlia. He spent the next several years making regular pastoral visits to his far-flung flock and teaching school at Atka. In 1835, his wife Anna Simeonovna Netsvetov became seriously ill, and Father Iakov decided to send her to Sitka where the best medical facilities in the colony were available. However, she died there of cancer in March, 1836, and in June that year, the new house burned down. Life during the next few years must have been very lonely for the ever-active missionary.

In May 1837, Father Veniaminov's wife Catherine stopped at Atka on her way home to Siberia to visit her family. She too would soon die while her husband was in St Petersburg, petitioning for permission and funds to publish his Unangan translations. Father Netsvetov administered Holy Communion to Matushka Veniaminov before she sailed to Okhotsk.

Sometime during the next five years, Netsvetov began work on his translations of the Scriptures into Atkan. Although this project consumed much of his time, he seems to have felt increasingly isolated and alone. He petitioned to be replaced at Atka, and the bishop in Irkutsk in principle approved, requiring him to remain at his post until a replacement could be appointed. Netsvetov waited for seven more years. Atka, however, became more enjoyable when his brother-in-law Gregory Terent'ev was assigned there. The next governor, Etolin, was also a personal friend, and by 1840 Veniaminov, his long-time colleague, had returned to Alaska as Bishop Innocent.

Encouraged by Veniaminov, Netsvetov applied himself to the work of compiling alternate translations for the Gospel of St Matthew in the Atkan dialect, which differs significantly from the dialect of Unalaska, and compiling the largest Unangan dictionary ever produced. In 1841, Father Iakov recorded in his journal that he had cured at Amlia a woman "possessed," stating that after he had read some prayers (probably exorcisms) she returned to normal. He brought her with him to Atka until he was convinced that she had been completely cured.

Beginning in 1842, Unangan was also employed in worship in the Atkan and Unalaskan churches, using Netsvetov's translations. By this time the Atkan school, whose staff included John Ladygin and Laurence Salamatov, had graduated dozens of Aleut and Creole students, who were productive members of the company staff, managing the local affairs, keeping the books, charting the coasts, and sailing around the world.

Father Netsvetov and the Yukon Mission

In 1842, Bishop Innocent Veniaminov opened the seminary at New Archangel, fulfilling Archimandrite Joasaph's 1795 goal of training indigenous Alaskan clergy on American soil. Renewed interest in Native languages and the expansion of the Orthodox mission into new regions also characterized the early years of St Innocent's episcopate. Father Iakov Netsvetov was called to Sitka, not to retirement as he had requested, but to be transferred first to Kenai, and later to the Kushokwin-Yukon Delta, which the bishop considered more important. Netsvetov brought with him his nephew Basil, Deacon Innocent Shaiashnikov (a former student at Atka) and subdeacon Constantine Lukin, son of Kolmakovskii manager Simeon Lukin and his Kodiak Alutiiq wife.

Netsevetov's Yukon journals reveal the difficulties he faced and the humility and dedication with which he overcame them. His eighteen years on the Kushokwin-Yukon inaugurated a period of Creole and Native Alaskan dominance of the Eskimo mission. His diaries represent the first detailed view of Alaskan Eskimo culture before radical changes disrupted the traditional lifestyle of the indigenous people on Alaska's two main rivers. Simeon Lukin's sons, Ivan and Constantine, both played active roles in the affairs of the Orthodox church after the sale of Alaska. The older, Ivan, managed his father's trading post until 1860, when he was sent by the company to locate the "English settlement" (Fort Yukon). Disguised as an Indian, and travelling with a party or Ingalik or Koyukon Indian friends, Ivan visited Fort Yukon several times, sending important information to company headquarters in Sitka after each trip. A few years later, Ivan served as guide and interpreter for the Western Union Telegraph Expedition, although his talents were hardly appreciated by the patronizing and often contemptuous American leaders. To them, the exceptionally well-educated Ivan was merely a "half-breed." Ivan Lukin was probably responsible for the construction of the chapel at Kolmakovskii Redoubt.

Ivan's younger brother Constantine, an expert hunter, was taught the "four R's" at home before being assigned to assist Father Netsvetov. He guided Father Iakov back and forth from St Michael's on the Bering Sea to Shageluk, hundreds of kilometers inland, by dog sled, kayak and canoe from 1845 until his dismissal in 1861. Throughout these years, Lukin and Netsvetov energetically dispensed medicine and vaccinated Natives to prevent the devastation that smallpox had brought to other parts of Alaska. Constantine probably served as a blacksmith at Russian Mission and built the first church in the Kuskokwim-Yukon Delta. The roots of Orthodox Christianity on the lower Yukon and Kuskokwim Rivers, therefore, reach back to the time of Father Netsvetov from St George Island and his Creole assistants, whose ancestors came from Kodiak.

The huge territory Netsvetov and Lukin served required additional personnel, and at Father Iakov's request, an assistant was eventually recruited for St Michael's Redoubt in 1849. Hieromonk Filaret, however, was not an enthusiastic volunteer but an unhappy misfit, sent to Alaska against his will, whose superiors apparently made use of the opportunity to rid themselves of this undesirable priest-monk by shipping him off to the American colony. Filaret seems to have hated Alaska and the Yukon from the start, and to have taken all his resentment and bitterness out on Netsvetov. After only a few weeks at Father Iakov's headquarters at Russian Mission, Filaret attacked his colleague with a pistol and later with an axe, and had to be bound hand and foot, then locked in a steam bath until he regained his composure. Constantine Lukin later escorted him to St Michael's, where he performed no priestly services for a year, and he was subsequently removed by the company to Sitka.

Netsvetov's next "assistant" was even worse. The truly insane Hieromonk Gavriil (Gabriel) arrived two years later. Although this unfortunate man's instability was apparent to all who met him, it took time for the bureaucracy to intervene. Defrocked and deprived of all financial support, Gabriel barricaded himself in his cabin at St Michael's Redoubt and refused to leave, even after he was ordered to sail to Sitka. He died in 1860 convinced that Netsvetov was trying to poison him.

Even more tragically, Gabriel's reports from St Michael's included ridiculous but serious accusations against Netsvetov and Lukin. No one who knew these Creole missionaries or their careers could take the allegations seriously, especially considering their source. But a new bishop from European Russia had just been assigned to Alaska. Completely unfamiliar with Alaskan history or conditions, Bishop Peter summoned Netsvetov and Lukin to Sitka.

Of course, Netsvetov was cleared of all charges, but in the course of the investigation, Constantine's irregular marital situation was uncovered. He had been living with a Yup'ik woman, technically the wife of Makar Nugagleksa, since 1851. Netsevtov must have been aware of this, but it is not known why he did not intervene. Perhaps he viewed this as one of those extraordinary situations defined by Bishop Michael of Irkutsk and reiterated by Bishop Veniaminov, in which missionaries were instructed to respect the local marriage customs. The administration in Sitka saw things differently. Lukin was removed from his position and his common-law wife returned to her legal husband. A few weeks later, Constantine died, either from an attack of appendicitis, an ulcer, or perhaps suicide, on June 7, 1862.

Archpriest Iakov relinquished his post to Hieromonk Ilarion in late spring 1862, and set out for St Michael's Redoubt (where a company ship would take him to Sitka), with only two sled dogs and very few provisions. Local Yup'iks prevented their pastor from attempting such a long journey with so few supplies and furnished him with several more dogs and additional food. Several hunters accompanied him to the coast to assure his safe arrival. In Sitka the bishop immediately recognized the venerable missionary and scholar to be incapable of the crimes the crazy Gabriel, now deceased, had accused him of committing.[9] When Netsvetov died on July 26, 1864, he was appropriately buried in a place of honor, at the entrance to the Tlingit chapel he had served his final year, a site marked today by a miniature stone "castle" quite near the present-day bishop's residence. His wife rests a few hundred paces away, in a forested area visible from the bishop's front door, her grave marked by a stone her husband erected to her memory. Although most histories of Alaska never mention him, Iakov Netsvetov was truly a remarkable and talented teacher, linguist, scholar and missionary, the "Aleut Apostle" to the Eskimos.

Netsvetov's immediate successor, Hieromonk Ilarion, remained for five years before returning to Russia in 1867, when Alaska was transferred to American rule. His diaries indicate, however, that he was a dedicated and energetic missionary who travelled throughout the delta. He visited the village of Quinhagak, where he reported that Hieromonk Iuvenalii had been killed by a Yupik hunting party.[10]

The three Bel'kov brothers, who were Creoles from St Paul Island, played dominant roles in the life of the Yukon mission in the following decades. The eldest, Nikolai Bel'kov, married Simeon Lukin's widow, Sophia, in 1859, thus uniting two prominent Creole families. The youngest, Zachary, continued the missionary and linguistic work of his predecessors for two decades, 1876-1896, supported in part by the middle brother, Anisum Bel'kov, who operated the trading post in the same village. This has been the source of some confusion and even slander, for by the end of the century, Jesuits who arrived in the region and who were unable to distinguish between the Bel'kov brothers, criticized the Orthodox missionary as being "more interested in commerce" than in his pastoral vocation.

9   Lydia Black, *Iakov Netsvetov: the Yukon Years* (Limestone Press, Kingston, Ont. 1984), introduction, p. xv-xx.

10 Wendell Oswalt, "Eskimos and Indians in Western Alaska 1861-1868" (*Anthropological Papers of the University of Alaska*, Vol 8, No. 2, 1960), p 110.

The Orthodox were, by that time, under almost constant attack by newcomers in every part of Alaska, most of whom had not expected to find any missionary competition in their area. When they encountered the Orthodox, they inevitably assumed a negative attitude toward the doctrines and practices of the Church in order to justify their own presence in the region. Bel'kov and others were also criticized for not being omnipresent among their flock, and for not providing regular weekly services in every village, although American evangelists soon found it impossible to serve all their chapels simultaneously also. They also criticized what they considered the superficiality of Eskimo Orthodoxy, reporting that natives had only learned how to participate in ceremonies and had little understanding of the ethical, moral or doctrinal aspects of Christianity. A century later, sectarians level the same charges against all the established denominations whose missionaries challenged their Orthodox predecessors in Alaska.

Father Zachary Bel'kov produced excellent translations of Orthodox hymns in Yup'ik which were, together with some of Father Netsvetov's earlier work in Yu'pik, published by the diocese soon after Bel'kov's death. Although his journals have never been published, the manuscripts survive in the Library of Congress. The entry for September 2, 1879, reads,

> Kuinhagmiut [Quinhagak]: Here Hieromonk Iuvenalii was killed with arrows by the local inhabitants. This happened before the establishment of the Russian American Company.[11]

Six years later, Father Vasilii Orlov recorded similar information, adding that a "104-year-old woman named 'Tutmalria' showed us the exact spot where this happened."[12] Rev. John Kilbuck confirmed these reports in his diary, proving that Hieromonk Iuvenalii had, in fact, penetrated Yup'ik territory and reached the shores of the Bering Sea.[13]

11 Bel'kov Journals (manuscript), Library of Congress, Alaska Church Collection, Box 246, Folder II; quoted in Oleksa, "The Death of Hieromonk Iuvenaly" (*St Vladimir's Theological Quarterly*, Vol. 30, No. 3. Crestwood, NY, 1986), p 262-263.
12 Orlov Journal (manuscript) Alaska Church Collection, D-27, p. 1, quoted in Oleksa, *ibid.*, p. 263.
13 Ann Fienup-Riordan, *The Yup'ik Eskimos* (Limestone Press, Kingston, Ont. 1988), p. 30.

7

The Development of an Indigenous
Orthodox Culture

The intermarriage between *promyshlenniki* and Alaskan Natives, the ability of many of them and most of their children to speak two languages, function in two cultures, and after St Innocent, to read and write in Russian and their own language, produced a unique American Orthodox society. Aleut denotes a cultural synthesis of European/Siberian and indigenous Alaskan elements, united in a common commitment to Orthodox Christianity. This culture provided nineteenth-century Alaska with some of its most remarkable leaders.

Explorers

In 1820, the *promyshlennik* Theodor Kolmakov founded a trading post at Nushagak which he named Fort Alexander, in honor of the tsar. It was here that Veniaminov first met Eskimos and baptized the first Yup'iks in the river. Kolmakov himself continued this process, baptizing others who came to him for instruction. Governor von Wrangell later permitted Kolmakov to establish another post in 1832, this time on the Kuskokwim. Kolmakov spent his last years exploring the region and promoting cooperation between various tribes. He awarded one chief a medal and named him officially "headman" in order to gain his trust and enlist him in the company's efforts. The old *promyshlennik* techniques were still useful.

Andrew Glazunov, under orders from Assistant Chief Manager Rosenberg, explored the lower Yukon and Kuskokwim river basins and established trade relations with the Yup'iks there as early as 1834. Theodor Kolmakov's Creole son Peter ranged far up the Kuskokwim River and collected large quantities of beaver pelts in 1839. He succeeded in discovering the shortest portage between the Yukon and Kuskokwim Rivers and attempted to link the new post at Ikogmiut (Russian Mission) with his

143

father's when he learned that the original Yukon settlement, established in 1842 by another Creole, Andrew Glazunov, had been destroyed. Together with another Creole, Matrozov, Peter Kolmakov explored the upper Innoko River as well.

In 1806, Simeon Lukin, a survivor of the first settlement at Sitka, was ransomed by Baranov and adopted by him. He was sent to study at St Herman's school in 1816, and three years later assigned to the Nushagak to serve as Kolmakov's interpreter. He followed Theodor to the Kuskokwim and managed the post there after Kolmakov's death in 1840. Because an important exploratory expedition visited Kolmakovskii Redoubt during Lukin's administration, documents praising his excellent rapport with the Natives survive. He himself penetrated deep into the interior on trapping and trading ventures, and his Creole son Ivan travelled the length of the Yukon River, spying on the British at Fort Yukon in 1863, and continuing upstream as far as Dawson City before returning home.

Lukin met Lt. Laurence Zagoskin during the latter's scientific survey of the Kuskokwim-Yukon Delta in 1842. Here is what Zagoskin wrote of him:

> The colonial administration was quite ignorant of the location of this place before our survey, but here one man—Simeon Lukin—was able to spread the Christian Faith among many savages, and to establish such good order among them that any changes could hardly be an improvement. Let us bear in mind that this man was a Creole, without scientific education. Is he not worthy of our greatest respect?[1]

> Lukin has always kept open house; we have seen a dozen natives in his little room who will wait silently for days at a time until he returns from his traplines. If a guest enters at mealtime, a piece of dry fish and the teapot of "colonial [tundra] tea" are divided among those present. As he knows their customs well, he never asks who a visitor is or why he has come...Lukin is available day and night; the visitor taps at the window and enters freely. [Free entry is still common among traditional Kuskokwim Yup'iks even today.]

> It was Saturday evening, the manager, according to the custom he has established, read some prayers and psalms in the store, which was arranged as a chapel. All the workers and their families attended. Let us remember that most of those present were newly baptized, and then it will be understandable how the much

---

1   Michael, Henry G., *Lt. Zagoskin's Travels in Russian America* (University of Toronto Press, Toronto, Ont., 1967), p. 250.

respected Lukin has succeeded in extending his influence over distant tribes—his safeguard was his piety: his Helper, the Protector of those who call on His name.

On Sunday morning we went to prayers; after dinner we checked one of the traps. I went to the manager [Lukin]. Forty whitefish were taken, and the manager thanked God that his men would have fresh fish for the feast day tomorrow [St Nicholas Day].[2]

Much of Pierre Pascal's description of the popular religious life of the Russian people applies here.[3] Lukin was not a clergyman, but he had been educated in Kodiak in 1817-1819, which means that Father Herman taught and inspired him. Lukin allied himself not with the exploitation of the Baranov era, but with the mission inaugurated by the monks of Valaam.

Two Kodiak Creoles, Gregory Kurochkin and Nikifor Talisuk, accompanied Zagoskin on his expedition. Talisuk had been born at Fort Ross, California, where the Russian American Company had unsuccessfully tried to grow enough food to supply its Alaskan outposts. The fort had been managed by the notorious Ivan Kuskov and staffed by dozens of Aleuts and Creoles. Zagoskin records that Talisuk was something of a cowboy, lassoing a stray dog on one occasion to rescue it from a porcupine. Other Creoles on Zagoskin's crew included Paul Akliayuk, also from California, Timothy Glazunov, Nicholas Shmakov, Peter Ustiugov and Prokopii Vertoprakhov.

The contributions Creoles and Native Alaskans made to the progress of the Russian American colony have been overlooked for decades, partly because these designations have often been misunderstood. A Creole was not only a person of mixed Russian-Native ancestry, but any Native who was a permanent resident of a town. It was a social rather than racial designation. As generations passed, all or most Native Alaskans in an area came to be Creole, although their genetic relationship to any Caucasian ancestor may have been very slight, or even non-existent. Simeon Lukin was ethnically Russian, a typical, traditional *promyshlennik* (although born in Alaska), married to Native Alaskan wives, with Creole sons. Zagoskin mistakenly called him a Creole, but Lukin, in fact, functioned as one, being bilingual and quite familiar with the customs of the indigenous people of his area.

2   *Ibid.*, p 208.
3   See Part I, Chapter 3.

Long before the sale of Alaska in 1867, Creoles constituted a vital
middle-management class in the "Russian" colony. In fact, they were the
majority of the urban population. Sixty percent of the residents of New
Archangel (Sitka), the capital city, and ninety percent of the citizens of
Kodiak were of Native ancestry. The hierarchical structure of Russian
society did not limit their mobility. Energetic men like Netsvetov could
become members of the hereditary nobility. By 1835, many Creoles were
sailing the globe for the Russian American Company, navigating its ships
and mapping the coastline, opening the frontier in the name of the tsar.
Their accomplishments have been ignored, partly because their Slavic
surnames made them indistinguishable from Russian or Siberian *promyshlenniki*. Alaskan history texts touch only lightly upon the first half of
the nineteenth century. They mention Shelikov, Baranov, Rezanov, but
seldom St Herman. Veniaminov and a few governors receive a few paragraphs to cover the years between 1820 and the sale. Virtually nothing
noteworthy happened during those fifty years. But what actually happened
was that the Creoles were managing the colony. To fill in the missing years of
Alaska's story will require research into the remarkable Aleut contributions to
the social, economic and spiritual development of the colony. Indeed, even
the term colony is misleading. *Promyshlenniki* had to apply for licenses to
operate in Alaska, and company employees after the establishment of the
monopoly were forbidden to settle permanently in America. Like workers for
modern multi-national corporations, Russians came for a relatively short tour
of duty overseas and returned home, never having intended to stay in Alaska.
There never were, in fact, more than nine hundred ethnic Russians at any one
time in the entire territory. The company had to rely on Native Alaskan
expertise and manpower in order to function at all.

Ilarion Arkhimandritov

Ilarion Ivanovich Arkhimandritov, the oldest son of a teamster from
Tomsk and his Unangan Aleut wife Natalia, was born around 1820 in the
eastern Aleutians, probably at Unalaska. The church register recorded his
baptism on July 13, 1827, along with the baptism of two sisters, Helen
and Paraskeva, He began his education in Veniaminov's Unalaska school
and continued his studies at the Kronstadt naval academy. In 1831, aboard
the America, he wintered in California and arrived in St Petersburg in

September 1833. It was not uncommon for teenagers to be included on such voyages. Lt. Davydov, for example, at the age of fifteen, had already completed his studies at Kronstadt, received his commission, and been shipped out.

After successfully completing his courses in cartography and navigational science, Arkhimandritov returned to Alaska on a voyage that lasted from August 1837 until April 1838. He was hired by the Russian American Company as a navigator with a salary of one thousand rubles, and in 1841 he received a gold medal and was knighted with the Order of St Anne for bravery, having heroically assumed command of the *Naslednik Alexander* when both its captain and first mate perished in a storm. Arkhimandritov rescued the crew, its passengers and cargo, and saved the – ship as well. His career had a brilliant beginning.

When the Russian biologist Elia Voznesensky came to Alaska to collect bird, plant and fish specimens for the Academy of Sciences in 1841, Arkhimandritov and another Creole, Filat Druzhinin, collected artifacts for him. From 1843 to 1860, he sailed several regular routes for the company, hauling passengers and cargo across the north Pacific, from Sitka to Kodiak to Atka to Kamchatka and return. Beginning in 1846, the company began using Arkhimandritov's training in cartography as well, assigning him the task of drawing navigational charts of Kodiak Island, Cook Inlet, and Prince William Sound. Travelling in a traditional *baidarka* along the shore, Arkhimandritov produced the maps of the southcentral Alaskan coast which were published later in former Governor Tebenkov's 1852 atlas.

During the Crimean War, Arkhimandritov's steamer, *Alexander II*, sailed under the American flag to avoid capture by the enemy British or French navies. Finally, after twenty-two years of faithful service, Arkhimandritov requested a raise. The governor granted him another thousand rubles, saying that his leaving the company's service would be a significant loss.

Then, in February 1860, Arkhimandritov's good fortune turned sour. As naval officer Golovin reported to his family in Sitka:

After the departure of the master of the Tsaritsa, on which we came to Sitka, this vessel was put under the command of a certain Arkhimandritov, a man of excellent qualities and experience, who sailed these seas his entire life...Then this incident occurred:

Near the island of Kodiak, there is a small islet, "Spruce," where a monk, Herman, one of the first missionaries to the colonies once settled. He lived there as an almost total recluse, later organized a school for orphaned Aleuts, whom he taught reading, writing, religion, and where he died in 1837, being held in great reverence by the Aleuts. They built a chapel in his memory on the island, and he was buried near it. When Arkhimandritov was sailing to Kodiak the first time, the wife of the former governor, Voevodsky, told him he should offer a *moleben* [prayer service] in this chapel every year before undertaking his first voyage. Arkhimandritov promised to but did not keep his word.

The first year everything went well. On his second voyage he again visited Kodiak and took on a cargo of ice for San Francisco. A few miles out of Kodiak, on a clear day, with excellent weather conditions, March 30, his vessel struck an uncharted rock. The impact was so severe that the water filled the hold almost at once. The crew, passengers, and Arkhimandritov himself abandoned ship in life boats. The vessel, kept afloat by the cargo of ice, was battered by the sea for three days, and finally beached at Spruce Island, directly opposite the chapel. There it sank, so that only the tip of her mast and the cross rail protruded above the water level, forming a perfect cross. Is this pure chance, or a reminder from Above? Judge for yourselves, but the fact is that since that time, Arkhimandritov's luck runs poor.

Governor Furuhjelm, a Lutheran, was so impressed with this incident that he decided to donate an icon to the Spruce Island chapel. We ourselves celebrated a *moleben* there after we arrived in Kodiak.[4]

The Governor gave Arkhimandritov a new assignment after the Spruce Island catastrophe, ordering him to chart the harbor. Paddling his *bidarka* again, Arkhimandritov spent the summer of 1860 mapping the coast of Kodiak, indicating all the hazards, rocks and reefs.

He was soon given another ship, which he sailed to San Francisco from Woody Island, near the main Kodiak settlement, so named because of the saw mill there. The mill's primary function, however, was not to produce lumber but sawdust, which was used to cover the huge chunks of fresh water ice the company cut from lakes near the shore. These were dragged across the beach, covered with sawdust, secured to ships, and towed to California, where, in the days before mechanical refrigeration, the ice was sold by the ton to meatpackers. The inspiration for this commerce came from an American ship's visit to Sitka in 1852. At that time the Americans purchased 250 tons of ice at $75 per ton, adding $121,956.04 to the company treasury.

4   *Morskii Sbornik* (1863), Vol. 6, p. 306-307.

For the next three years, Arkhimandritov traveled throughout the North Pacific and Bering Sea, even visiting Honolulu during the winter of 1865-66. On a trip to San Francisco, he met Carolina Peters, whom he married in a Protestant ceremony. He then brought his bride to Sitka, where they were wed in St Michael's Cathedral. The following spring, he was sent to the Aleutians, the Pribilov Islands, and St Michael's, north of the mouth of the Yukon, to gather information for a new atlas of the colony, and later sailed the *Nakhimov* to Ayan, on the Siberian coast.

After the sale of Alaska to the United States, Arkhimandritov settled in San Francisco, where he organized a political group of former Alaskan and Russian immigrants who opposed tsarist rule in Russia, the "Pan-Slavic Society." In association with a Ukrainian nationalist and missionary, Rev. Agapii Goncharenko, the society published the *Alaska Herald* to propagate its views. In something of a party purge, Goncharenko was expelled from the society in March 1868, and Arkhimandritov disappeared. It was rumored that Arkhimandritov had been abducted by tsarist agents and exiled to Siberia, but he resurfaced in Alaska, working for the Alaska Commercial Company at Unalaska. There he was elected by the Aleuts to serve as liaison with the Americans, whose language and customs he so much better understood. He died at Belkovskii in December 1872, ending one of the most fascinating careers of any Aleut seaman in the service of Russian America in the mid-nineteenth century.

Alexander Kashevarov

Philip Kashevarov, Alexander's father, was probably the same local teacher at Kodiak who befriended Archimandrite Joasaph when the monks from Valaam first arrived. The Alaskan branch of the Kashevarov family originally settled in Kodiak, but within two generations, there were Kashevarovs throughout the territory.

Alexander Philipovich Kashevarov was born in Kodiak in 1809. His mother, a Kodiak Aleut, probably raised her children to speak Alutiiq, as the Sugpiaq language came to be called by its own speakers. This transfer of name, of self-identity, seems to have coincided with the increase in the Creole population. As Creole inter-marriages with Russians and other Creoles occurred, the "pure" Sugpiaq and Unangan tended to identify with the new, more socially prestigious, social class. The name Aleut was applied to both Sugpiaq and Unangan, the Sugpiaq often distinguished from the latter by being called "Kodiak Aleut." By the middle of the century, the terms "Aleut" and "Creole" had become synonymous, although the census listed Native Sugpiaq or Unangan separately as "Aleut" and the "Creoles" as a distinct social class, which included many Natives who had no biological ties to Russians. All tradesmen, merchants, or company foremen were also Creole, regardless of race. Statistics that indicate the continuing decline of the Aleut population after 1820 can be misleading, for while the number of Aleuts did decrease, the Creole population increased dramatically. The Aleuts did not die, but rapidly became Creole. After the sale to the United States, when the social class no longer existed, the process was reversed: all Creoles became Aleuts.

The Creoles as a class tended to include large numbers of bilingual, biliterate townspeople. In the Aleutian Islands, due to the educational efforts of St Innocent Veniaminov, Chief Ivan Pan'kov, and Father Iakov Netsvetov, many villagers were able to read both Russian and Unganan. On Kodiak, Alutiiq had been taught in the schools and used in church services since Father Gideon's time, and Sophia Vlasov, St Herman's assistant, was herself a bilingual Creole. It was into this bicultural environment that Alexander Kashevarov was born.

After completing elementary school at Kodiak, Alexander, like Ilarion Arkhimandritov, was sent to the Kronstadt Naval Academy. In 1828, at the age of nineteen, he returned to Alaska aboard the *Elena,* captained by Lt. Khromchenko. This voyage took him around the Cape of Good Hope, across the Indian Ocean and on to Sitka in just eleven months. During this journey, from May 22-26, Kashevarov mapped some of the Marshall Islands. It was the start of a brilliant career.

Again with Khromchenko, in 1831, Kashevarov sailed to Copenhagen, Portsmouth, England, and the Canary Islands. After a leisurely stop in Rio de Janeiro, their vessel, the America, was damaged in a storm off the tip of Africa. They spent a month in Sydney, Australia, repairing the ship before setting sail for the Gilbert and Marshall Islands. Delivering their cargo to Petropavlovsk, Kamchatka, and Sitka, they returned to St Petersburg via San Francisco, where they spent most of January 1833, and Cape Horn, with rest stops in Rio and Copenhagen again.

Five years later, in July 1838, Kashevarov was sent to the Arctic coast of Alaska to map the shoreline. Aboard the brig *Polifem*, crewed by thirteen Russians and Creoles and ten Aleuts, and accompanied by another ship commanded by Creole Nicholas Chernov, he sailed to Cape Lisburne, where the party transferred to a large *baidara* (skin boat) propelled by twenty one oars. They paddled along the shore, mapping the coast as they went, until ice made it impossible to continue. Using smaller, three-hatched *bidarkas*, they proceeded beyond Point Barrow, where the Inupiaq Eskimo gathered twenty kayaks to oppose the intruders. Kashevarov decided not to risk a battle with them and returned to his ships in Kotzebue Sound.[5]

For the next twenty years, Kashevarov served the Russian American Company in various capacities. He sailed the *Aleut* between Siberia and Kodiak, and by 1840, he was first mate aboard the *Okhotsk*, surveying the Asian coastline. In 1850, some of his maps were published in the Atlas of the Eastern Ocean, compiled by Tebenkov. That same year, Kashevarov was promoted to the rank of Lt. Captain and appointed commander of the Siberian port of Ayan. When, in 1852, a band of Russian refugees, persecuted Old Believers, arrived there. Kashevarov supplied them with food, lodging and clothing.

Sometime before 1861, Kashevarov retired to St Petersburg. As a Major General in the service, he was a respected member of the nobility, with a distinguished and colorful career to his country behind him. During the debate on the future of the Alaskan colony, he published several articles opposing the renewal of the company charter. The board of directors, of course, tried to present the company's activities in the best possible light, but Kashevarov openly criticized them, writing:

> Are we who were born in Russian America really supposed to consider forever the best interests of the Russian American Company as we have been taught from our childhood, and smother within ourselves every natural striving, every idea about the interests of our native land?[6]

Primarily because of Kashevarov's opposition to the renewal of the company's twenty-year charter, the government postponed any immediate decision on the request and dispatched Captain P. N. Golovin to

5   For a map of this expedition, see Golovin's *The End of Russian America* (Oregon Historical Society, Portland, 1979), p. 136.

6   *Morskii Sbornik*, Vol 54, No. 7 (1861), p. 19-20.

Alaska to inspect conditions there. When this report was published in 1862, Kashevarov attacked it as unbalanced and too favorable to company interests. His objections to Golovin's findings forced the government to re-examine the report. The committee decided that Kashevarov's criti-cisms were well-founded, and recommended that the company petition for renewal of its charter be denied. Thus the Creole from Kodiak, Major General Alexander Kashevarov, played a critical role in the ultimate decision to sell Alaska to the United States. He did not live to see this, however. He died in St Petersburg in 1866 at the age of 57.

Aleut Missionaries

In the nineteenth century, Father Iakov Netsvetov accomplished extraordinary missionary feats during his many decades in the Atka and Yukon districts. Bishop Innocent Veniaminov had planned to send him to Kenai, but then realized that only a single man without a family could manage at so remote a post as Ikogmiut. Father Iakov spent almost twenty more years in the Yukon Delta among the Eskimo and Indian peoples of the frontier, and became the first Unangan Aleut to bring Christianity to his linguistically distant cousins on the mainland.

Theodor Kolmakov and his assistant Simeon Lukin had already begun the process of evangelizing the Yup'ik on the Nushagak a generation earlier. Lukin, as Zagoskin reported, was conducting abbreviated services at Kolmakovskii Redoubt in 1842, prior to Netsvetov's arrival. The old *promyshlennik* pattern was repeated. The conversion of the Yup'ik was from the beginning the combined effort of Russians, Sugpiaq and Unangan Creoles.

Very early in the history of the colony, Native and Creole converts to Christianity cooperated with and often initiated the evangelization of neighboring tribes. Not only did adults bring their relatives and children for instruction, but many eagerly sought the clergy and requested baptism without any such encouragement. The essentially oral nature of this process complemented the traditional educational approach of the pre-contact Unangan and Sugpiaq. The people intently listened to the new sacred stories and repeated them to their children, passing down the tradition the same way the pre-Christian faith had been transmitted for centuries. None of this required a trained clergy. The priests' function was limited to the celebration of chrismation, matrimony, burial and, of course, the eucharist. Many of these could be performed in an abbreviated form by laity when circumstances dictated. Teaching, as ever, remained a function of the family, the head of each household responsible for communicating the tradition to the next generation. This pattern continued both by design and necessity in Russia and Alaska. It explains the survival of Orthodoxy during the seven decades of communist rule. In a sense, then, each Orthodox parent served as a teacher and missionary within the family. It is not surprising that some would fill this role within a wider community as well.

In very recent times, when the younger generation has become literate and their elders remained unschooled, the transmission of essential religious and spiritual practices has been disrupted. The more formally educated youth consider their book-learning superior to the unwritten heritage of their unlettered parents. High school and college graduates, well-versed in secular affairs, have little or no understanding of the spiritual worldview of their ancestors, and often lack the linguistic capability to gain it. Elders, on the other hand, are continually frustrated in their efforts to pass their religious and cultural heritage on to their literate offspring, who usually show little interest in learning "the old ways." Instilling a positive, receptive attitude toward the oral tradition and devising ways to communicate the spiritual tradition in written form constitute major problems for modern Alaskan catechesis.

Artists

In his "Notes on the Islands of the Unalaska District," Veniaminov wrote, "The local church of the Lord's Ascension was founded July 25, 1825, consecrated June 29, 1826. Inside, the church has a rather fine iconostasis with finely wrought columns and carved gilded frames of Aleut workmanship."[7]

Modern ethnologists have mourned the "loss" of Aleut culture under the supposed influence of Russian and Siberian contact. Certainly many customs and traditions, including slavery and inter-tribal warfare, were

7   Veniaminov, *op. cit.*, p. 239.

abandoned at an early stage, so that Veniaminov was unable to find informants for songs and dances as early as 1825. Those ceremonies, associated with pre-contact Unangan religion, seem to have been lost during the first generation following Father Makarii's visit. Masks were usually produced for a given performance and then destroyed afterward, so that once the ceremonies were no longer performed, the regalia associated with them were no longer made. If, however, carving had been employed for religious purposes in the past, the same talents could now be used in the church. Frames for icons and entire icon screens were produced by Aleut artists whose names, unfortunately, have not been recorded.[8] Father Netsvetov painted icons at Atka and at his mission post on the Yukon. Others made vestments, altar coverings, crosses, and various liturgical utensils. Every Aleut chapel contains examples of this kind of locally produced folk art, some of it modern, some of it a century old.

Toward the end of the Russian era, P. N. Golovin reported that at Sitka the school trained students to become "scribes,...navigators, apothecaries, or machinists, or Tlingit language translators, portrait painters, tailors, leather workers...or craftsmen."[9] Moreover, even under the harsher rule of Baranov, Aleuts in Sitka proved themselves talented musicians, comprising a chamber orchestra for festive occasions at the governor's mansion on "Castle Hill," which also boasted of a piano in Baranov's time.[10] This musical interest continues to the present time. During the hearings conducted by the United States Congress investigating the relocation and internment of Aleuts during the Second World War, several evacuees lamented the loss of their icons and musical instruments when their homes were looted by American troops stationed in the islands to defend them from possible Japanese invasion. Most Aleut homes today include at least one guitarist, and Aleut choirs are among the best in the diocese.

Vasilii Kriukov painted, or, to use the traditional term, "wrote," fine icons for the Unalaska church. Veniaminov wrote of him,

> ...several Creole boys have taught themselves to draw...Vasilii Kriukov without a teacher learned to draw so well that he pained very fine icons and finally made excellent water-color portraits. It was enough for him to see a person two or three

8   See, for example, Lydia Black's *Aleut Art* (Aleutian-Pribilof Association, Anchorage, AK, 1982), plate 16.
9   Golovin, *op. cit.* (1979), p. 60.
10 Hector Chevigny, *Russian America*, p. 131.

times and he would bring that person's image alive, covering the whole spectrum of facial expressions.[11]

Kriukov's icons are authentically Aleut, a combination of the traditional style of the Eastern Church with characteristics of western Renaissance painting, and yet distinctively Alaskan. The faces of certain figures betray certain Aleut characteristics, and the script on the pages of the open Gospel Book in the icons of St Luke and St John resembles Unangan writing. In an icon of St George, a typical Aleutian volcano rises in the distance. Kriukov used local materials in his work: driftwood and local pigments. His art, therefore, is more than color and line. It is an offering of Alaska itself, its soil and its life, transformed by an Aleut iconographer into a proclamation of the faith. Kriukov's icons are visible prayers, hanging today in the Cathedral of the Ascension at Unalaska in the chapel of St Innocent of Irkutsk, where they will remain for future generations of Alaskans to revere.

Writers

With the introduction of literacy in Native Alaskan languages, many Aleuts and Creoles became avid writers. Father Iakov Netsvetov's journals, preserved at Kodiak today, testify to the extraordinary care taken to provide clear and accurate records for the company and church bureaucracies. The publication in 1848 of the Alutiiq Gospel of St Matthew, and of the primer and short catechism the following year, all prepared by Elia Tizhnov, gave new impetus for Native language literacy in Kodiak, a tradition that survived well into the twentieth century in some communities.

Netsvetov's successor at Atka, Father Laurence Salamatov, studied at Sitka, and returned to his hometown to become the most important Atkan writer of the nineteenth century. Salamatov completed translations of all the Gospels and composed a catechism in 1862. Only one of his translations was ever published: the Gospel of St Mark was printed using a new orthography in 1959, by a Norwegian linguist, Knut Bergsland.

At Unalaska, Father Andrew Siztsov began work on translations of the Gospels of SS Mark, Luke and John and the Acts of the Apostles. His work was completed by his successor, Father Innocent Shayashnikov, who

11 Veniaminov, *op. cit.*, p. 164-165.

had served briefly with Father Netsvetov on the Yukon. Shayashnikov himself wrote a book in Unangan entitled *Brief Rule for a Pious Life*, which was published in 1902, the year after his death. Father Andrew Ladochnikov translated Orthodox prayers and hymns into Unangan for a book printed by the diocese in 1898. This work became a model for similar translations in Yup'ik and Tlingit during the next decade. The Aleut people themselves raised the money to pay the cost of publishing these and other books in their own language.

On Kodiak Island and in Prince William Sound, the Alutiiq speaking population continued to translate Orthodox hymns, but none of these were ever compiled or published. Instead, following a much more ancient pattern, they circulated orally, with translations from one village passing to others through traveling choir members. Many Chugach Alutiiq people, despite the difference between their dialect and Kodiak's, became familiar with translations produced on the island. Afognak village was the bridge between the two traditions. The Alutiiq oral tradition there, and later at Port Lions, was especially vital, due to the work of Tikhon Sheratin, and later, his nephew, Sergei. Perryville and English Bay were also centers of this Alutiiq Orthodox translation work. The fact that none of these hymns were published does not minimize the fact that bilingual Creoles and Aleuts perpetuated their cultural and religious heritage for a century after the sale of Alaska. Certainly well into the 1960's, Aleut children were still attending "Aleut" or "Russian" school after finishing their classes in the public or "American" school. The church bell summoned them to reading lessons in Cyrillic characters, and parents insisted that their children attend these sessions every weekday afternoon. Church readers Innokentii Shugak, Larry Ellanak and Vladimir Melovedoff represented the last generation of these Kodiak bilingual teachers. On the mainland, Father Nikolai Moonin provided the same sort of leadership at English Bay, while Emil Kosbruck translated and taught Alutiiq on his own initiative at Perryville. In the Kodiak area, women have assumed responsibility for conducting services in most villages in the last two decades: Olga Panamaroff in Karluk; Lucille Lubova Davis in Larsen Bay; Betty Katherine Bernsten and Stella Stephanida Zeedar in Old Harbor; Lubova Eluska in Akhiok; and Barbara Boskofsky assisting Larry Ellanak in Ouzinkie.

Nikolski also became a center for Aleut literacy with Afenogin Ermelov producing secular works in Unangan and English, including stories for the 1932 *Alaskan Sportsman* monthly magazine. Ermelov's diary, in Aleut, was copied by the local school teacher, Jay Ransom, and survives today. Father Gregory Kochergin, originally from Nikolski, translated texts from Russian into Aleut and Yup'ik. He served as a storekeeper, manager, and bureaucrat for the United States government at Nushagak until his death in 1948. Kochergin was one of the last quadri-lingual Aleut writers. Well into the twentieth century, Aleuts were typically bi- and tri-lingual. Sergei Sovoroff continued the Nikolski tradition, serving as an important informant for Father Paul Merculief in the 1970's. Aleuts delighted in their multi-cultural heritage. As recently as 1945, an article in *American Anthropology* stated:

> The ability to write their native language has injected into the family of almost every native [Aleut] an atmosphere of study and a delight in the realm of the mind. Although his reading must be more or less restricted to the printed volumes of religious material, his writing may conform to anything passing through his thoughts, and what one can write will directly affect the reading of some other person.[12]

Under the auspices of the Orthodox Church's educational ministry, Native Alaskans assumed prominent social and cultural positions in Russian America during the final decades of company rule. This heritage survived for over a century after Alaska had become American territory, and provides Orthodoxy with a central place in Aleut society today.

The 1860's

During the final decade of Russian rule, the Aleut population assumed a dominant role in the life of the colony. The 1860 census indicates that the population of the capital city, New Archangel consisted of 452 Russians (366 of whom were adult males), 569 Creoles and Aleuts, and three men of other nationalities. In the Kodiak District, which included Kenai and the Alaska Peninsula, there were 67 Russians, and 3,019 Creoles and Aleuts. Only four ethnic Russians lived in the Eastern Aleutians, with 1,766 Creoles and Aleuts, while in the western Aleutians, 960 Creoles and Aleuts lived with four Russians in five villages. Statistics no longer distin-

12 Quoted from Richard Dauenhauer, "The Spiritual Epiphany of Aleut," *Orthodox Alaska*, Vol. 8, no. 1. Kodiak, AK. (1979), p. 24.

guished Sugpiaq and Unangan Aleuts, for both were settled in the Kuril Islands, where one Russian, ten Creoles and 154 Aleuts were counted in 1860.

A major reason for the rapid depopulation of Kodiak Island was the impression of the Sugpiaq into virtual slavery during the Baranov years, and their dispersion to the far corners of the North Pacific. While Unangan were also deported from their islands to Kodiak and Sitka, Alutiiqs were shipped to Urup Island, just north of Japan, to the Pribilovs, in the Bering Sea, to Sitka, Fort Ross, California, and even Hawaii, as well as the Alaskan mainland. Also, as Aleuts married Russians and Creoles, the number of people listed as Native declined, no longer because of exploitation but because they were being increasingly absorbed into the distinct Creole social class. In 1862, Golovin predicted that "in a few decades the Creole population will become dominant in the colonies and replace Aleuts whose numbers are diminishing."[13] In general, however, Golovin did not have a very high opinion of Creoles. He wrote:

> There are some very fine people among the Creoles, but they are the exceptions, and I am talking about the group as a whole...Education and rank does not always benefit their crude natures...Several of them are very good alert *promyshlenniki*. They raise cattle, plant gardens, build small ships, trap furs, and trade in lumber.[14]

Despite these positive contributions, Golovin maintained that Creoles "have been and continue to be useless."[15] Golovin also reported, contrary to his negative stereotyping of Creoles, that a metal shop, machine shop, foundry, sail-making factory, a wharf for building and repair shops, and even a local chamber orchestra at Sitka, were all staffed by Creoles and Aleuts. At Kodiak, the flour mill, blacksmith shop, tannery and lumber yard, as well as the metal works and schools were operated by Creoles. They were also active in the ice business and continued in this trade until the sale of Alaska. Golovin boasted of the fine work the company was doing, without, it seems, noticing who was doing it.

During the 1860's, Kodiak Island's main industry continued to be the fur trade. Hunting was listed as the main occupation for most of the men there. Of the 515 adult males on the island, 63 were employed by the

13 Golovin, *op. cit.*, p. 17.
14 *Ibid.*
15 *Ibid.*, p. 15.

company at Old Harbor, Sun'alleq, near Three Saints Bay. Sea otter hunting had brought only 350 pelts a year regularly for the past twenty five years, but beaver, fox and muskrat pelts accounted for a larger share of the profits as the years passed.

Aleut Society in 1839 and 1870

When Father Veniaminov traveled to St Petersburg in 1839, he was asked to prepare a report on the condition of the church in the American colonies. His assessment of the four parishes indicated a wide divergence between Sugpiaq and Unangan piety at that time. In 1870, one of the first Americans to reside at Kodiak recorded his impressions of life there, and these present a different picture of the Kodiak Aleuts by that time. Here are extracts from those two rather detailed accounts of life in the Aleutians and on Kodiak. They depict an indigenous Orthodox society in which education and spiritual life centered on the church.

While Kodiak is the largest parish, Father Veniaminov began,

...spiritually it is the least advanced. According to the Kodiak office, the parish included 6,338 members: 114 Russians, 400 Creoles, 1,719 Kodiak Natives, 1,628 Kenai Indians, 2,006 Yup'iks and 471 Chugach. These figures illustrate the difficulty for one priest attempting to confirm and strengthen the faith of parishioners scattered over more than 1,600 kilometers among the Kodiak parish's thirty-six settlements, along both sides of the Alaska Peninsula, as well as around Cook Inlet and Prince William Sound [which V. called, Alaska, Kenai Bay and Chugatsk Bay respectively]. As a result, priests have rarely been in many places since the time of Father Iuvenalii.

All those who have been to Kodiak unanimously agree that the Aleuts there almost never go to church. They cling to their shamans openly or in secret, and few fulfill their [sacramental] duties to the Church...The smallpox epidemic which killed many Kodiak Aleuts clearly shows that they do not believe in Russian superiority or in Christianity. They ran away and hid, refusing doctors willing to help them. More than 700, or one third of the population, died...The Unalaska Aleuts, in contrast, gratefully accepted help and assisted the doctor as much as possible. Of 1,200, only 80 who were not reached in time—or one-fifteenth—died.

Because information is scarce, I can add nothing more about the Kodiak parish. Probably the Kodiak Aleuts lack faith because they know little of Christianity, not because they are stubborn or hostile. The Kodiaks at Sitka voluntarily went to confession while I was there. Many confessed intelligently and with feeling, particularly those who had been instructed by Father Herman, from the Valaam mission. The Kodiak parish merely needs better organization.[16]

Although Veniaminov tactfully does not mention it, the years of exploitation under Baranov also took their toll. Kodiak Alutiiqs only gradually became devout Orthodox Christians, in contrast to the Unangan, whom Veniaminov knew best.

None of the Aleut virtues delighted and gladdened my heart so much as their enthusiasm, no, craving for God's Word. The most inexhaustible preacher would weary before the Aleuts grow inattentive or lose their eagerness. For example, when I arrived in a settlement, everyone dropped his work, no matter how important, and gathered around me to hear a sermon. They listened with amazing concentration. They were not distracted nor did they look around. The most loving mothers were deaf to the cries of their children who were left behind if they were not old enough to understand.[17]

Before they had written or printed language, Aleuts who knew no Russian would sit an entire day, gazing at the Slavonic Psalter or the Lives of Saints. When they saw the first printed edition of the catechism which I translated, even old men began to study the alphabet in order to read their own language, and now more than one in six can read.

Father Netsvetov intended to make special translations for the Atka natives, but instead he used my translations, written in Unalaskan. He needed only add commentaries [footnotes]. The Unalaskans and Atkans speak different dialects of the same language, and therefore my translations were adequate for both parishes. In his preface to the catechism, Father Iakov states that "by reading the same dialect, they might eventually develop a common language and become Christian brothers." He has also translated the first chapter of Luke, and the first two chapters of the Acts of the Apostles with commentaries for the Unalaskans.[18]

After noting that, as of 1839, four schools and four orphanages served about one hundred boys and fifty girls in his parish, Veniaminov continues:

In church and at prayer, they stand remarkably still. During the entire service, even for the four hour service during Holy Week, even the children stand motionless, so that after they leave it is possible to count attendance by looking at the places they stood...Some know how to pray from the heart. They do not do so before others or in church, but usually they do so in their dwellings, behind closed doors. I have noticed how at church those who truly pray do nothing to attract attention.

...in Unalaska there were never any murders, fights or quarrels. This is not an

16 Veniaminov, "Condition of the Orthodox Church in Russian America," *Pacific Northwest Quarterly*, April (1972), p. 41-54.

17 Bearne, *op. cit.*, p. 49.

18 *Ibid.*

exaggeration; even young children control not only their tongues but their actions. Refusal to speak is the usual revenge, and this can sometimes last for days, but not beyond confession and communion. If anyone manages to catch something after three or four days of hunger, he divides it with those in need, and keeps only enough for his own family. He frequently shares even this portion. Aleuts are so long-suffering to the point of insensitivity. There is no difficulty an Aleut could not endure, no affliction he could not bear...When ill, he never cries or moans, even in the most extreme pain.[19]

In 1870, Lt. Eli Huggins describes life at Kodiak in a series of letters and journal entries which describe a considerable improvement in the spiritual condition of the parish there since Veniaminov's time.

Creoles all belong to the Greek or Orthodox Church, dissent and skepticism being alike unknown. The Creoles of Alaska are the most devout people at church I have ever seen. The entrance of strangers, however novel in appearance, never slows the rapidity of their crossings and bows, nor distracts their attention from the altar and the officiating clergy. The Orthodox have a great many holidays, but those which all are expected strictly to observe are not very numerous. They seldom celebrate their own birthdays, but a sacred day to each individual is his "name day," a day of the saint for whom he is named [and therefore the annual commemoration of his baptism]. These "name days" are a serious tax on a large family.[20]

When the priest enters any house, he pauses at the door and invokes a blessing on all the occupants before entering. When he shakes hands with any of his flock, he takes their hand into his left, makes the sign of the cross with his right hand, and solemnly repeats the words, "In the name of the Father, and of the Son, and of the Holy Spirit," both the priest and the parishioner removing their hats until this ceremony is over. When any Russian learns of the death of a friend or acquaintance, by letter or otherwise, he or she makes the sign of the cross and devoutly says, "May he receive the heavenly Kingdom." They have other customs equally devout and beautiful.[21]

In the best room of each house and sometimes in every room is a picture of some saint, usually the Virgin and Child, painted on wood and framed, like all church pictures, in metal. In front of this picture stands a wax candle which is lit on important holidays. The more devout never enter a room without turning to this picture and crossing themselves. Most of the people can read, and each house contains one or more prayer books, besides which I did not see a dozen other books on the island.[22]

19 *Ibid.*
20 Eli Huggins, *Kodiak Afognak Life, 1868-1870* (Limestone Press, Kingston, Ont., 1981), p. 12-13.
21 *Ibid.*, p 42-43.
22 *Ibid.*, p. 27.

Every year in May...a fleet of several hundred *bidarkas* is assembled at Kodiak for hunting sea otter...Nothing could induce the expedition to start before receiving the formal blessing performed by the priest, a ceremony that lasts two or three hours.[23]

On January 21...the Natives on Woody Island are anxious to have cold weather so they can have employment cutting ice. The day before yesterday [Epiphany] they sent a delegation to the priest, requesting him to go and bless the lake, so that it would freeze [sic]. He went and got the people together and a procession was formed which marched to the lake, chanting, some of the people carrying lighted wax candles and censers. I did not witness the ceremonies and do not know just what they were, but the priest was gone all day. It turned clear and cold that night, and the lake has been freezing steadily ever since.[24]

...Although the Russians and Creoles in other respects assume a haughty tone with Natives, they would think it un-Christian to make them worship in a separate church or even in a separate part of the church, the "negro pew" is, I believe, a purely American invention. The church in Afognak was built by voluntary labor of the congregation, no money being required except for glass and nails.[25]

The Creoles are generous and hospitable, and perhaps as honest as other people, but have little idea of punctuality and fidelity in business appointments as understood by Americans. They rarely refuse by a decidedly negative answer to comply with any request, but instead make a qualified or conditional answer. "Tomorrow" is heard more frequently in their mouths than any other word, and they never seem more happy as when they have just succeeded in putting off the decision on some troublesome question.[26]

There are no temperance societies among them, but confirmed drunkards are rare. They are fond of music, and nearly all play some instrument, generally by ear, though I met some cultivated musicians among them...Nearly every Sunday, as well as on holidays, the *crème de la crème* assembled at the hospitable home of the governor, every room of which was thrown open...The priest used to assist at these parties, spending much of his time in the refreshment room, his face beaming approval at the door of the dancing hall...The Kodiak priest...was a middle aged Creole, fond of his ease and rather too fond of the fiery beverage called "vodka" but amiable and benevolent...A good deal of his time was passed in neighboring villages where he exercised an excellent influence. Rather indulgent toward private vices, he strove to inculcate among his flock benevolence, good will and kindly relations.[27]

After a century and a half, then, the Aleut peoples had become devoted members of the Orthodox Church, but had not abandoned certain as-

23 *Ibid.*, p. 14.
24 *Ibid.*, p. 21.
25 *Ibid.*, p. 25.
26 *Ibid.*, p. 11.
27 *Ibid.*, p. 12.

pects of their traditional way of life. They had rather created an indigenous Orthodox culture, the fruit of the Valaam mission and the labors of Fathers Veniaminov and Netsvetov.

The Sale of Alaska

While some modern histories have raised new questions about the motives for the Alaskan Purchase, for the most part the accepted versions of the story seem accurate. Russia apparently realized she could no longer defend so distant an outpost. The Crimean War jolted the empire into recognizing that her resources were limited, and that the social, educational, economic and military needs for maintaining and defending such a far-flung empire were beyond her means. As her recent opponents had leaned toward supporting the Confederacy during the American Civil War, Russia alone had supported the Union. Tsar Alexander freed the serfs as Lincoln had freed the slaves, and both had been assassinated for their trouble. The late 1860's, therefore, were a time of warm Russian-American relations, and the tsarist government offered Alaska to Washington, not only to prevent the British from seizing the colony during some later conflict, and not only to earn a few million badly needed dollars for the Russian treasury, but also as a gesture of friendship to the land of Manifest Destiny.

Secretary of State Seward enthusiastically pursued the secret negotiations that culminated in the treaty signed late at night in his Washington home on March 30, 1867. Articles II and III ceded to the United States

all public lots and squares, vacant lands, and all public buildings, fortifications, barracks, and other edifices which are not private, individual property. It is, however, understood and agreed that the churches which have been built in the ceded territory by the Russian Government shall remain the property of the members of the Greek Oriental Church resident in the territory as may choose to worship therein...and the inhabitants of the ceded territory, according to their own choice, reserving their natural allegiance, may return to Russia within three years; but if they should prefer to remain in the ceded territory, they with the exception of the uncivilized tribes, shall be admitted to the enjoyment of all the rights, advantages, and immunities of citizens and shall be maintained and protected in the free enjoyment of their liberty, property and religion...[28]

Article III was to be violated time and again in the following decades,

28 The Treaty of Cession, quoted from David H. Muller, *The Alaska Treaty* (Limestone Press, Kingston, Ont. 1981), p. 2-3.

and the Aleuts who certainly considered themselves civilized were to wage a losing battle for the cultural and religious liberty and protection which the Treaty of Cession had guaranteed to them.

The Transfer Ceremony

At 3:30 PM on October 18, 1867, the official ceremony marking the transfer of sovereignty of Alaska from Russia to the United States took place. 259 American soldiers under the command of General Jefferson C. Davis (no relation to the President of the Confederate States), Governor Prince Maksutov and his wife, and several Tlingit chiefs were present. General Lovell N. Rousseau, the official American representative at the event, filed this report with the Secretary of War in Washington:

> The command of General Davis, about 250 strong, in full uniform, armed and handsomely equipped, were landed about 3 o'clock and marched to the top of the eminence on which stands the governor's house, (Baranov's Castle) where the transfer was made. At the same time, a company of Russian soldiers were marched to the ground and took their place upon the left of the flagstaff, from which the Russian flag was then floating. The command of General Davis was formed under his direction on the right... The United States flag to be raised on the occasion was in the care of a color guard—a lieutenant, a sergeant and ten men of General Davis' command—the Prince Dimitri Maksutov and his wife, the Princess Maria Maksutov, together with many Russian and American citizens and some Indian chiefs were present. The formation of the ground, however, was such as to preclude any considerable demonstration.
>
> It was arranged by Captain Pestchurov and myself that, in firing the salute on the exchange of flags, the United States should lead off, but that there should be alternate guns from the American and Russian batteries, thus giving the flag of each nation a double national salute, the national salute being thus answered the moment it was given. The troops being promptly formed were, at precisely half-past three o'clock, brought to a "present arms" the signal was given to the Ossipee (Lt. Crossman...in command) which was to fire the salute, the ceremony was begun by lowering the Russian flag. As it began its descent down the flagstaff, the battery of the Ossipee with large, nine-inch guns, led off the salute, peal after peal crashing and re-echoing in gorges of the surrounding mountains, answered by the Russian battery (on the wharf), firing alternately. But the ceremony was interrupted by the catching of the Russian flag in the ropes attached to the flagstaff. The soldier lowering it continued to pull at it, tore off the border by which it was attached, leaving the flag entwined tightly around the ropes. The flagstaff was a native pine, perhaps ninety feet in height. In an instant, the Russian

soldiers attached to the flagstaff attempted to ascend to the flag, which was whipped around the ropes by the wind, and remained tight and fast. At first, being sailors as well as soldiers, they made rapid progress, but laboring hard, they soon became tired, and when halfway up, scarcely moved at all, and finally came to a standstill. There was a dilemma; and in a moment a "boatswain's chair" so-called, was made by knotting rope to make a loop for a man to sit in and be pulled upward, and another Russian soldier was drawn quickly up to the flag. On reaching it, he detached it from the ropes, and not hearing the calls from Capt. Pestchukov below to "bring it down," he dropped it below, and in its descent, it fell upon the bayonets of the Russian soldiers.

The United States flag was then properly attached and began its ascent, hoisted by my private secretary, George Lovell Rousseau, and again salutes were fired as before...Captain Pestchukov stepped up to me and said, "General Rousseau, by authority of His Majesty, the Emperor of Russia, I transfer to the United States of America the Territory of Alaska," and in a few words I acknowledged the acceptance of the transfer, and the ceremony was at an end. Three cheers were then spontaneously given for the United States flag by the American citizens present, although this was no part of the program, and on some accounts I regretted that it occurred.[29]

For most of the next twenty years, the American government paid little attention to its newly acquired territory. Most of the Russians, who had never totalled more than 900 persons throughout the entire region, returned to their homeland. The only professional people who remained in Alaska were, for the most part, Aleuts. They were the ones who continued to operate the schools, churches and trading posts. They served as translators and bureaucrats. Financially supported by the Missionary Society that Veniaminov founded as Metropolitan of Moscow in 1870, the Orthodox clergy continued their evangelical work during these years of Congressional neglect. In 1871, a U.S. Senator criticized federal neglect of Alaska stating that

...the Russian clergy made Christians of ignorant people, built churches, established schools and even at the present time, the rays of Christianity, be it said to our shame, reach there not from Washington, but from St Petersburg.[30]

In 1887, twenty years after the transfer of sovereignty, the Orthodox Mission was operating seventeen schools with an annual budget of twenty thousand dollars from the Mission Society. While this support suddenly

29 *Ibid.*, p. 132-133.
30 Ivan Barsukov's biography of Veniaminov, p. 711 (Moscow, 1883), quoted in Afonsky, *op. cit.*, p. 70.

and in some cases catastrophically ended during the 1917 Russian Revolution, Aleut schools continued to function informally throughout southern Alaska for another fifty years, but not without opposition and even persecution.

Bishop Veniaminov and the Sale

A few months after Alaska had been transferred to American rule, Archbishop Innocent Veniaminov wrote from Siberia to the Ober-Procurator of the Holy Synod:

> Rumor reaching me from Moscow purports that I wrote to someone of my great unhappiness about the sale of our colonies to the Americans. This is utterly false. To the contrary, I see in this event one of the ways of Providence by which Orthodoxy will penetrate the United States, (where even now people have begun to pay serious attention to it).

Were I to be asked about this, I would reply:

A. Do not close the American diocese—even though the number of churches and missions there has been reduced by half, (i.e., five).

B. Designate San Francisco rather than New Archangel the residence of the vicar (bishop). The climate is incomparably better there, and communications with the colonial churches are just as convenient from there as from New Archangel, if not more so.

C. Subordinate the diocese to the Bishop of St Petersburg or some other Baltic diocese, for once the colonies have been sold to the American Government, communications between the Amur and the colonies will end completely and all communications between the headquarters of the Diocese of Kamchatka and Alaska will be through St Petersburg—which is completely unnatural.

D. Return to Russia the present Bishop and all the clergy at Sitka (except the readers and wardens) and appoint a new bishop from among those who know the English language. Likewise, his retinue ought to be composed of those who know English.

E. Allow the bishop to augment his staff, transfer its members and ordain to the priesthood for our churches converts to Orthodoxy from among American citizens who accept all its institutions and customs.

F. Allow the vicar bishop and all the clergy of the Orthodox Church in America to celebrate the liturgy and others services in English (for which purpose, obviously, the service books must be translated into English).

G. To use English rather than Russian (which must be sooner or later replaced by English) in all instruction in the schools to be established in San Francisco and elsewhere to prepare people for ordination and missionary work.[31]

Veniaminov welcomed the possibilities that the sale of Alaska represented for the growth of the Orthodox Church in the New World, despite the reduction in the number of clergy in Alaska after the sale. He did not foresee any widespread apostasy, nor the decline of the church after the transfer, but predicted its growth years before he, as founder of the Orthodox Missionary Society, would be in a position to support the Alaskan mission again. His optimism about the future of Orthodoxy in America was grounded in his decades of experience among Native and Creole Christians in Alaska. He knew that the Church was firmly established among them, and he could therefore confidently recommend that the diocesan headquarters be moved to California. As Metropolitan of Moscow, Innocent implemented his plan, approving the transfer of the American see to San Francisco and appointing an English-speaking bishop there before his death in 1879. Bishop Nestor, who later drowned during a second pastoral visit to Alaska in 1882, spoke several foreign languages, and his successor, Bishop Vladimir, celebrated services and preached in English, commemorating the President of the United States instead of the Russian imperial family. He insisted that his priests learn and serve in English as well. Veniaminov's goal of providing translations of Orthodox services in English was partially realized with the publication of the Liturgy of St John Chrysostom in 1876. In fact, Bishop Vladimir was able to carry out much of Veniaminov's program, visiting immigrant communities in New York, Chicago, Detroit, New Orleans and San Francisco, as well as touring the Alaskan diocese three times and re-establishing a pastoral school at San Francisco where Alaskan clergy were trained. During a visit to the capital, Bishop Vladimir was received by the President of the United States, and reported to him directly on conditions in Alaska.

At the same time, the Holy Synod of the Church in Russia appropriated funds to support the American mission, more than thirty-eight thousand rubles in 1872, and increased to fifty-two thousand in 1874, and seventy-four thousand in 1894, reaching ninety thousand by the end of the century. These funds paid the salaries of the clergy at Sitka, Kodiak

31 Veniaminov *Letters,* Vol 3, p. 139-140; quoted in Oleksa,(1987), *op.cit.,* p. 251.

Unalaska, Russian Mission, Nushagak, the Pribilov Islands, Kenai, Belkovsky, Juneau, Chuathbaluk, and Nuchek, in Prince William Sound. Most of the clergy were Aleuts, Creoles of Sugpiaq or Unangan descent.

Bishop Nikolai (Zerov) governed the American Church for most of the 1890's, greatly accelerating the growth of the Orthodox mission both in Alaska and the "lower 48." He accepted into the Orthodox Church over twenty Uniat parishes that had decided to return to Orthodoxy now that they had the freedom to do so in the New World. He ordained Native clergy and expanded the educational role of the Alaskan mission to include forty-three schools and two seminaries at Unalaska and Sitka, for the training of indigenous clergy, and two more pastoral schools at Minneapolis and Cleveland, to educate American-born clergy to serve in other parts of the country. By 1902, the Orthodox Diocese of Sitka consisted of 11,758 members, 17 priests, one deacon and dozens of readers, with 87 Russians, 2,257 Creoles, 2,147 Tlingits, 2,406 Aleuts, 4,839 Eskimos and 22 others of various ethnic backgrounds. There were forty-five schools, two pastoral schools and five orphanages, eight brotherhoods, four temperance societies, and in San Francisco, the diocese was publishing the *American Orthodox Messenger* in Russian and English. Most of its monthly issues contained articles about Alaska from 1896 to 1907. By that time, Alaska was but one of several dioceses and missions on American soil, and the church had its headquarters in New York City. Its ruling bishop's official title was "Bishop of the Aleutian Islands and North America." The connection with the Aleuts as the historic foundation on which the entire church was built has never been abandoned.

On the eve of the Bolshevik coup in 1917, the Orthodox Church in the United States consisted of five bishops, 461 parishes, served by 309 priests and almost 600,000 members, including a Serbian mission with 36 parishes and 36,000 members, an Arab mission with 32 parishes and 150,000 members, and an Albanian mission with 30,000 more. There were by this time over a half million Orthodox Christians in the United States, most of whom were immigrants from the Old World, and totally unaware of the history of the Alaskan Church. All they knew about Kodiak, Kenai or Juneau was what they read in the monthly *Messenger*. Sadly, despite the expansion and acceleration of many of the mission's activities, most of the news from Alaska was not good.

PART III

The Supression of Alaskan Orthodoxy

8

Conflicting Worldviews

The American Schools

The primary proponents of assimilationism as public social and educational policy in Alaska were the Reverend S. Hall Young and the Reverend Dr. Sheldon Jackson, both Presbyterian ministers with close personal ties to officials in Washington, D.C., including several presidents.

Young wrote in his autobiography:

> One strong stand, so far as I know I was the first to take, was the determination to do no translating into...any of the native dialects. I realized...that the task of making an English-speaking race of these Natives was much easier than the task of making a civilized and Christian language out of the Native languages. We should let the old tongues with their superstitions and sin die—the sooner the better—and replace these languages with that of Christian civilization, and compel the Natives in our schools to speak English and English only.[1]

Sheldon Jackson, the first general agent for education in Alaska, determined the direction of public school policy from 1885 to 1906. Jackson had been active in Alaska since 1877, and he was determined to establish Mission Schools as "Protestant Forts" to protect the Natives from the military, as well as from sourdoughs and bootleggers. Basic to Jackson's philosophy were two fundamental goals: the establishment of Protestantism in Alaska and the replacement of all Native languages with English exclusively. He maintained an office in Washington, D.C., and stayed in close contact with influential Protestants in both the church and government, including President Benjamin Harrison, William Cleveland (brother of President Grover Cleveland) and John Eaton, the Federal Commissioner of Education. The Presbyterian Church paid Jackson's salary through 1907.

Since the Grant administration a decade earlier, the federal government had assigned various Indian reservations to specific Christian de-

1   Quoted in Michael Krauss, *Alaska Native Languages: Past, Present and Future* (Alaska Native Language Center, University of Alaska, Fairbanks, AK, 1972), p. 23

nominations and paid the salaries of the missionaries who operated the public schools on these reservations. Jackson imported and imposed this preexisting structure on Alaska. He orchestrated the educational effort, combining church support with federal funding. Congress appropriated only twenty-thousand dollars for the establishment of schools in the first year of Jackson's tenure. With so little money to work with, Jackson believed that only committed missionaries could be recruited to serve as teachers in the new territory. The major American Protestant denominations accepted Jackson as the coordinator for mission strategy in Alaska, giving him two major roles to play.

In Alaska, boarding homes were established by federally funded Protestant missions whose goal was to "recreate" young Natives in the likeness of their white mentors. Schools also aimed at preparing students for jobs as laborers, miners, teamsters and agricultural workers. As one Commissioner of Education expressed it, "We have no higher calling in the world than to be missionaries to these people who have not yet achieved the Anglo-Saxon frame of mind." However, when the American teacher/missionaries met the literate, Christian Aleuts, there was bound to be trouble. These Natives had embraced the "wrong" kind of Christianity and adopted the "wrong" alphabet. The conflict between opposing groups raged throughout the southern half of Alaska from about 1870 until about 1916. Many cases were reported in the *Orthodox Messenger*, a monthly publication of the diocese, printed in New York in both English and Russian. Documented clashes occurred at Kodiak, Nushagak, Sitka, Unalaska, and St Paul Island.

At Kodiak, the Baptist Mission and the public school cooperated to impress Orthodox Aleut children into the Woody Island boarding program. Mr. Roskor, the Superintendent of the Baptist Home, reportedly resorted to forcing his way into Aleut homes and compelling parents to sign away custody of their children. The North American Commercial Company, the successor to the Russian American Company founded by Shelikov, transported students to Woody Island "free of charge." The Aleut students remaining in Kodiak were taught to pray in the Protestant tradition and to sing Protestant hymns at the public school. The pastor of the Orthodox parish complained to the superintendent that such religious practices at the public school were illegal. He requested that they be discontinued, and it seems that they were. An Aleut Orthodox mother, Mrs Olga Shmakov, had to file suit in federal court to recover her son, who, she alleged, had been kidnapped from her home by the Baptist missionary. The boy was ordered returned to his parents, but Mr. Roskor went unpunished for abducting him.[2]

At Nushagak, in March 1896, the Orthodox priest requested permission to visit the Moravian Church's Boarding Home at Carmel to administer Holy Communion to the Orthodox children residing there, if they could not return to their villages for Holy Pascha. The administrator replied:

> Such which attend the mission school cannot go, neither can you come here to administer the Holy Sacrament. This is in accordance with the rules of the government, and the direct request of the ex-governor of Alaska.[3]

The close cooperation between the government and the churches is obvious from these statements.

At Sitka, a Tlingit Orthodox woman died, and her dying wish was to be buried according to the rites of the Orthodox Church. Her husband and two of her younger children wanted her to be buried as she desired, but two others sons, residing at the Presbyterian Mission school, allegedly requested a Presbyterian funeral. Governor James Sheakley, Rev. A. E Austin, and the U.S. Federal Marshal, W. E. Williams, seized the body, removed it from its original Orthodox coffin and took it to a neighboring house. When Hieromonk Anatolii, the Orthodox priest, protested, he was insulted and told to leave town. After the burial, the headmistress of the Presbyterian mission attempted to coerce the widower to relinquish custody of his younger children and enroll them at her school, but the Orthodox priest again intervened and prevented this.

In 1897, a similar incident occurred at Unalaska. An Aleut boarding student at the Methodist Mission, the Jesse Lee Home, suddenly died and was buried by the Protestant staff in the Orthodox cemetery, but her priest and family were not notified. In spite of the fact that a federal agent had assigned Aleut children to the home to attend school with a promise from the administration that their Orthodox religious tradition would be

2   Michael Oleksa, "The Suppression of the Aleuts" (*St Vladimir's Theological Quarterly*, Vol. 28, No. 2, 1984), p. 103.
3   *Ibid.*, p. 104.

respected, the mission administration insisted that it had acted in accordance with the wishes of the girl's father. When he, an American Protestant, returned to Unalaska and learned of his daughters death, the Orthodox priest asked him if he had instructed the Jesse Lee Home staff to convert his children to Protestantism. He denied ever requesting such things and immediately removed his two remaining children from the home.

In another case, the Jesse Lee Home sought custody of a child on the grounds that her Aleut mother was an alcoholic who neglected her maternal responsibilities. The local pastor, Father Alexander Kedrofskii, secured an affidavit from a magistrate in Kodiak, where the mother was residing, affirming that she was of sound moral character. The matron of the home, Mrs Agnes Newhall, insisted, however, that she had documents from another Kodiak judge, testifying to the mother's incompetence. Later, when this was proven to be false and Father Kedrofskii confronted her, she only grinned.

This provided the background for a very illuminating correspondence between Father Alexander and Mrs Newhall, published in the *Russian-American Orthodox Messenger* in 1898.[4] Father Kedrofskii initiated the correspondence with a request that he be permitted to visit the boarding school. He complained that his church should not be called "Russian."

...if there is a "Russian" or "American" religion, I know of none. I know only that there is a Christian religion, to our misfortune divided into two...If you happen to address someone with a question about religion, do not ask "Do you want to have a Russian or American religion."[5]

In response, Mrs Newhall asserted that her home was devoted to the "advancement of Christ's Kingdom and the uplifting of fallen humanity," with special interest in the children of Alaska. She wrote:

We assume complete charge of the children while under our care. As for religious instruction, it is wholly under the direction of the home management and according to the Protestant faith. Your request to visit the home for religious instruction cannot be granted...No children are allowed to attend the Greco-Russian Church...In case of death, services and burial are conducted by the home management, except in such cases as we shall decide otherwise. Interference in these respects shall not be tolerated.[6]

4   Reprinted in Oleksa, *Alaska Missionary Spirituality, op. cit.,* p. 330.
5   *Ibid.,* p. 330.
6   *Ibid.,* p. 331.

The policies of the Methodist home were the same at the Moravian Mission at Nushagak. In the next section of her letter, Mrs Newhall expressed her personal opinion of the Aleuts and their "moral" condition:

Is it enough to take the name of Christ upon our lips to witness the forms and ceremonies week after week, and still go on in sin and wickedness? We think not. Is not dishonesty, profanity, adultery, fornication, lasciviousness, strife and drunkenness rife? Is it not an insult to God and the cross of Christ for such workers of iniquity to call themselves Christians? We think so.[7]

Clearly Mrs Newhall did not have a high regard for the Aleuts or their religion, and considered it her mission to "uplift" them.

An outraged Father Kedrofskii replied with a lengthy letter, almost a full sermon, containing numerous Biblical quotations. He began by noting that the Jesse Lee Home had been established at Unalaska for more than ten years, but had disguised its identity under the name, "a home attached to the public school," until 1898. He noted that many of the students assigned to the school were taken by force from their homes by civil authorities, with "breaking open doors and beating of parents." Even then, he wrote, it was promised that the children's religion would be respected. He accused the management of the Home of "deceit and craftiness" and quoted three New Testament passages condemning such behavior.

Father Kedrofskii continued that in the past children from the home were allowed to attend Sunday and holiday services, that they attended Orthodox church school after liturgy, and that during Christmas and Paschal seasons he had visited them in the Home. Now that the Home had shown its true colors, the management was changing its policy, but he considered this to be "dishonorable."

Referring repeatedly to Mrs Newhall as a "most worthy" or "most respected matron," he disagreed strongly with her assessment of Aleut Christianity.

You, respected matron, hear of the sinning but not the penitence, and of the sinning you hear exaggerated accounts. No, it is possible that you exaggerate yourself, which would be natural to a certain extent...for you stand as sentry, as it were, over us, and exaggerate our shortcomings...If we are to speak of the depravity of the Natives, we must not forget that the blame for it falls to a great extent on the strangers who bring here the evil example of their lives...Are they

7 *Ibid.*, p. 332.

– [the Aleuts] to be blamed because their homes are invaded at night—by depraved
strangers, newcomers, who bring liquor with them for evil purposes?...The
Aleuts are not hardened and persistent sinners; they are people with humble
infirmities, with broken and contrite hearts [Psalm 51:17] as I, their spiritual
father, very well know. I do not dare to think that I am better, purer, than they
in the eyes of God...[8]

Against the accusation that the Aleuts were only outwardly religious,
Father Alexander replied,

– How do you account for this "outward religiosity" of theirs?...It is not hypocrisy,
for they do not know how to sham. It cannot be habit—just try to get into the
habit of standing for two hours at a time (at church services) or the habit of
giving your last penny for a good cause...No; this outward religiosity of theirs is
the fruit of an inward and sincere disposition of the heart, and that is why they
may enter the Kingdom of Heaven *before us.*[9]

Father Kedrofskii's personal humility and love for his flock is striking.
He accused the "most worthy matron" of exaggerating when she called
the Aleut homes "brothels of sin."

From what do you conclude that the Natives of this region lead such very sinful
lives? Coming to the list of the sins which you say prevail among them, I must
– inform you that some of those sins do not exist among them at all; others do
exist, as you say, though not everywhere, and others again exist in no greater
degree than, I dare say, we shall find them in *ourselves,* you and I, if we take the
trouble to "know ourselves." ...The alleged total depravity of the Natives causes
you deep sorrow, yet do tell me, from your conscience, is the moral life of the
– people from where you came any better than theirs? How do you explain what
we read in the newspaper headlines?[10]

After several more paragraphs, in which Father Kedrofskii lectured
Mrs Newhall on the piety of the Aleuts and his (and her own) spiritual
struggle, he finished his letter by returning to the issue of Irene Titoff, the
girl who had been secretly buried the previous fall. Calling her his
"spiritual daughter," he asked, "What need then had you to take her from
the faith of her church and give her a new faith—yours?" He lamented
that it was so obvious that the staff of the Jesse Lee Home were "completely unacquainted with the tenets of our Church" and offered to send
books about it "in the English language," so that they could, in the future,
avoid bearing false witness against their neighbor. He concluded by

8   *Ibid.,* p. 335.
9   *Ibid.,* p. 336.
10   *Ibid.*

stating that he did not blame Mrs Newhall personally for all that had transpired, because she was "under authority."[11]

This correspondence is probably one of the most graphic illustrations of the conflict between rival mission and school philosophies, and of the human toll it took.

The Pribilof Islands represent an extreme case of total federal domination of an Aleut population. Government agents used physical punishment and even incarceration to force Aleut parents to enroll their children in the federal school. In 1873, Mr MacIntyre, the Treasury Agent, arrested a father who had refused to send his son to the "American School," locked him in the cellar of the company house in handcuffs, and fed him bread and water for four days until he consented to send his son, who had also been confined in a closet and fed the same diet, to the federal school.[12] Aleuts did not resist learning English, but struggled to maintain their own traditional languages, Unangar, and Russian. The government began imposing fines on parents whose children did not attend the federal school. Attendance improved, but Aleut resistance continued.

American missionaries and federal officials alleged that Orthodox clergy opposed the introduction of English, but as early as 1871, Bishop Paul had begun the process of adapting the curricula at the Orthodox schools to English. At Sitka, in fact, English was offered as early as 1845. Church services were published in English in 1872,[13] and in 1876 Bishop Nestor reported that, beginning at seven years of age, Pribilof Aleut students were taught "in the American language."[14] English was added to the curriculum at Unalaska in 1879, at Kenai in 1893, and at Nushagak in 1894. The Orthodox school at Seldovia began offering English language instruction in 1896, and at all the twenty-three new Orthodox parish schools which opened between 1890 and 1904, teaching English was a primary objective.

In 1910, however, federal agents at St Paul were still complaining that

11 *Ibid.* p. 339
12 Dorothy K. Jones, *A Century of Servitude* (University of Alaska Press, Anchorage, AK, 1980), p. 28.
13 Microfilm: Documents Relative to the History of Alaska (University of Alaska, Fairbanks, AK), Roll 2; page 373.
14 Svetlana Feodorova, *Russians on the Pacific and California* (Limestone Press, Kingston, Ont., 1973), p. 266.

only five or six Aleuts there could speak English well, and continued to blame the Orthodox school and Aleut parents for insisting on the use of Aleut in village affairs. Some time before 1916, the government forcibly closed the Orthodox parish school.

Elsewhere in the news:

> Circa 1912—the U.S. Government closes the Orthodox Church school St Paul, Pribilofs, by force, for the crime of teaching Aleut. There will be no Natives teachings Natives native, or in the Native languages.[15]

The Orthodox Response

As early as 1885, Orthodox priests were pleading for an end to the persecution they felt the federal government had begun of their church and their flocks. Father Nicholas Metropolskii wrote on May 21:

> I write this report at the request of the parishioners and I beg the ecclesiastical consistory to consider it and to petition the Russian Ambassador in Washington for intercession on behalf of the Orthodox people of Alaska. After 1867, the members of the Orthodox Church in Alaska have not had the rights enjoyed by other American citizens. Last year, the American authorities set up a civil government in Alaska...Now it is being rumored that...Dr. Jackson is endeavoring to remove them and replace them with his supporters. If he attains his aim, not only the white but the Indian members of the Orthodox congregation will suffer greatly here. Our school at Sitka was and is attended by children of Roman Catholics, Jews, and people of other denominations. We taught and still teach them Russian and English free of charge and do not force them to study church rules and regulations...

The literate Native population did not endure this harassment silently. In 1897, for example, the Aleut and Tlingit people of Sitka brought their situation to the attention of the Imperial Russian ambassador in Washington, D.C. They mentioned the disruption of the Tlingit Orthodox burial by the governor and the federal marshal and said "similar and even worse outrages" occurred everywhere in Alaska. Writing on behalf of "the Orthodox Natives, numbering no less than 482," who are "subjected to vexations of every description," they complained that they could not obtain justice in courts "and other official places where Presbyterian influences reign supreme." They specifically requested that the ambassa-

15 Richard John Dauenhauer, *Glacier Bay Concerto* (Alaska Pacific University Press, Anchorage, AK, 1980), p. 39.

dor protest the abuses to which the Orthodox Natives were subjected by the Presbyterian Mission and the U.S. federal government, and ask the Russian government to appoint a representative to reside at Sitka to protect the religious and civil rights which had been guaranteed in the 1867 treaty. The petition was signed in English and in Russian by men and women named Chernoff, Larionoff, Paramonoff, Simeonoff, Chichenoff, Kashevarof, Bourdukofsky, and Shishkin, and was published in the *Russian-American Messenger.*

That same year, a petition was mailed to President McKinley, asking him to 1) restrict the Baranoff Packing Company from blocking rivers and streams that had been traditionally used by Tlingit subsistence fisher- men; 2) order Governor Brady to desist from constructing roads through the Tlingit village and desecrating their cemetery, and 3) prevent the introduction of American saloons. The local Tlingit chiefs signed their names in Cyrillic characters.[16]

As Bishop Nicholas was leaving Alaska for a new assignment in Russia, he also appealed to President McKinley for protection from "the abuses of officials who...are sent to Alaska exclusively on the recommendation of...Sheldon Jackson." He pleaded, "Alaska must be delivered from that man. By his sectarian propaganda, he introduced dissension, enmity and inequity where these evils did not exist before." The bishop also cited the 1867 treaty as the legal basis for respecting the legitimate place of the Orthodox Church in Alaska and asked why the government was

> trying to drive her out by every means possible, legal and illegal. Will you be acting consistently if, while waging war for the liberty of Cuba, Puerto Rico, and the Philippines, for their human rights, you ignore these matters at home, in part of your own country?...And so, Mr. President, be indulgent and gracious to poor, hapless Alaska.[17]

The *New York Tribune* attacked Bishop Nicholas for his "blind and unwarranted prejudice against this Protestant country and its excellent schools" and a Presbyterian monthly in Pittsburgh labeled the bishop's criticisms unfounded and unfair:

> A bishop of the "orthodox" Greek Church...has lodged a complaint with Pres. McKinley...abusing the public schools of this country and insulting the Ameri-

16 The texts of both petitions are reprinted in Oleksa, *Alaska Missionary Spirituality, op. cit.*, p. 322-326.
17 *Ibid.*, p. 327.

can People...The people of Alaska who have such a combination of ignorance and insolence in their spiritual leader are to be pitied. It is by means of men of this character that they have been brought to the degradation with which they are now afflicted.[18]

The Orthodox press was even more critical, however, of Dr. Jackson when his *School Report of 1898-99* was issued and the Orthodox schools were not even mentioned. The accomplishments and contributions of twenty-eight federally funded mission schools were so exaggerated that editorial pages in nearly every Alaskan newspaper mocked the report. In July 1900, the *Orthodox Messenger* noted that most of Dr. Jackson's schools had been founded in villages where Orthodox schools already existed, "in the midst of the Orthodox population," and therefore "not in accordance with the needs of the people, but only with the purposes of the [Protestant] missions in mind." The editorial also alleged that all the employees of the Presbyterian missions received salaries from the federal government that year.[19]

The Rev. William Duncan, founder of the "model" Christian Indian community of Metlakatla, near Ketchikan, also criticized Jackson's school system. He opposed separating children from their parents and quoted a federal marshal as saying that "not long ago, of twenty Indian inmates in his jail, nineteen had been students in boarding schools. The young men, disgusted with work, gradually sank into laziness and vice." Duncan added that the marshal reported that the girls had become prostitutes. Duncan believed that each community should have its own school where the children would be taught in their own language and remain at home with their parents. The school should, the Orthodox editorial commented, "do all those things which Dr. Jackson and his assistants now so strenuously oppose."[20] Actually, in Duncan's model town the indigenous language, Tshimsian, was also eventually suppressed as "heathen."

The assimilationist educational and social policies of the American Protestant missions forced the Tlingits of southeastern Alaska to reconsider their initial unreceptive or hostile attitude toward Orthodoxy. While St Innocent Veniaminov had greatly admired Tlingit culture and devoted years to developing cordial relations and learning the Tlingit language,

18 Microfilm, Personal communication, Paul Garrett.
19 Oleksa, "Suppression," *op. cit.*, p. 111.
20 *Ibid.*, p. 258.

very few Tlingit embraced Christianity during the Russian period. After the sale of Alaska, only 102 Russians and Creoles remained at Sitka, and bishops there were pessimistic about the future of the Orthodox mission as the Presbyterian assault began in 1878. However, in the 1880's, Tlingit chiefs themselves petitioned the Orthodox bishop for teachers and clergy and encouraged their people to accept baptism. At Sitka, eighty persons were received into the parish in 1881, and fifty more adults were baptized between 1882 and 1885. By 1892, a majority of Sitka's Indian population had become Orthodox.

Several factors combined to attract the Tlingits to Orthodoxy. After the chiefs had expressed their interest in the faith, the cathedral parish assigned Father Vladimir Donskoi to serve as a missionary priest for the Tlingit community. Donskoi organized informal weekly meetings, participated in traditional Tlingit feasts, and defended Tlingits from some of the more coercive tactics of the Presbyterians. He learned to speak Tlingit and translated a short collection of prayers and hymns, which the mission eventually published. The poorly staffed Orthodox parish school trained Tlingit readers and choir directors in two and sometimes three languages, and soon attracted more students than it could accept. The Orthodox clergy tended to tolerate, if not to approve, many Tlingit traditions which the Presbyterians condemned as heathen. The Orthodox used persuasion rather than excommunication or suspension when new converts "lapsed" into pre-Christian behavior. Both Russian/Creole and Tlingit cultures provided ample opportunity for socializing, especially feasting. Tlingits were invited into the homes of "respectable" Aleuts, many of whom had maintained prestigious social positions after the 1867 sale. The traditional Tlingit emphasis on social rank and protocol could be satisfied with such inter-ethnic intercourse. During Pascha 1887, an eyewitness described the community celebration in this way:

> Tlingits of both sexes dressed up for the occasion, visited homes of their godparents, and offered congratulations, for which they received eggs, kulich, (sweet Easter bread)...and Paskha (a special cheese-cake), or simply bread. They like the customs of the Orthodox people and are introducing them into their own homes. Their own tables are now decorated with holiday food.[21]

21 Sitka diary of Stepan Ushin, 1874-1895, Alaska Church Collection, Library of Congress, quoted in Sergei Kan, "Russian Orthodox Missionaries and the Tlingit Indians of Alaska, 1880-1900" (May 1983), pp. 19-20.

In most of Alaska, winter was a traditional season for holiday feasting and visiting, and the Orthodox clergy were sensitive to the cultural parallels. They were also aware of the importance of protocol and social status in traditional Tlingit life, and baptized leading chiefs, such as Qatlian, with great pomp and public ceremony, no doubt much to the dismay of the Presbyterians. In turn, the American missionaries turned increasingly to the civil authorities to enforce assimilationist policies. When potlatching[22] was officially outlawed, the Orthodox bishop was given a ceremonial paddle as a token of unity and solidarity. In Orthodox communities, memorial feasts continued to be held at the burial and on the fortieth day following the death, despite the legal ban on such "pagan festivities."

About 1899, Sheldon Jackson reacted angrily to Bishop Nicholas' letter to President McKinley. Jackson claimed that the "days of the Orthodox Church are numbered" and that "twenty-five years from now, there will not be any Orthodox church members left in Alaska." In 1900, however, he was forced to include the School Report of the Orthodox Mission in his own annual report, but this proved to be only a minor concession to mounting public pressure.[23]

Within two decades, the number of federally-funded monolingual schools and the decreasing financial support from Russia for the Aleut bilingual schools ended this uneven struggle. The Russian Revolution and civil war suddenly and completely ended all funding for the remaining Aleut schools. In a few scattered and determined communities elders and teachers continued to teach children the four R's for another thirty or forty years. Ultimately, however, Sheldon Jackson's assimilationist, monolingual policies completely dominated Alaskan education.

Every few years, experienced village teachers returned to their home states, and new recruits came from outside Alaska to replace them, without any cultural orientation or historical perspective to prepare them for rural Alaska. Such experiences led teachers coming to the Pribilofs to

22 Potlatch: A memorial feast conducted by northwest coast Indians at which names, gifts, and food were awarded, and by which clans maintain their social status and prestige. The central role of traditional oratory at the Tlingit *Koo.eex'* is best described in *Haa Tuwunaagu Yis*, by Nora and Richard Dauenhauer (University of Washington Press, Seattle, WA., 1990), p. 3-155.

23 Oleksa, "Suppression," *op. cit.*, p. 111.

consider their students "stupidly dull," and to demand the suppression of the "Russian School" which met only once a week. The remedy for Native language related "disabilities" seemed obvious to the territorial commissioner of education in 1903. He ordered all teachers to bring with them works of English literature, supposing that Shakespeare, Scott and the like would "furnish exactly the material...to arouse and kindle the sluggish minds of the Natives with sentiments and motives of action which lead to our civilization."[24] As the years passed and new instructors came and went, this attitude came to prevail among village teachers and Alaskan educators in general. The idea that Native language bilingualism impedes progress in school and befuddles the mind has a long history in the state, and resurfaces periodically in the Alaskan press.

Although Aleuts were in a better position to resist the assimilationist policies of Jackson and his allies, succeeding generations came to accept their externally-imposed identity as "just dumb Aleuts." Increasingly dependent on federal and state programs and funding as the determining factors in their lives, Aleut communities became apprehensive about their future. As generations have passed, the accomplishments of 19th-century Aleuts have faded from popular memory, and people have begun to blame themselves for their marginalized social position. This provides the context for many of the serious social problems—alcohol and drug abuse, domestic violence, child abuse and neglect, and even suicide—which affect most such communities today. The government responds to these problems with more money, more programs, more imported expertise. In this way, it only perpetuates the dependence and the cycle is complete.

As recently as 1968, attempts to permit the use of Native languages in Alaskan classrooms were frustrated by the State Commissioner of Education who said that bilingual education "would undermine the authority of the teachers." In 1965, the federal government invited the Assembly of God Church to establish a mission on St Paul Island against the unanimous objections of the Aleuts. The government maintained that it favored the introduction of this denomination "for the religious diversification of the Aleuts." Assimilationism, it seems, is far from dead.

In the 1970's, Native parents began to oppose the federal and state

24 Quoted in Richard Dauenhauer, "Conflicting Visions in Alaskan Education" (University of Alaska, Fairbanks, AK, 1980), p. 20.

school systems, which continued to remove teenagers from their villages to distant high school boarding programs.

> When they [the students] come back educated, they are no longer the same children we once saw leave for school. Some of them are strangers to their own people, but much worse, they are strangers to themselves.[25]

The Supreme Court decision in Lau v. Nichols in 1974 declared that bilingual education is a legal right of minority children. In addition, the "Molly Hootch" case in Alaska a few years later mandated local high schools for Native Alaskans. Some aspects of the Aleut educational philosophy are being revived.

The effects of the suppression of Aleut schools and the educational philosophy they represented remain in force. The government continues to impose standards and goals on a Native population which is trying to maintain a separate cultural identity in a rapidly changing world. The only difference now is that the public schools rather than federally-supported parochial schools have been assigned this task. A peaceful and reasonable settlement of this problem can come about only if both sides recognize that the necessary course is to combine in the classroom the "best of both worlds" (as the Aleuts did over a century ago), or if Native society deteriorates to such a point that the indigenous peoples of Alaska cease to exist.

The nineteenth-century Aleut experience demonstrates that such a synthesis of traditional and modern cultures can be achieved. To inaugurate such a philosophy in education and in society in general requires more than the popular desire to do so. Certainly this is precisely the wish of the vast majority of Native Alaskans today. Indeed, the goal of most Third and Fourth World cultures around the globe is to integrate those features of the global culture which are most useful and relevant to local needs, and at the same time to retain what is most precious and necessary in the traditional culture. Every nation, and indeed every individual human being, needs to adapt to and to relate to the larger society in which they live, while simultaneously maintaining their own unique identity. The Aleuts proved the feasibility of this by maintaining a continuity in worldview during their transition from pre-Christianity to Orthodox Christianity. They adapted new technology and retained much of the old.

25 *Must One Way of Life Die for Another to Live?* (Yupiktak Bista, Bethel, AK, 1970), p. 70.

They used ancient talents and techniques for new purposes. They added two new languages to their social repertoire without abandoning their mother tongue. As long as they were intellectually and culturally free to accept or reject what was extraneous or foreign, and to retain what they saw as important and meaningful of what was authentically their own, Aleut culture could develop and thrive.

There is increasing sympathy for such a vision among Alaskan professionals. Some school districts have mandated bicultural curricula, seeking to integrate aspects of traditional indigenous culture into the classroom. This is, of course, a reversal of the assimilationist policies so violently enforced as recently as the 1950's, but the success of such a program will almost certainly be limited. The overwhelming majority of public school teachers in Alaska are unfamiliar with local traditions, and they are often unaware that an alternative worldview even exists in their community. Many come to realize that such differences exist but become all the more determined to eliminate them, to create a homogeneous population, an American identity based on the concept of the "melting pot," the imposition of Anglo-Saxon norms and values on everyone else. Popular sovereignty, allowing Fourth World tribal peoples the autonomy they need to combine the best of two worlds without being forcibly assimilated into the dominant one, has been accepted and approved by one Alaskan governor in 1990, only to be rejected by the next administration a year later.

Since the public school has been the battleground on which the struggle for cultural autonomy and spiritual integrity has been fought for over a century, the question arises as to whether it is an appropriate institution for creating such a cultural synthesis. If multi-cultural education is reduced to net mending and nouns, in other words, to handicrafts (as cultural education), and vocabulary lists (as bilingual education), indigenous peoples might better dispense with both. If, however, each community, each family, can resolve to define and maintain its traditional spiritual values, and the educational establishment acknowledges the importance and cooperates in supporting and enhancing the local culture— not just as subsistence economic activities or traditional crafts but the essentially spiritual worldview which these presuppose—if, in other words, there is real rather than nominal control of local schools by proponents of pluralistic multiculturalism, and a commitment to cooper-

ate in creating a new multicultural vision, something like the Aleut
Synthesis could emerge again. This reorientation of educational and social
priorities appeals to most "minority" communities in the United States;
but rural Alaska, geographically removed from major urban centers, with
a small but homogeneous indigenous population, has perhaps the best
chance for implementing it.

At present, then, there are several layers of difficulty to be overcome.
There is the maintenance of the traditional spirituality and worldview.
There is the adequate training of educators, especially indigenous professionals, in which students acquire competencies demanded by the modern work place without losing a positive sense of their traditional identity.
There is the willingness and flexibility of modern institutions to adjust
appropriately to allow for cultural differences and local needs. There is
community awareness of the problems and a determination to deal with
them, resolving them by a consensus of the Native population, without
philosophically capitulating to external pressures and norms. There is the
development of instructional materials for students across the entire
curriculum, at all grade levels and in all subject areas. Finally, there is the
indigenization of the entire teaching profession in rural Alaska. All this
must be accomplished in the midst of tremendous social and economic
upheaval. It will not be easy.

Those who designed the great cathedrals of Europe in the Middle Ages
were only able to lay the cornerstones. They had to have the faith that
succeeding generations would continue the work, bringing it to its ultimate completion, sometimes centuries later. Nothing worthwhile, say the
Holy Fathers, can be done in one lifetime.

9

Alaska's Enduring Orthodox Heritage

Despite the hostility of the government and the ignorance of sectarian polemicists, as well as the much-reduced level of external financial support for the mission, Alaskan Orthodoxy has more than survived. As Orthodox Natives have moved to other villages, they have brought their faith with them and often constructed new chapels. Such, for example, is the history of several new parishes on the lower Kuskokwim. Atmautluaq was founded by villagers primarily from Kasigluk, a predominantly Orthodox community, and Nunapitchuk, a predominantly Moravian town. Both the Moravians and the Orthodox built new chapels at the new settlement, the latter naming their church for St Herman of Alaska. When villagers from Kwigillingok decided to relocate, they initially took their little church with them to the new site, but later built a splendid new building there, furnished with an iconostasis that came to them all the way from an Orthodox parish in New Britain, Connecticut. The few remaining Orthodox in Kwigillingok then built a new chapel for themselves, with the help of their relatives who had moved to the new village. In the Yukon Delta, the small Orthodox community at Mountain Village decided that they needed a church of their own and recently erected one there. Even villages with less than five Orthodox households almost always have an Orthodox church. Such fidelity to Orthodoxy cannot be explained on the basis of the mission's greater material, financial or professional resources. Rather, there continues to be a deep commitment to this ancient faith at the popular level, the basis of which seems to derive from the cosmic dimension of the Orthodox worldview as celebrated in Orthodox public worship.

The Alaskan Church in the Twentieth Century

With the closure of the Unalaska seminary after the Bolshevik Revolution in Russia in October 1917, Orthodox Alaska was left without a training center for church leaders. Some graduates of the San Francisco school returned to their villages late in the nineteenth century, transmitting their knowledge along traditional, Native Alaskan lines, especially from uncle to nephew. The late Sergei Sheratine of Port Lions, for example, was trained by his uncle, Tikhon Sheratine, who had completed his studies in California in 1899. Archpriest Basil Sifsof, who finished his schooling at Unalaska, was further prepared for his ministry by his father-in-law, Basil Backford. Archpriest Nikolai Epchook, originally from Netsvetov's original Yukon Delta headquarters, "Russian Mission," learned much from the Aleut clergy who resided in the area, and he was ordained after spending some months at Unalaska. He, in turn, trained his son, Archpriest Vasilii Epchook, and Archpriest Nikolai O. Michael, at Kwethluk.

Subdeacon Matthew Berezkin, an Unalaskan Aleut, attended the seminary in his hometown, married, and was ordained to the priesthood. Early in the century he was assigned to Kolmakovskii, on the Kuskokwim, but his Unangan wife deserted him after the death of their infant daughter near Chuathbaluk. Reduced to lay status, Berezkin remarried at Napaskiak and labored for nearly forty years, translating scriptural and liturgical texts and training readers and singers in English, Yup'ik and Slavonic years after his eyesight failed. These translations became part of an extensive corpus of oral folklore which includes all of the hymns for Orthodox vespers, most of matins, and the fixed sections of the eucharistic liturgy. Choirs memorized the words and sang entire services by heart in their own language.

"Starring"

About 1905, the only Ukrainian missionary to serve in western Alaska, Father Iakov Korchinskii, probably introduced the singing of Carpatho-Russian folk carols, *koliady*. Winter was the ancient traditional season for feasting and distributing gifts, associated with the Bladder Festival, and the Yup'ik quickly adapted the caroling customs to their own needs. In any case, the Yup'ik celebration of *Selaviq*, derived from the Slavonic "*Slava*" represents an obvious synthesis of Orthodox liturgical, Ukrainian folk, and ancient Eskimo traditions.

"*Selaviq*" (also called "Starring") is observed differently in different parts of Alaska. In southeastern Alaska, where the traditional potlatch or memorial feast is still conducted with speeches, feasting, traditional dancing and gift giving, caroling has much less cultural importance. The format consists of the singers, gathered around a large, pin-wheel style "star," singing the verse from the Gospel of St Luke, "Glory to God in the highest and on earth peace...," the Christmas troparion and kontakion, and concludes with the invocation of "Many Years," the Orthodox hymn for blessings and long life, sung in English, Slavonic and Tlingit. A few treats might be offered to the guests, a warm beverage for the adults, and perhaps candy for the children in the entourage. The entire household ceremony, however, is only slightly more elaborate than most typical American Christmas caroling. The reason for this seems to be that the Tlingit have combined the Orthodox practice of prayers for the departed on the fortieth day after death with the Tlingit memorial feast. So widespread is this fortieth-day feast among the Tlingit that it is generally believed to be an ancient Tlingit custom.[1]

The Alutiiq and Unangan Aleuts enjoy the house-to-house visitations and festive atmosphere of "Starring," during which they sing the same hymns in Slavonic, English and sometimes in their Native language as well. Not many folk carols have been translated into these languages, and none have ever been published. However, a large corpus of Christmas liturgical music was anonymously translated on Kodiak Island and circulated widely, again through oral transmission and memorization, among the Alutiiqs of Prince William Sound, on the mainland, where this tradition has recently been discovered and recorded by Jeff Leer, an Orthodox linguist.

Another aspect of the pre-Christian winter festivities has been preserved among the Unangan and Alutiiq Orthodox. After the "Starring," "masking" or "masquerading" begins. In some villages, such as English Bay or Port Graham, elaborately disguised participants gather in the community hall or recreation center for a type of Halloween party, during which each tries to guess the identity of the others. In other towns, the "masqalataqs" come door-to-door, and the residents of each house attempt to identify them. These "maskers" were, until recently, considered frightening, and children would run to hide from them. A biblically-in-

1   Dauenhauer and Dauenhauer, *op. cit.* (1990), p. 34.

spired explanation for this practice recalls the massacre of the innocent children "two years old and under" by King Herod's command, supposing that the soldiers who carried out this order were disguised. The custom more obviously derives from the pre-contact winter festival, during which the participants wore, according to Netsvetov's Atkan reports, masks which were often terrifying. In the past, those who wore the masks were required to bathe and be blessed with the newly-sanctified water of Epiphany before they were allowed to participate in church functions. Masked dancing represented, until this century, a relapse into paganism, but by now, it is another unique Aleut custom the Orthodox enjoy.

It is among the relatively recently baptized Yup'ik that the greatest variety and creativity in adapting Orthodox faith to local customs appears. Among the Nushagak and Iliamna peoples, *Selaviq* includes less feasting in each household (and, for that matter, less actual singing), than among the Yup'ik of the Kuskokwim-Yukon Delta, but much more inter-village travel. The singers, following their village "star," visit each Orthodox household in their own community, and then travel by sled and snow-machine, and more recently charter airplane, over the frozen tundra and river ice to neighboring villages. At each residence, they are welcomed with refreshments, and a generous donation is made "to the star," that is, to the parish the singers represent. By visiting several hundred homes, the singers enjoy not only visiting their extended family and friends throughout the region, and consuming a substantial amount of traditional foods, but also raise thousands of dollars for the annual budget of their village church.

The Kuskokwim/Yukon holiday tradition differs considerably, and perhaps reveals its pre-Christian ancestry most vividly of all the regional variants. *Selaviq* in this deanery requires months of preparation, since the berries needed for holiday *akutaq* (a whipped Eskimo dessert made with fruit, oil, sugar and in recent times, mashed potatoes), must be picked during summer, and groceries for the banquet, as well as hundreds of dollars in gifts (caps, gloves, scarves, socks, towels, and similar items) must be ordered in advance from catalogues or purchased locally. Until very recently, "Starring" in most villages on the first two days continued from late afternoon or early evening throughout the night, and sometimes well into the next morning, before the exhausted singers would collapse into bed for a few hours' sleep. On the third and final day, singing continued until the last homes were visited, even if this meant an all-night, all-day marathon. The final singing of the entire repertoire of *selavircuutet* (starring songs) occurs at the parish cemetery, where the three-barred cross grave markers have been illuminated with lanterns for the entire three-day period. This pattern has been slightly modified by episcopal decree to allow singers to participate in the festal liturgies of the first two days, the Feasts of the Theotokos and of St Stephen the first martyr. Starring on those days begins earlier in the afternoon and ends at midnight, and the large number of homes now requires *Selaviq* to continue for several more days beyond the original three-day event. Each passing year, more food and gifts are distributed, indicating a level of material prosperity never before attained in rural Alaska.

A group following the "Star" (or even several groups following several stars) will enter a house singing "*Slava v vyshnikh Bogu...*" (Glory to God in the Highest...), sometimes in Slavonic, sometimes in Yup'ik. The order and number of hymns and *koliady* varies from village to village, but in most, the troparion, kontakion, and sections from the canon (a lengthy hymn sung at festal matins) with at least one *koliada* and "Many Years," represent a bare minimum. In larger homes, the performance is much expanded to include more of the canon, and as many as five *koliady*, each with three to ten verses! These songs are sometimes followed by a sermon, either by a member of the household or by a special guest. Immediately following the final chorus of "Many Years" (during which there may be a shotgun salute fired outside the window) the oldest men and church leaders sit down to a traditional Yup'ik festal dinner: dried and smoked salmon, moose, caribou, seal or beaver stew, canned fruit, jello, fried or freshly baked bread, *akutaq*, tea and coffee. Children receive handfuls of candy or similar treats, much as on Halloween in American culture. As the first sitting finishes their last cups of tea, the gifts are distributed. The next sittings follow in order until all the adult men have eaten. The women and young children, and finally any adolescents, then eat in turn, each receiving appropriate gifts from the hosts, until all have eaten as much as they wanted or could have. The time elapsed between the entrance of the singers until the last guests have eaten is normally several hours. The "Star" then exits, and the crowd follows it to the next house,

where the singing and feasting begin again. The amount of food con-
— sumed during the three-day *Selaviq* in a typical Orthodox community is
almost incredible.

Most Yup'iks consider *Selaviq* a "Russian" tradition, since the feast and
the hymns are either Orthodox liturgical selections or Ukrainian carols.
The custom of following the "Star" also originated in Eastern Europe,
although the "Stars" there were traditionally icons mounted on a pole,
rather than the large, spinning, tinsel-decorated pin-wheels all Alaskans
know. The feasting and gift-giving, however, constitute the remnant of
the ancient Yup'ik winter festival in Christian garb, and it is for this reason
that many non-Orthodox Eskimos participate in the celebration.

Although Aleut "masking" is unknown among the Yup'ik, similar
household feasts are held on other religiously important days—after a
baptism or wedding, on the annual name day of living or deceased
members of the family. On the Feast of the Apostles Peter and Paul in July
(Julian Calendar), for example, parents with children named for either
saint, or with fathers or grandfathers who bear these names, prepare a
lavish banquet, sponsoring a day-long "open house" to which certain
village leaders are summoned in a particular order, beginning with the
clergy and older parish council members. The parish name day is also
observed by the entire community with a similar dinner, in more recent
times including performances of traditional Eskimo dancers. Many families invite friends and relatives for a feast on Pascha as well, but none of
these observances rival *Selaviq* in quantity and quality.

The cultural continuity between modern Orthodox observances and
their pre-Christian counterparts nowhere indicates a superficial commit-
— ment to the Gospel, but rather derives from the fact that to communicate
the Christian Gospel in any indigenous language requires the use of terms
and concepts with which the people are familiar. The very word
Netsvetov used for the concept of deity, *agayun*, has obvious pre-Christian meanings which were associated particularly with the Bladder Feast:
the *agayun* is the reality behind the mask, the force that animates and
enlivens it. All communication requires the use of mutually intelligible
terms, but words in one language, with all their poetic allusions and
lexical associations, never translate exactly into another.

The Eastern Orthodox Church has always recognized this as an inevi-

table outgrowth of the linguistic diversity of Christian preaching manifested at Pentecost. Nevertheless, she has also preferred to encourage
cultural and linguistic pluralism everywhere, while, at the same time,
striving to bring all nations to Christ, to the truth. It required eight
centuries to christianize Hellenism, to mold Greek culture and classical
philosophic language into an appropriate tool for the articulation of the
Gospel, to define and redefine words until they became *theology.* The
same process was undertaken in Russia, and that nation received the
Orthodox tradition in its own language and cultural context, inevitably
emphasizing certain aspects of it, while paying less attention to others.
The Orthodox Church recognizes that the same will be true as the same
faith comes to America. No single nation or culture can ever fully manifest or become the ultimate expression of truth, or will ever be a totally
Christian, completely "catholic" embodiment of the Gospel. No individual except Jesus Christ Himself ever will. However, each person and each
nation is called to strive to embody, to "incarnate" the Word of God, each
in its irreproduceable, absolutely unique way, realizing that in this world
the task is unattainable and will be consummated only in the Kingdom to
come. Every individual believer strives to attain to the stature of Christ
without ever fully realizing it. Likewise, each must seek this impossible
goal while recognizing that the process, begun at baptism, in its corporate
as well as personal sense, has no end. Even in the Kingdom of God, the
continuing growth and transformation, "from glory to glory," constitutes
an infinite and never-ending transfiguration of the human personality, for
to be "in Christ" is to be without limit.

Cultures themselves have no such eternal value. However, every
human persons develops within a cultural context. The positive characteristics of each culture, insofar as they provide the context for personal
development and spiritual growth, acquire eternal significance. Part of the
essential uniqueness of the saints derives from their historical and cultural
peculiarities. St Gregory the Theologian is forever a "Greek" saint, just as
St Sergius of Radonezh is eternally "Russian," St Sava Serbian, St Innocent Veniaminov an Alaskan. As fully man, Jesus Christ is forever a
Galilean, a perfect Jew, although at the same time, as God, there is in Him
"neither Jew nor Greek" (Galatians 3:28).

Conversely, without a positive cultural identity, the ability of any individual to fulfill the potential for divinity, to become all that he or she was called to be from all eternity is severely limited. Indigenous peoples whose cultures have been disrupted and denigrated by technologically superior societies inevitably suffer traumatic demoralization and almost irreparable spiritual damage. The same can be said of Russian Christians, who in the name of "modernization" were systematically deprived of the very means for perpetuating their spiritual tradition, and must now attempt to rebuild it. The Church has always understood her mission, therefore, in cultural as well as personal terms; for each person's language and culture constitute an indelible and permanent foundation and context for that person's understanding of the world, as well as his or her self-identity. One must love one's neighbor as one's self, but no one can love himself and despise his ancestry, his race, or his cultural heritage.

Certainly the Church is enriched by the new perspective a particular culture contributes to the entire *oikoumene*. The affirmation of the life force, the *inua/yua* of the Eskimo, as a sacred reality, as *logoi* related to Christ, the Divine Logos, constitutes the essence of the Alaskan Christian spiritual and theological experience. The cosmos is the symbol of God. Whatever is true, noble, or beautiful is Christ.

The Difficult Decades, 1920-1970

The twentieth century has not been kind to the Orthodox Church. The Russian civil war and the brutal persecution of Christians in the Soviet Union that followed deprived Alaskans of all spiritual and financial support. The turmoil into which the various Orthodox jurisdictions were plunged because of the chaos in Russia distracted immigrant communities from any involvement in the Alaskan mission for fifty years. The collapse of the Ottoman Empire brought temporary political freedom to Greece and the Balkans, but the Nazi occupation of the region and the Bolshevik victory in Russia prevented these traditionally Orthodox countries from playing any significant role between the two world wars. In Palestine and Lebanon, the Orthodox population was caught in the cross-fire between the Israeli army and warring Maronite as well as fundamentalist Islamic militia, and beset by proselytizing fundamentalist Protestant missionaries. The secularized Turkish state views the presence of the Ecumenical Patriarchate in Istanbul either as a menace or as a nuisance. Consequently, it has imposed crippling taxes and burdensome restrictions on the few thousand Orthodox who remain. With all the major centers of Orthodox Christianity so oppressed or restricted for most of the century, no spontaneous assistance came to Alaska from 1917 until 1968.

At the time of the Russian Revolution, one of Alaska's hierarchs, Bishop Philip (Stavitskii) was in Russia. He never returned. Arrested in 1928, and almost certainly imprisoned in the Gulag during Stalin's reign, he reappeared as Bishop of Stalingrad in 1944, and died as Archbishop of Astrakhan in 1952. There were at that time in Alaska fewer than a dozen priests, many of them elderly, and no functioning seminary within four thousand miles.

One of the most prominent Creole families, the Kashevarovs, supplied the Alaskan mission with several priests during the years immediately following the Revolution. Father Andrew Kashevarov not only served St Nicholas parish in Juneau, but founded the territorial museum and historical library, publishing one of the first biographies of St Innocent Veniaminov in *Alaska* magazine in 1927. A teacher at the seminary in Sitka, where he learned Tlingit, Father Andrew, in keeping with his Unangan Aleut heritage, could also could read and write English, Aleut and Russian. Other Kashevarov brothers ministered to flocks in Kodiak, Nushagak and the Aleutians.

Left to its own resources, the Alaskan Church not only survived but grew. This is due almost exclusively to the devotion and determination of the Alaskan Orthodox people themselves. There had been Aleut clergy since 1828 and after 1920, nearly all clergy were Native. Father Sergei Repin, guided and assisted by Agafangel Backford, continued to travel by dog sled and kayak from his headquarters at Egegik, on the northern shore of the Alaskan Peninsula, visiting Orthodox communities throughout Bristol Bay, the Nushagak, Kvichak and Iliamna regions. Trilingual, he also worked on translations from Slavonic into Yup'ik and English, as his predecessor, Father Gregory Kochergin had done at Nushagak, near Dillingham. Kochergin, in fact, continued to operate a parish school where he taught history, arithmetic, Russian, English, and catechism, and produced some extraordinary manuscripts of liturgical texts in Unangan and Slavonic. These, unfortunately, were never published.

The Pribilof Islands nearly always had resident priests, usually local men who had studied at Unalaska. Fathers John Orlov, Elary Gromoff, and Michael Lestenkov celebrated services in Slavonic, Unangan and English, and transmitted Unangan Orthodox spiritual and cultural values to two generations of Aleuts. Their spiritual children serve as clergy, readers, singers and choir directors today in Sitka, Tyonek, Unalaska, Nikolski, the Pribilofs and Anchorage. Villages which enjoyed consistent pastoral attention during the middle years of the century have tended to produce more clergy and church leaders for the diocese in the next generation.

Several young Aleut men traveled to South Canaan, Pennsylvania, to attend seminary and prepare for lives of service to the Alaskan mission in the middle of the century. At the age of seventeen, Father Elary Gromoff's son, Ismile, journeyed from St George Island by boat and continued by train across the continent to St Tikhon's Seminary. He returned to serve among the Unangan and Alutiiq Orthodox for nearly forty years. In 1980, he was appointed to a Congressional commission, headed by former Supreme Court Justice Arthur Goldberg, investigating the impact of the internment of Aleuts during the Second World War. Father Michael Oskolkoff from Ninilchick served at Eklutna and Anchorage for many years, while his nephew, Father Simeon Oskolkoff, another graduate of St Tikhon's Seminary, labored at Cordova, Tyonek, Tatitlek, Homer, Anchorage, Juneau, Sitka and Eklutna during his pastoral career. Father Paul Merculief also completed studies at South Canaan, and became well acquainted with the rich folklore of the Unangan people during his years at Nikolski. He was among the first faculty recruited to teach at St Herman's Pastoral School when it opened at Kenai in 1973, and later served in Anchorage and Tyonek. Originally tonsured reader by Bishop Amvrosii in 1966, Father Nicholas Kompkoff not only served parishes across the south-central and southeastern regions of the state, but was elected president of the statewide federal school board in the early 1970's, and later to various leadership positions within his Native corporation, refounding and rebuilding the village and parish at Chenega before his death in June 1987.

Of the thirty ordained clergy in Alaska in 1991, twenty-three were Natives, and two of the seven non-Native priests had married Yup'ik wives. Father Nicholas Molodyko-Harris has labored for a quarter century to found and build the cathedral community of St Innocent in Anchorage. Native Alaskans have formed the nucleus of this church since the beginning, with George and Mary Bourdukofsky, their son Deacon Peter and his wife Katherine, Anna, Dimitri and Iliodor Philemonof, Anna Lazanas, Lubova Davis, Bill and Alice Bouwens, and Anatoly and Michael Lekanof among the founders and consistent supporters of the parish. Archpriest Eugene Bourdukofsky, another graduate of St Tikhon's, and his wife Mary have served St Michael's Cathedral in Sitka with distinction for nearly two decades. Aleuts continue to play a leading role in the life of the diocese.

Yup'ik Orthodox also assumed responsibility for the continuation of their spiritual tradition in their region. In the Kuskokwim-Yukon Delta, Father Vasilii Changsak, the successor to Father Zakharii Bel'kov, traveled widely with Father Nikolai Epchook. Hieromonk Amphilokhii Vakulskii established his headquarters at Russian Mission, and even after being consecrated bishop of Alaska in 1924 preferred to live on the Yukon, celebrating liturgy in Yup'ik. In fact, Bishop Amphilokhii took Alaskan Eskimos with him on his year-long sojourn to the Siberian coast, where, in 1909-1910, there were thousands of Orthodox Chuckchi who benefited from the Alaskan mission to Russia. Father Nikolai's son, Vasilii, who remembered sitting on Bishop Amphilokhii's lap to learn Slavonic hymns as a boy, served Egegik, South Naknek, New Stuyahok, Dillingham, Lower Kalskag and his hometown, Kwethluk, during his lifelong ministry. His Bright Week funeral during April 1991 was a joyful and triumphant tribute to this generation of priests who so devoutly and courageously served Christ and their people during these difficult decades.

A church reader from Kasigluk, Charles Zachary Guest, was ordained to the holy priesthood by Bishop John Zlobin in the 1950's. The energetic Archpriest Zachary traveled throughout southwestern Alaska, frequently as far inland as Nikolai and Telida, in the shadow of Mt McKinley. His remarkable talents as an engineer and carpenter were widely appreciated, and villages eagerly sought his advice and assistance in building new churches. One of his first construction projects was at Eek, where only two Orthodox families resided. Nevertheless, these two households together with Father Zachary constructed an attractive log chapel, the first of nearly twenty churches this missionary priest would build during his thirty years of service to the Orthodox church and the Yup'ik people.

The former U.S. postmaster, Nikolai Ooliggaq Michael, succeeded Archpriest Nikolai Epchook in the early 1960's, as the Russian Mission reader, Gabriel Gabrieloff, was ordained to serve on the Yukon after Father Changsak's death. Neither man was seminary-trained, but their commitment to the church and their years of experience convinced the diocesan bishops at the time of their qualifications. As archpriests, both men built new churches in their respective villages, contributing funds and months of physical labor to the effort. In the next generation, Kwethluk and Russian Mission, with a total combined population of perhaps five hundred parishioners, produced six priests and two deacons.

Subdeacon Matthew Berezkin at Napaskiak made St Jacob Church there a major liturgical center. With the approval of Fathers Changsak and N. Epchook, he translated additional hymns into Yup'ik and organized regional church conferences on the two rivers each summer, thereby creating a vehicle for the dissemination of the new material every year. Every August 1-2, the feast of the Prophet Elijah on the old calendar, clergy, church committee members, chiefs, ladies' auxiliary officers, wardens, altar servers, church school teachers and choir members and directors gathered at a predetermined village. Each day began with the celebration of vespers and eucharistic liturgy. If the bishop was able to attend, the conference would start with a thanksgiving service to welcome him. Each service included several sermons, so that the people from villages without resident priests had an opportunity to gain a basic understanding of the faith. The annual topics presented by the priests were "faith," "marriage," "repentance," and "communion." When asked why these four subjects were always retained, they answered, "This is the way we have always done it." Lay preachers, "Chiefs," were invited to preach on the conference theme verse, a text selected six weeks earlier at the planning meeting at Kwethluk on the feast of Saints Peter and Paul.

On the first two days of the conference, after a long, solemn hierarchical liturgy and a quick brunch, participants divided according to their ecclesiastical function or interest. Wardens and altar servers would gather in one house, sisterhood members in another, choir members and directors in another, clergy in the church, and so forth. Each shared with the others the new ideas, new translations, continuing problems, concerns and unresolved questions that had arisen in the last twelve months. Vespers or vigil was followed by confessions, socializing and steam bathing. On the third day, everyone gathered after the festal liturgy and breakfast in the largest available building, usually the school gymnasium, to present reports on the topics they had discussed in the separate groups, and pose questions to the bishop and clergy for final approval or resolution. This final session could last up to seven or eight hours, with most of the participants sitting patiently on the hardwood gymnasium or multipurpose room floor. On the Yukon, the same procedures were observed on the Feast of the Transfiguration, and later on the Feast of SS Peter and Paul. In more recent times, a conference has been organized August 26-28 on the Nushagak, and on October 4-6 at Iliamna Lake. Thousands of Orthodox laity annually participate in the regional conferences and derive tremendous educational and spiritual benefit from the experience.

During the last twenty years, conferences have been the occasion for most ordinations, so that many Orthodox priests share common anniversaries in their vocation. This only further contributes to the festive atmosphere at conferences, making them an opportunity for reaffirming common commitments and interpersonal ties. Regional conferences are, next to *selaviq* and Pascha, the most important annual observances in rural church life.

Parish and Family Life

Alaskan churches are usually homemade affairs. The funds to build a new temple are collected from the villagers themselves by a group of responsible elders who make their rounds, accepting scores of very small donations, usually once a month for many years. While the lumber, roofing, and insulation are purchased from supply companies, the candlestands, lecterns, icon frames, altar table, table of oblation and even chandeliers are often hand-made locally. The interior is painted and the icons decorated in a folksy style, often with embroidered or crocheted coverings. These, as well as altar covers and vestments, are designed and created by village women. Everyone has an opportunity to contribute time, energy, resources or talents the project.

If clergy and readers have tended to dominate the public liturgical life of the parish, *matushki* (priests' wives) and older women have traditionally played the central role in the parish and nuclear family. Among the matrilinear Tlingit, children receive their tribal name through their mother's clan, while among the Eskimo, women usually perform the naming rites. In pre-contact times, girls were secluded at the time of their first menses and forbidden to participate in public ceremonies during menstruation. This practice coincided with Old Testament prohibitions. Consequently, in many communities menstruating women either refrain from attending services or remain in the narthex, despite regular assurances from the bishop and parish clergy that this practice has no doctrinal basis. In eighteenth-century Russia and throughout the Middle East, the concern that no blood be shed within the Christian temple, where the "bloodless" sacrifice of the eucharist is offered, produced similar restrictions. Wherever the traditional and the Orthodox attitudes have overlapped, they have tended to reinforce each other. When challenged, the women respond, "But this the way we have always done it."

"The way we have always done it" includes the way each day begins. In many pious Orthodox homes, the family members wash, dress and pray silently before the icons. This is repeated in the evening. Most rural Alaskan homes have an "icon corner" that extends over the better part of a major wall in the main room of the house, and sometimes along most of one wall in every room. The family is thus visually surrounded by Christ, the Virgin, the angels and saints, especially Alaska's Father Herman, in its daily activities. The house is still a microcosm of the Christian universe, since it replicates the Church. The oil lamp hanging before the icons is lit on the eves of major feasts, or whenever the family is preparing to receive the sacraments. During *selaviq*, the icon corner is illuminated and decorated with Christmas wrapping paper and ornaments, and whenever a church-related service is celebrated in the home, the people all face it.

The annual sanctification of water at Theophany has special meaning in rural Alaska, where the river or sea represents the source of life and livelihood for the traditional hunting and fishing communities. Cross-shaped holes need to be cut through the thick river ice in order to perform the rites in late January, but hundreds of faithful participate in the celebration, carrying water to their homes where the village priest comes during the following week or two to read prayers for the blessing of the dwelling and the household members. This also reinforces the perception of the interior of the house as sacred space. Heaven is not another, totally distinct and distant, "spiritual" reality. It is this world purified, sanctified, made "new."

Every meal begins and ends with the sign of the cross, which in the Alaskan tradition is usually made twice. In many Aleut villages, an Orthodox follows the Russian custom of greeting the icons first, before addressing any of his hosts, just as those who enter the church venerate the icons before taking their place among the congregation. Children leaving for boarding school may receive their parents' blessing, and men departing for a hunting trip usually carry with them a small icon hung around the neck in an embroidered or beaded pouch. Everyone generally wears their baptismal cross, removing it only when absolutely necessary, such as in the steam bath. In putting it back on, the owner makes the sign of the cross and kisses it. The sound of church bells signals a moment of silent prayer, people making the sign of the cross. Three tolls of the bell announce a death in the community, and some will proceed directly to the church.

Funerals in Alaskan villages are community events. There are no anonymous professionals who make the necessary arrangements for a price. As always, everything depends on interpersonal relationships. All Tlingit clans are divided into two moieties, Raven and Eagle, and when a member of an Eagle clan dies, members of the various Raven clans cooperate to provide everything needed for the funeral and burial rites. Forty days later, the relatives of the deceased, members of the various Eagle clans, invite those who assisted them to a memorial meal, at which they reciprocate for all the donations of time, talent and money the opposite moiety provided for them in their time of grief. Among Aleuts and Eskimos, the community as a whole contributes materials, time, and know-how to assure the proper and respectful burial of their neighbor.

The priest is notified whenever someone is gravely ill, and everything is done to allow the dying to receive the holy mysteries. The oil lamp is lit and prayers for the dying read aloud. Elders express their wishes at this time, an oral will and legacy of wisdom for their family. When the end comes, the priest and choir assemble in the home and celebrate the first brief memorial service at bedside. The body is washed and dressed for burial, a coffin constructed of plywood, painted or covered with cloth, and decorated with ribbon and artificial flowers. Twice each day, the priest returns to the house for the same short Panikhida. During the first night, the community keeps vigil, sitting silently with the surviving family, a reader chanting the Psalms quietly until dawn. On the second night, the Acts of the Apostles and the Epistles of St Paul are read. The open coffin is temporarily closed on the third day as the body is transferred to the church for the funeral services.

The text of the Orthodox burial rite is relatively fixed, but Aleuts and Yup'iks have added some Alaskan features. In keeping with Orthodox tradition, the coffin is usually open, and the community comes to bid farewell to the departed by venerating an icon he or she holds, and sometimes kissing the "crown" (a paper headband, representing the "crown of glory" each Christian who has "fought the good fight" hopes to receive). All bless the body with the sign of the cross, tracing it three times with their right hand or with the icon they have already venerated.

An Alaskan village funeral allows the family and friends to grieve, to accept the reality of their loss, and also to affirm their faith in Christ and his victory over death. The procession with the body, therefore, in popular Alaskan practice, parallels the rites of Holy Friday, when the Shroud (in Slavonic *Plashchanitsa*, in Greek, *Epitaphios*) depicting Christ's "lifeless yet life-bearing Body" circles the church three times. The three-barred wooden cross used to mark the grave is carried at the head of the procession, and at the grave site, it is placed into the ground as the coffin is lowered. The final "Memory Eternal" is sung slowly as the church bell tolls. This usual climax of the burial service is augmented in village Alaska by several additions. Everyone assists in the actual burial, at least nominally, by placing a handful or more of earth into the grave. As the congregation rushes forward to do so, they sing Paschal hymns, and the bell rings triumphantly as it does all day on Pascha. "Having beheld the resurrection of Christ," they joyfully chant, "let us worship the holy Lord Jesus, the only sinless One...for behold, through the Cross, joy has come into all the world...Having endured the Cross for us, He has destroyed death by death." And another Paschal hymn is sometimes added:

Before the dawn, Mary and the women came to the grave and found the stone
rolled away from the tomb.
They heard the angelic voice, "Why do you seek among the dead as a man Him
who is Everlasting Life?
Behold the clothes in the grave and go proclaim to the world: The Lord is risen,
He has slain death...

These hymns are repeated until the grave is filled and the cross marker
firmly in place. The people then sing a three-fold "Lord have mercy,"
make the sign of the cross three times, and return to the home for a
memorial meal. A similar banquet is held each year on the name day of
the departed.

Matushka Olga

A short biographical sketch of a contemporary Alaskan woman will
perhaps serve to bring many of the unique qualities of Alaskan spirituality
into focus. The life and death of Matushka Olga Michael, wife of Archpriest Nikolai O. Michael, characterizes in many ways the traditional
ideals of her people and faith, including a cosmic dimension unknown in
most of the outside world.

Olga (Arsamquq) or Olinka was not a physically impressive or imposing figure. She bore six children who lived to maturity, delivering several
herself, without assistance from even a midwife. Her sons and daughters
cannot recall that she ever raised her voice to them. Real People do not
shout. With a large family and a husband often traveling to one of the
dozen parishes entrusted to his pastoral care, Matushka was always busy,
but not only with her own household chores. In addition to sewing Father
Nikolai's vestments in the early years and crafting beautiful parkas, boots
and mittens for her children, she was constantly sewing or knitting socks
or fur outerwear for others. Hardly a friend or neighbor was without
something Matushka had made for them. Parishes hundreds of miles
away received unsolicited gifts, traditional Eskimo winter boots ("muk-
luks") to sell or raffle for their building fund. All the clergy of the deanery
wore gloves or woolen socks Arsamquq had made for them.

As her children grew up and married, Matushka Olga had more than
a dozen grandchildren upon whom to lavish her hand-crafted treasures,
but she never restricted her generosity to her own relatives. Week after

week she diligently prepared eucharistic bread, the prosphora, serving as
the principal agent by which the created universe was transformed into an
offering to God at the village liturgy. Her knowledge of services was
exceptional. Not many Orthodox today have committed to memory the
entire service for a major feast, but Matushka Olga knew the hymns of
Palm Sunday, Holy Week and Pascha in Yup'ik by heart. Whenever a
visiting priest entered her house, she hurried to don her scarf and approached with her right hand on top of her left, palms upward, requesting
a blessing.

Increasingly freed from domestic chores as her remaining daughters
assumed more of the load, she traveled with her husband to regional
conferences, sharing her experience and wisdom with another generation
of *matushki*. She enjoyed visiting other parishes during *selaviq*, but was
always glad to return home to Kwethluk. Through her lifetime, the village
underwent radical changes. From a circle of small, semi-subterranean sod
dwellings, it had become a large, typical Eskimo town, with a diesel
generator, a grade school, high school, community center, Head Start
program, clinic and a grocery store. Public radio and television from
Bethel, seventeen miles down river, brought news and images of the world
into every Yup'ik home. Wood stoves gave way to oil, dog sleds to
snowmobiles.

Some years ago, Matushka began to feel weak and ill, but refused to
concern any of her family about her condition. She did not improve, and
her daughters noticed her loss of weight. Finally persuaded to visit the
Bethel hospital, she was sent on to Anchorage for additional tests. The
specialists diagnosed terminal cancer. It was too late, they said. There was
nothing they could do.

Matushka Olga received the news without bitterness or emotion, and
returned home to prepare for the inevitable. Her family resolved that
medical science would not have the final word, and two daughters left
their bedridden mother for Kodiak, where they offered prayers at both
Monk's Lagoon and at the reliquary of St Herman. Upon their return to
Kwethluk, they found their mother's bed empty. She was outside, hauling
buckets of water from the village well in order, no doubt, to do a load of
laundry, or perhaps to scrub the kitchen floor.

For nearly a year her condition returned to normal, but by conference time the following August, Matushka was too weak to walk to or stand in church unassisted. Bishop Gregory awarded her the highest recognition bestowed on laity in the diocese, the St Herman Cross, draping the red, white and blue ribbon and the enamelled cross, bearing in the center the icon of Alaska's first saint, around her neck at the end of the feastday liturgy.

Her condition continued to deteriorate over the next several months. She began to prepare for death, instructing her family how to do the things she had always done for them, and how to distribute her few material possessions among themselves and her neighbors and friends. She had her wedding gown cleaned and asked to be buried in it. She told her sons and daughters not to grieve for her, and expressed regret that she had taken a granddaughter into her home, not because she loved her less, but because she feared that the granddaughter might mourn her grandmother's passing too deeply. As the end drew near, the grandchildren from distant Mount Edgecumbe High School were summoned home. An early winter storm delayed them. By the time they arrived, she was gone.

News of her death spread rapidly across western Alaska. Planeloads of mourners began to arrive as the evening Panikhida was sung in the house. That night, a strong southerly wind blew forcefully and continuously, melting the November snow and river ice. Yup'ik neighbors from nearby villages came to Kwethluk by boat, an impossibility at that time of year under ordinary circumstances.

Hundreds of friends who came from as far as Lake Iliamna and the Nushagak, as well as from the Yukon and Upper Kuskokwim villages, filled the newly-consecrated church on the extraordinary spring-like day of the funeral. Upon exiting the church, the procession was joined by a flock of birds, although by that time of year, all birds have long since flown south. The birds circled overhead, and accompanied the coffin to the grave site. The usually frozen soil had been easy to dig because of the unprecedented thaw. That night, after the memorial meal, the wind began to blow again, the ground refroze, ice covered the river, winter returned. It was as if the earth itself had opened to receive this woman. The cosmos still cooperates and participates in the worship the Real People offer to God.

Conclusion:
The Church's Mission to Alaska

For over two centuries Alaska has been the object of Christian mission. Orthodoxy has become an indigenous Native Alaskan faith, during the first eighty years defending and supporting the Aleuts, in the second eighty educating them and advancing their cause, and in the last eighty being itself supported and propagated by Natives. The early success of the mission can be attributed to the sympathetic attitude which the monks from Valaam and Konevitsa monasteries adopted toward traditional culture and their forceful, indignant opposition to Baranov's exploitation. The blossoming during the second period was due to the enlightened educational efforts of St Innocent Veniaminov and his Aleut colleagues. The third period was the age of unsung Native heroes of the faith, Aleuts, Creoles, Eskimos and Indians, who opposed the assimilationist policies of the United States federal government. The survival of the Orthodox Church in Alaska constitutes something of a modern miracle.

In most of rural Alaska, the Orthodox Church is perceived as the one Native institution for which the local people are themselves responsible. The schools, except for the Aleut-Russian classes which continued in some villages into the 1960's, are an agency of state or regional government. Out-of-state or even international interests control the fishery and lumber industries. In most areas, a single urban center, with its non-Native majority, dominates the social and political life of the region. Politically, socially, economically, and even intellectually, the Native peoples of Alaska are in bondage, their lives and destinies largely controlled by newcomers or outsiders whose main concern, like Baranov's before them, is to extract from rather than contribute to Alaska's well-being.

Since the late nineteenth century, confident that they knew what was best for Native Alaskans, federal officials removed adolescent children from their homes and communities and transported them to distant boarding schools where they were instructed in the ways of modern America. Village schools required English only as the language of instruction, even though the public school teacher (who was, in the early years also a Protestant missionary) was the only person in town who spoke that language. Initially, parents enthusiastically sent their sons and daughters to the mission or public schools, confident that they would return with the "White Man's" knowledge. Instead, the students had their self-identity irreparably damaged by being badgered and bullied to conform to the teacher's norms, and severely criticized, humiliated and even beaten when they failed or refused to do so. Many left school, their self-esteem destroyed, believing that they were unfit to be full citizens of the world's greatest democracy. They referred to themselves as "just dumb Natives," not remembering the amazing exploits and significant contributions their great-grandparents had made during the Aleut years, in 1830-70. The schools and missions, supposedly instruments of enlightenment, taught three generations of Native Americans to be ashamed of being what they inescapably and eternally are. Aleuts renounced or concealed their Native identity, preferring in some places to emphasize their Russian cultural heritage. Then came the Cold War, and there was no prestige in that either. Instead of maintaining the essential unity and balance of the two unique traditions and affirming the intrinsic value of each, Aleuts were forced to deny both. The Native soul was being torn apart.

What enabled Alaska Native peoples to endure and survive was their essential spirituality. Tragically, this inner strength was undermined by programs inspired by a desire to uplift the poor, assist the weak, sustain the downtrodden. In the late 1960's, the Great Society discovered that rural Alaska was, per capita, the most impoverished region of the country. Although the Natives had successfully managed to survive in the Arctic for centuries, they were suddenly and unexpectedly inundated with non-reciprocal institutional assistance—welfare checks, food stamps, and an entire bureaucracy to sustain and perpetuate these programs. As one elder testified a few years after this torrent of "help" rained down on them, "Our language has no word for wealthy or poor. We did not know we were poor until these outsiders came and told us." Another added, "Poverty has only recently been introduced to Native communities."[1] Indeed,

1   *Must One Way of Life Die for Another to Live?* (Yupiktak Bista, Bethel, AK, 1970), p. 9.

the elders protested the tremendous levels of unsolicited financial help which the government, without consultation or explanation, decided to provide. They recognized that this would lead to a crippling dependence, saying, "Welfare programs should not be administered as general hand-outs that encourage people to become dependent upon a government check and lose their sense of motivation."[2]

A few years later, a regional health corporation hired a community psychologist with remarkable cross-cultural experience to work with the Native people in the area. He made a preliminary tour of several villages, asking the elders, through an interpreter, what it was they wanted him to do. He reported to his agency that in every community the elders responded as if with one voice: "Help us to become less dependent."[3]

The cycle of intellectual and emotional dependence began early in this century when the government, and in some instances the churches, founded the first monolingual schools. The thinly veiled message they delivered, no matter what their positive contributions might have been, was: "Since you Alaskans are so culturally backward, we have come to your remote village to enlighten you. We will teach you the three or four 'R's and train you in some sort of productive work. When you have completed school you will be qualified for a job somewhere else." In fact, the official school philosophy promulgated in 1900 stated:

> If the Native population of Alaska can be brought under the influence of Christianity and be given a rudimentary English-language education, it follows that the white population (comprised of immigrants from the other states) could employ them in mining, transportation, and the production of food.[4]

The ultimate goal of American public education was to produce Native laborers. Alaskans could assimilate into the dominant culture, but at the lowest level.

This was also the age of the boarding schools, and the first generation confidently went off to distant dormitories expecting to gain enough of the new knowledge to win acceptance for themselves and their people. But when they returned to their villages, they were, as one elder put it, "no longer the same children we once saw leave for school. Some of them

2   *Ibid*, p. 20
3   Dr. Robert Alberts, personal communication.
4   Dauenhauer, "Conflicting Visions," *op. cit.*, p. 20.

are strangers to their own people. But much worse, they are strangers to themselves."[5] Basic cultural values conflicted, as one high school graduate later observed: "The purpose of Western education is for the individual to find ways to excel and promote himself...whereas the purpose of native education has always been for the individual to find ways to serve his family and people."[6] Initially, being the village student to complete twelfth grade seemed a noble achievement. Unfortunately, the educational process tended to mold the minds according to secular values and train the body in skills that were of little or no use in the traditional village context. The "educated" person was caught between two worlds, fitting comfortably into neither of them.

This situation continued for decades. The first generation of students and parents were anxious and confused. The second generation became frustrated and indignant. Unschooled elders still made the important decisions that affected everyone's lives, while distant, nameless bureaucrats established programs and procedures disruptive or destructive of traditional ways. A conflict between the old, spiritual wisdom, and the new secular knowledge arose within the hearts and minds of a new generation of Native Alaskans.

The essential elements of the "old wisdom" included meaningful survival, founded on a fundamentally spiritual apprehension of reality. The basis for the most of the "new knowledge" rested firmly on scientific naturalism, the view that science has not only succeeded in controlling or manipulating the world, but has "proven" that the visible universe, composed of measurable physical quantities of atoms and molecules, constitutes the totality of reality. In other words, the real struggle was between a traditionally sacramental vision of life and a radically secular one. The critical issue was, therefore, neither social nor political nor economic but theological.

The inner turmoil, anger, frustration, and bitterness so many Native Alaskans experience gradually erupts, manifesting themselves first of all in recklessness, resulting in "accidents" and eventually suicide. Native people begin to believe that their situation is, to some significant extent, their own fault, that they are to blame for their lack of "success" or "adjust-

5   *Must One Way, op. cit.*, p .70.
6   *Ibid.*

ment" to the modern world and that, due to some innate inferiority, "Natives can't." Once this false notion, consciously or unconsciously, took root in the soul of Alaska, anti-social and self-destructive forces were unleashed that today threaten the survival of individuals, families and communities. For the first time in history, the natural world, the harsh environment and the merciless elements are not the deadliest foe whose unpredictable power confronts Native peoples. The main threat to the well-being of Natives has become Natives themselves.

The dominant society has not stood idly by, watching the dramatic rise in crime, suicide, and "accidents" among Native Americans. It has mandated increased financial and professional assistance. Programs to prevent various abuses and addictions have been devised. Counselors, social workers, bureaucrats, administrators, lawyers, doctors, law enforcement officers, and clergy have rushed to the rescue. "Help" has arrived.

Unfortunately, this institutional, depersonalized help only perpetuates and aggravates the original dependence which lies at the root of the problem. The more imported help, the more money, the more energy the dominant society pours into rural Alaska (and this is the experience now of several decades), the worse the very problems these programs and dollars are supposed to address become. Traditional people have an ancient tradition of helping each other. There has never been anything demeaning about accepting assistance from a relative or neighbor, a fellow villager, for everyone recognizes that sooner or later that benefactor will require help himself. Reciprocity developed and strengthened precisely those relationships which Native peoples cherish. But this new kind of help comes impersonally, anonymously and non-reciprocally, and thereby de-personalizes and humiliates the recipients, setting up the chain of emotions, anxieties, frustrations and hostilities that instigated the cycle of dependence in the first place. Hence, the more such "help," the worse the problem.

What is *mission*, then, in this context? What is the "Good News" the Church needs to bring to Alaska today? The greatest threat to the spiritual and material well-being of an Alaskan Native child being baptized today is not that he or she will be attracted to some exotic heresy. Modern Arians, Nestorians and iconoclasts abound, it is true, and these posed a real threat to the very survival of the Orthodox mission until relatively recent times. To be attracted to some form of sectarian fundamentalism, however, presupposes an interest in and an experience of some sort of spiritual reality, and the necessary openness to the spiritual dimension of life is precisely what is being systematically undermined. Dependence on and domination by "outside experts" perpetuates a self-destructive cycle from which, it seems, there is little hope for deliverance. It is seculariza-tion that is killing Aleuts, Eskimos and Indians.

Christians cannot stand silently by, witnessing the destruction of sisters and brothers. In Orthodox villages, the people *are* the Church. The Church is not essentially a state-wide or national institution, important as the canonical structures of the Church may be. The Church is the community of believers assembled to praise, thank and worship God who has called them out of non-existence into being and eternal communion and life with Him. The Church is that community which *remembers* Christ, and "all those things which have come to pass for us: the cross, the tomb, the resurrection on the third day, the ascension into heaven, the sitting at the right hand, and his second and glorious coming."[7] It is in this context, remembering all that has happened and simultaneously remembering what will be, that Christians act. In the face of injustice and oppression, it is a betrayal of Christ to remember only His suffering, and to apply this as the only appropriate Christian metaphor, the model for appropriate human response to evil. Too often, when confronted with such situations, the Church has urged silent suffering now, assuring those who humbly bear their present humiliation of some eventual, eternal reward. But Christians are also called to remember the future and to act with the Second Coming, the Kingdom of eternal love, freedom and justice, as the other guidepost, orienting and directing their lives. The Church acts and lives in the tension between what has gone before and what will be, the former being the revelation and foretaste of the latter. The Church and individual believers act *as Christians*, whenever they bring their remembrance of both this sacred past and the future, in Christ, the Christian "Metaphor," to bear on a particular situation. It is the creative tension between these two poles that enables a Christian to act, and which makes the action Christian.

The Church must be herself—blessing, sanctifying, and restoring

7   Offertory Prayer, Liturgy of St John Chrysostom.

fallen humanity, celebrating, making active and accessible that joyful vision of the Kingdom which is the content of her "Good News." This must be done meaningfully, intelligibly, and as beautifully as possible. No absolutizing of old Greek or Russian rubrics (often missiologically inadequate even for the time and place they were published) will restore worship—in Alaska or anywhere else—to its full and proper function as the visual and artistic expression of Christian Metaphor of all that has been already accomplished and of the Kingdom which is to come. There is a certain security, perhaps, but little faithfulness to Christ and the proclamation of His Reign, in merely repeating old liturgical formulae. The very conservative hierarchy of the pre-revolutionary Russian Church were, in fact, very dissatisfied with their *typikon,* and were anxious to restore worship to express the Church's vision more adequately, to enhance the Church's mission. Many of the reforms (preaching regularly, celebrating services in the vernacular, reading the prayers of the anaphora aloud, keeping the royal doors open, encouraging regular and frequent participation in the sacraments, reviving the evening celebration of the Liturgy of Presanctified Gifts during Great Lent, electing laity to parish, diocesan, and national councils and promoting their participation at every level of church life) which they recommended in 1905 have been implemented in American and in Alaska. Orthodox in the New World should be confident of, not embarrassed, by these positive steps toward renewal. Worship in the American Church is intelligible, meaningful and beautiful in ways that are not yet true in the Old World, but this too is part of the American Church's mission. The American Mission has, on this level, led the way for the older patriarchates to consider and follow, for it was only in the United States that many of the proposals and decisions of the 1917 Church Council were ever implemented. The liturgical renewal begun in Russia has blossomed in America. Much of the work the newly liberated Orthodox Churches in Eastern Europe must undertake to revitalize Christian life has, by the grace of God, already been accomplished here.

Devout pastors who are equipped and inspired to labor tirelessly to impart the three-fold Christian experience and vision of the world as essentially good, fallen away from God into sin and corruption, and redeemed in Christ, can inspire their flocks and transfigure their lives.

The training of such church leaders is absolutely essential.

For Alaska to recruit and educate her own will, for the foreseeable future, require the prayerful and generous support of Christians elsewhere.

Fundamental as this dimension of the Church's mission is, it is not all. The Church cannot affirm the infinite value of each human person at each baptism, each chrismation, through every rite of blessing and sanctification every Sunday on one hand, and allow the "fallen world" to undermine her proclamation of the resurrection on every other level, Monday through Saturday, on the other. The Church's mission extends to the whole cosmos and everything and everyone in it. To reveal to human beings their essential and eternal priesthood requires also the restoration of creation to its fundamentally spiritual significance. The Church cannot concentrate exclusively on the salvation of souls and let the world go to hell.

There is (not to be too simplistic) only one effective means of breaking the cycle of dependence that with each passing year accelerates and kills not just the body but the soul of people. The mission of the Church must be to reverse this cycle at its starting point, to transform dependent people into competent "experts" in their own right, to "help" only insofar as it is necessary to move the dependent population from their condition of dependence into a position of responsibility. Native Alaskans need to be trained, as the Aleuts a century ago were, to assume leadership roles in their communities and institutions, and especially in the Church. This means education.

Schools and missions have been at the heart of the current tragic situation, of course. The entire vision and philosophy of education must consequently be quite different. The goal must not be to "re-make" the Native Alaskan in the image of someone else. Neither the "Lower 48," nor the "latest research," nor "Europe," nor "Japan" can be the criterion against which rural Alaska is judged. Justice Berger recommended "self-determination" as a necessary political and social goal. It must be a spiritual and theological objective as well. The Church must condemn and renounce all cultural imperialism, within itself first of all, and then in society. Alaskan Native culture needs to be brought to the altar, but it must be brought by Native Alaskans. Alaskan spirituality, rejoicing in the essential goodness and eternal spiritual significance of the cosmos, needs to be affirmed—but primarily by Native Alaskans. Native leadership in all aspects of rural Alaskan society needs to be supported, encouraged, promoted and defended, but first of all by the Native people themselves. And the Orthodox Church, as an overwhelmingly Native Church, must here accept moral responsibility. This is the challenge Alaska presents to the Church. This is the Church's mission to Alaska.

The Church leaders whom history has called the "Holy Fathers" of the Patristic age struggled courageously to remain faithful to Christ and the Gospel within the difficult social and political context of their times. They sought to apply the eternal truths of the Christian Metaphor to the crucial issues of their day. It is useless and even reprehensible to quote the Fathers as ancient authorities and invoke their blessing on projects—even the building of churches, seminaries, or schools—that have little or nothing to do with the salvation of a single human soul or the transfiguration of one cosmic element, while refusing to face the major theological issues of one's own era. God has always supplied the Church with saints and prophets who fearlessly addressed the crucial problems confronting Christians in each age, no matter the personal cost. If there is a "mission to Alaska," therefore, it will require suffering and sacrifice. It will require the cross. But Alaska has already produced and glorified several saints, and many more yet officially unrecognized holy people—the Matushka Olgas of the North—known only to God.

> Surrounded then by so great a cloud of witnesses...let us run with patience the race that is set before us, looking to Jesus Christ, the author and finisher of our faith; who for the joy that was set before him endured the cross...and set down at the right hand of the throne of God. (Hebrews 12: 1-2)

Alaska's Mission to the Church

As an indigenous Native American institution outside the orbit of American secular culture, the Orthodox Church in Alaska by its very existence signifies an important ecclesial reality for the universal church. In the Johannine Biblical tradition, and in the theology of the Cappadocian Fathers, as in the writings of Metropolitan John Zizioulas today, the Church has always understood her mission in relational terms. The Gospel radically transforms perceptions of reality, and eternally alters ⁓

human relationships to God, to others and to the created universe. For traditional Alaskan Natives, relationships are everything.

Salvation defined as *theosis* (an infinite and eternal process of growth and transformation, a struggle to overcome all that divides each person from God, neighbor or the cosmos) requires progress in love—the development of relationships. The unity of God is not essentially a unity of substance, but a personal unity-in-love of the Father, Son and Holy Spirit, the infinite and inexhaustible love each, in total freedom, shares with the others. This is the paradigm, the prototype for human existence. Human persons are challenged, with Christ as the model and the means, to enter into the same kind of unity with God and others, to establish a community of love of total self-giving for the sake of the other, founded not on a common human nature, but on the free cooperation of each human person.

No one is irrevocably and permanently saved by entering into a sentimental, emotional or pietistic "private" relationship with their "personal savior," for to be united to Jesus Christ of necessity brings each person into communion with the totality of all that exists. No one in the Kingdom can be isolated from all the others. No one will be alone with God for all eternity. *Unus Christianus, nullus Christianus*—one Christian, no Christian. The twin commandments to love God and one's neighbor represent two aspects of the same truth, for life everlasting means living forever with both. Thus, for the Eastern Fathers, heaven and hell are the same reality: those who have entered a loving relationship with God will experience ecstasy being forever with Him; those who have despised or rejected His love will find being forever with him to be eternal torment. He will be all in all. He will, in His love, embrace everyone and everything. For some this will be heaven, for others hell. The difference will be within, in the attitudes each has developed during his or her life in this world. Relationships are all that really matter. It is a fundamental Christian truth Native Alaskan Christians understand very well.

The baptismal rite communicates and celebrates a vision of sanctified life. In the exorcisms and the Great Blessing of Water, the fallen condition of creation is acknowledged and the world is restored to its original beauty. In the immersion, vesting with a cross and "robe of light," chrismation and tonsure, and, at the culmination of the initiation, in the eucharist, the reality of the Kingdom is manifested. Too often the mystery is misinterpreted in a narrowly legalistic way, in terms of justification, inherited guilt, or quantified grace, but the baptismal liturgy provides a wider, more cosmic and eschatological context. The Native people know better.

The importance traditional Alaskans attach to naming parallels the biblical concept of the name. The name a person bears establishes his or her place in the community, and, in traditional Russian practice, creates a personal relationship with a saint with whom the newly illumined Christian hopes to share eternity. The name day celebrates an occasion on which not only the living but the departed who share a holy name which has been sanctified by a spiritual ancestor in the faith all join. In Christ, those who share the name are all united in a communion of love. Like ancient tribal titles, Christian baptismal names express something of the God-given goodness of each person. They are not only a means for distinguishing one child from another. The name establishes *relationships* with others, with God and with the saints, who "throughout the ages have been well pleasing to Him."

Alaskan Orthodox can affirm with Florensky and Ouspensky the spiritual power and necessity of beauty. Both correctly identify divine truth with beauty, and they insist that ecclesiastical art and architecture serve to convey the cosmic and eschatological as well as scriptural dimensions of the faith. In most Alaskan chapels, to be sure, the most westernized style of iconography imported during the last century falls sadly short on two or even all three levels. This situation should, of course, be corrected as quickly as it becomes pastorally possible.

There is another dimension to beauty that must not be overlooked. Doctrinally inadequate as much of Alaska's church art may be, most village churches contain the work of local artisans. A thousand Matushka Olgas have sewn and embroidered, scores of carvers and painters have offered their folk art to beautify the village churches of Alaska. Many of these offerings lack any artistic or historical value, but their production was motivated by humble piety and genuine love. Like the tattered and often soiled hand-made greeting cards grade school children make for their parents, these may not be masterpieces, but God does not need any human offering, not even bread and wine. No earthly gift is ever necessary or adequate. The childhood cards become parental treasures nonetheless, and the Church accepts the offerings of all her children, for she must never sin against love.

A recurring theme of this volume has been the relationship between the indigenous peoples of Alaska and their land, that portion of the planet they have for centuries considered home. The Apostle Paul, St Irenaeus of Lyons, St Gregory of Nyssa, and St Maximus the Confessor in ancient times, together with Pascal, Arseniev, Soloviev, Florensky and Schmemann in more recent years, have all affirmed the spiritual significance of the cosmos. This Alaskans understand. The tribes of Israel were not alone in their belief that God had given them their own promised land. Native Americans everywhere consider themselves attached to and a permanent part of their homelands, people *of* the land. Their view of the world derives from an integrated, holistic vision of reality, in which economic, social, political and artistic experiences are unified in an all-encompassing spirituality. Orthodoxy has not destroyed but enhanced this understanding. It is precisely this continuity in spiritual worldview that expedited their initial conversion to Christianity on one hand, and explains their long-term commitment to the Church on the other.

Alaskan Orthodoxy reminds the Church, perhaps especially in America today, of the cosmic, integrated and therefore *ecological* dimensions of the Gospel. How narrowly the average Orthodox parishioner comprehends the function of worship in the life of the Church! How little of the vision of the world, or rather of the cosmos, seen from the perspective of the Kingdom, in which Christ is "all in all," penetrates the consciousness of the faithful! The secular fragmentation of the world into various spheres or specializations has convinced modern society that these various compartments—economic, social, political, spiritual, sexual, public, private—actual exist, and that each individual has so many "lives" to live. Each sphere operates according to its own norms and logic, no one of them integrating or connecting them. Religious life operates in a world of its own, without intruding upon or disrupting any of the other isolated spheres. Yet theology, the rational reflection upon genuine spirituality, claims precisely to be that one "field" which integrates and brings meaning to all the others.

Traditional Native Alaskans have always known that all life derives from and depends upon the spiritual for its value and meaning. If today among some there are tremendous social problems—alcoholism, drug abuse, domestic violence, crime and suicide—this situation arises because modern society is challenging and undermining this traditional worldview on a global scale. Alaskans are not the only ones forced into a dependent relationship to forces and powers they can neither control nor understand. This is the fate of modern man as social, political and economic power is increasingly concentrated in the hands of an oligarchy in both the East and West, Europe, Russia, America and Europe. If Native Americans have been reluctant to assimilate, to trade their integrated and comprehensive vision of the world for a fragmented and secular one in order to reap some material rewards, this should be understood as an essentially spiritual critique of the modern world. Their refusal challenges and indicts. By standing in solidarity with them, the Orthodox mission joins its voice to that challenge, that indictment. Some may be afraid to speak boldly on behalf of the right to political and social self-determination for indigenous peoples, for they love the praise of men more than the praise of God, but the secular conception of humanity is a lie about God, about human beings, about the created univrse.

So long as there are Native peoples refusing to surrender their identity, their uniqueness, their souls, to the modern world, their resolve and their very existence comes as a challenge and a judgement. This is Alaska's mission to the Church.

Alaskan Orthodoxy, unlike dioceses in the lower forty-eight, has remained canonically united, with one bishop exercising jurisdiction over a geographical region in which various tribes and cultures live. Unity is based on plurality of culture and identity of faith, doctrine and liturgy. Assimilationism into mono-lingual Anglo-American society has been resolutely rejected. While there must be room for those with no personal connection to any ethnic Orthodox heritage to enter and enjoy full membership in the Church, and "pan-Orthodox" English-speaking missions are essential to the growth and mission of American Orthodoxy, unity can never be constituted on the basis of cultural homogeneity, an American melting-pot church. Converts to Orthodoxy need to give serious attention to the influence the Christian faith has had on traditional Orthodox societies, even at the level of pious folk customs. Besides, there will be, as long as there is a Greece, Greek-Americans with close personal and communal ties with their homeland, and they will demographically constitute a majority of Orthodox Christians in the United States. With the fall of the Iron Curtain, this same dynamic applies to other traditionally Orthodox groups, and it seems there will always be some individuals and communities who will identify themselves as Albanian, Ukrainian, Eritrean, Russian, Bulgarian, Serbian, Arab, Romanian, or Copt. These must not be viewed as a hindrance to canonical unity or a nuisance to administrative efficiency. Alaska reminds America that it is only by embracing each person in his cultural context that Orthodox mission has historically succeeded. Multilingualism will be the social norm in America in the next century. It will also necessarily be the norm within the Church. May the Alaskan model serve to inspire Orthodoxy unity in the New World.

A united Orthodox Church in America, comprised of all the various national and ethnic jurisdictions, but with a Greek-American majority, would most certainly be oriented toward Constantinople as the Ecumenical Patriarchate, first among equals among Orthodox hierarchs in the world. The Alaskan Church, on the other hand, has virtually no cultural, historical or geographic links to the Hellenic centers of Orthodoxy. Its entire history has been closely tied to events and personalities in Russia. Essentially indigenous as it has become, most Native Alaskans still call their church "Russian Orthodox."

The more strenuously the dominant culture has attempted, in violation of its own highest principles, to coerce Native Americans into assimilating, the more entrenched Native traditionalists have everywhere become. There are more Amerindians speaking their native languages today than ever before. Some tribes, it is true, have become extinct, others have been legally and officially "terminated" by federal decree, no longer recognized as tribes by the government. Others, however, have multiplied and persevered. There survival and determination represent a dynamic indigenous spiritual force.

For the Orthodox Church, this should come as no surprise. A more physically brutal but parallel relationship between the traditional spirituality of the Russian people and Marxist-Leninism resulted not in the extermination but the rebirth of Orthodoxy in the former Soviet Union.

Consistency demands that the Orthodox Church be equally supportive of both the self-determination of indigenous peoples and religious liberty for Russian or Albanian Christians. The Church, even in the midst of the Cold War, issued numerous public pronouncements and appeals on behalf of oppressed, persecuted, exiled and imprisoned victims of Communist tyranny, but remained inexplicably silent in recent years on Alaskan issues. Those who venerate the relics of St Herman are morally obligated to follow his heroic example.

Ultimately, the success of the Church's mission to Alaska and Alaska's mission to the Church are intrinsically correlated. Insofar as the Church communicates and makes active the presence of the Kingdom of God already in the lives of the people and in the cosmos, to that degree will Alaska be liberated, transformed, "saved." But insofar as Alaska is freed and transfigured, she will challenge the Church at large to fulfill her eternal mission. There is, in the last analysis, no one-way mission. To proclaim the Gospel, to celebrate the truth, to reveal the Kingdom, is always to establish a relationship between those who proclaim and those who hear the message, and both are changed in the process. The Christian, as defined by Father Alexander Schmemann, is one who, wherever he looks sees Christ and rejoices in Him. He is in the cosmos, filling all things. He is in Scripture, inspiring all words. He is at the right hand of the Father, reigning in glory. On this three-fold biblical and patristic faith, the catholic Church is founded, and the gates of hell shall not prevail against it.

In 1794, the first Orthodox missionary monks arrived at Kodiak to found what they believed would be an indigenous Orthodox Church in the New World, not an overseas ecclesiastical colony of the Russian, Greek or Syrian Churches, nor a church "in exile" from some other place. The Church is always a pilgrim church, in exile only from heaven. The monks and their successors succeeded in transfiguring the wilderness, making at least one small corner of it, Spruce Island, an authentic American "holy land." They recognized as integral to their mission the defense of Native people who were being abused, exploited and enslaved by an unjust regime. The mission understood its function in cosmic terms: to sanctify, here and now, this land, these people, and bring them to the unity-in-love which is the goal of all authentic Christian mission. The history of the Alaskan Church confirms the eternal and indestructible character of the Church's vision, integrating into her worship the cosmic, scriptural and eschatological dimensions of the faith. For in the breaking of the eucharistic bread the Church actualizes in Christ the unity of the world, the Church, and the Kingdom, remembering all that is past and all that is to come, confessing His death and proclaiming His resurrection till He comes.

O Christ, Great and Most Holy Pascha! Wisdom, Word and Power of God! Grant that we may more perfectly partake of Thee in the never-ending Day of Thy Kingdom!

Appendix I:

The Oath Of Allegiance Controversy

On January 1, 1801, a confrontation between the monastic mission and the colonial governor over the administration of the oath of allegiance to the new tsar erupted at Kodiak. Two versions of this controversy have survived, one composed by Hieromonk Gideon in 1805, the other Alexander Baranov's account. Allegiance to the tsar bestowed a form of naturalized citizenship, and the monks were anxious that their newly baptized flock be protected by the civil legislation and legal protection to which subjects of the emperor were entitled. The incident epitomizes in many ways the relationship between the clergy and the management during the early years of the Russian American Company's rule.

Father Gideon's Report

In accordance with the imperial manifesto published in 1796, the Kodiak people should have been brought to swear an oath of loyalty to the Russian Throne. As a result of being sent great distances by the company and the lack of time, this had not been done. Therefore, on January 1, 1801, Hieromonk Afanasii sought Baranov's permission to do this. In return, the hieromonk was shouted out and driven off with a warning not to return. Then some twenty men from various villages gathered with their chiefs to ask Baranov to release them from the obligation of any further distant hunting trips by the Sitka party, promising in return to hunt near their villages, but they were chased away and threatened with dire consequences. Then all were ordered to prepare for the spring hunting expedition. They were very bitter and desperate, and dared inform the missionaries that they did not want to go on this expedition, because many of their relatives had died on previous ones and some of their villages were deserted. If Baranov were to have them killed as a result, they had brought new parkas along, and they asked the missionaries to bury them afterwards in their new clothes and bear witness to the murder of innocent people.

On hearing this, the clergy and the officers who were present were horrified, and tried to talk them into patience, assuring them that His Imperial Majesty would be favorably disposed. When the Natives had calmed down, they suggested that they swear an oath of allegiance to the Sovereign. They readily agreed to this, and promised to obey in all things. Thus they set off for the church, accompanied by the same two officers, and the administration of the oath was conducted by Father Afanasii.

As they left the church and were getting into their *baidarkas*, Baranov's deputy, Kuskov with his hunters, seized one of them, a leading chief, and took him to the barracks, where he was put in irons and flung into a dark cell where even the windows were boarded shut.

The hunters chased the others but failed to catch any. Baranov wanted to arrest another of them, the archimandrite's godson, who had come to visit the priests. To assure their friend's safety, the clergy decided to escort them to their boats. Father Afanasii went to his *baidarka* first, and was arrested by some of the company men. Baranov himself, in a towering rage, began to call Father Afanasii a runaway serf, and the other clergy and officers rebels. Father Herman tried to calm the manager down, and asked him to state, in decent language, what his complaint was. Baranov shouted, "Now you have found some kind of oath and turned all the Americans against us!"

The humble elder replied, "The imperial manifesto was made public to all: if the religious mission has acted illegally at all, then the matter should be reported to the government..."

Baranov said he would have them all put in irons and taken to Unalaska, that the mission house would be locked and boarded up so that no one could get to them and they could not get out. This made everyone afraid, and they all expected to be arrested on Baranov's orders and beaten. They hardly dared leave the house..and for the same reason, they did not dare to go freely to church, and consequently for more than a year they conducted all services in their house.

When time came for the otter hunting party, Kuskov armed a *baidara* not only with rifles but with cannon, and set out for the village inhabited by the Natives who had sworn the oath...Arriving at the village, [foreman Kondakov]...shouted: "Come out to meet us! The priests are coming...to get you to swear the oath!"

...For the reasons described above, as well as the fact that the Americans no longer dared to visit the priests openly, and the priests feared to have the relations with them that their work demanded—when they would have been able to install Christian teachings—the success of the Religious Mission did not come up to expectations...[1]

That is quite an understatement. Most Alaskan history texts speak of the early decades of competing *promyshlenniki* as the most oppressive and destructive period, and the Baranov era as an improvement, when law and order were imposed and justice established. This is, of course, what Shelikov and his shareholders wanted everyone, especially the government, to believe. Their aim was to work systematically, to exploit the country's resources methodically. In doing so, they relocated, enslaved, exploited and killed thousands of Native Alaskans.

Baranov, in a letter to his colleague E. G. Larionov, dated March 22, 1801, had a very different interpretation of this incident and its consequences.

New Year's Day a new thing happened. After the liturgy, the clerk...and several hunters were at my place drinking tea when the hieromonk ran in, very excited, and shouted that I must not send the bird hunting crew this year, and that all people on the island had to take the oath of allegiance immediately. After giving him some tea, I answered that because the bird crew would be leaving in May, there would be plenty of time, but to gather the people for the taking of the oath of allegiance right away was inconvenient for the hunters and the islanders...It is not their custom to bring food supplies when coming here [to Kodiak] and we were all liable to starve if they were summoned.

1   Bearne, *op. cit.* p. 149.

Suddenly he called me a traitor to the emperor, and accused me of interfering with the people's swearing the oath. I was sorely vexed at being called such a name because I make the interests of my country and the glory of our Monarch top priority in all my activities. I asked if he had an order from the bishop. I asked why they could not wait for the Archimandrite to return. He answered that they did not have a special decree but that the original manifesto was issued for "all loyal subjects" and they consider the islanders to be such...Before leaving he told me that those men who live openly with unmarried girls would not be admitted to the church, according to the ecclesiastical rule. I am certain there is no such rule, but because of this, I have not attended services since then.

Finally during Lent they discontinued services altogether and conducted them only four times, on Sundays. They do not promise to have Holy Week services...They entice people not to recognize my authority, but to join them in the ruin of the company's gains and objectives...They promised the islanders freedom and independence to live according to their own customs if they would swear the oath of allegiance.

After calling the people of Ugashik village (the chief there is their godson) to take the oath of allegiance, they sent messengers to other villages to declare their independence and freedom. According to them, the Natives would not have to work for the company's crews but could hunt for themselves...I told the Natives that before the company built their present settlements they had lived in primitive conditions, and after civilizing them for eighteen years, the company had provided a secure and quiet existence for them. They would not listen to me, and the priests took them to the church and made them take the oath of allegiance...

...I saw in this a clear evidence of revolt...To meet the danger...I ordered the arrest of the chiefs who were leaving without settling their accounts, and whose behavior was that of former times, full of arrogance and independence. My men managed to seize only one of them,...but even one chief's arrest had a good effect on the others. Now foreseeing danger, I ordered hostages from the villages on the southern half of the island. The arrested chief is under guard.

The clergy became very excited...they called us robbers, traitors and mutineers...In the meantime, I learned that the rebel from Ugashik...had come secretly at night to visit the priests. I ordered a guard to wait for him and catch him on his way home, but the monks found out my intentions and at night they dressed one of the hieromonks in the chief's clothes and put him into the chief's *baidarka*, so that the guards arrested the hieromonk instead of the chief. He was set free without any fuss, but at this point a real riot began. The fathers all ran out with their cassocks tucked up high and their sleeves rolled up, as if ready for a prize fight, cursing and swearing. I went out to them and did some shouting myself, and told them frankly that if they did not stop inciting rebellion I would use extreme and disagreeable measures—house arrest or deportation to Unalaska.

Even after this they did not improve their behavior. They quit going to church altogether and claim that...they are afraid of us, but during the night they prowl around and seize our servants, taking them under their protection, and marrying them in the bathhouses.

From all this you can see what a peaceful and pleasant state of affairs prevails here with these restless fellows. To write everything would fill a library.[2]

2   Pierce, *History of the Russian American Co.*, Vol II, (1979), p. 124-127.

Such was the "union of church and state" in old Kodiak. In private communications with the company's board of directors, Nikolai Rezanov repeated Baranov's version of this episode, stating:

> At the time of the coronation of the emperor, the monks, without any word to the manager, sent out orders, calling all the Natives to Kodiak to take the oath of allegiance. There were no provisions at Kodiak, and if the manager had not stopped the people from gathering by sending his men to the villages, several thousand of them, gathering in Kodiak, would have killed everyone from starvation alone...Sometimes, unknown to the manager, they would set off uselessly to make converts...the monk Iuvenalii went to propagate the faith. He baptized some by force, married them, took girls away from some and gave them to others. The Americans endured his rough ways and beatings for a long time, but finally they decided to get rid of this reverend and killed him. He deserves no pity...[3]

Rezanov's account is replete with distortions and fabrications. The incident occured five years after the coronation of the tsar, and the monks were certainly justified in their suspicion that Baranov never intended to allow the Natives to swear the oath. That the clergy were inciting the Natives to assert their freedom and that the company insisted that they obey Baranov's orders indicates where the real issues lay. Hieromonk Iuvenalii traveled alone and unarmed, so that it was beyond his personal strength to force anyone to submit to baptism. Two centuries after his visit, the villages he baptized have remained overwhelmingly loyal to Orthodoxy. The historical evidence substantiates the monks', not the company's account. Had the Kenai, Chugach or Iliamna people been forced to accept Christianity, they would have abandoned it as soon as the missionary left town. Instead, they have remained steadfast in their allegiance, not to any earthly tsar, but to the King of Kings and His Church. The martyr St Iuvenalii did his work well.

Appendix II

Two Missionary Journeys

Extracts from Father Iakov Netsvetov's Yukon Journals

1851

May 18: I myself...am preparing these days for a journey upstream along the Kvikhpak [Yukon] to the distant upstream settlements which I have not yet visited and did not reach on my previous journey up the river in 1847, in order to preach the word of God to the wild ones whom I have not yet met. I am squeezing out the time (though it is inconvenient, because there is much I have to do in connection with the church construction here). I am allotting until at least the first of June for the trip, going as far upstream as circumstances and available means will permit, remaining for a time wherever I should meet with the people, though I know that usually they are not to be found in their settlements in assembly there, but are dispersed through various localities, along many creeks and lakes. I have been moved to decide on this not only by the misfortune visited upon the Nulato outpost [it had been burned when warring Indian factions fought there], but also because everyone, especially along the Yukon, is afraid of an attack on the part of the wild ones, as allegedly those who perpetrated the crime intend to sail down the river and attack not only the Russian dwellings but the Native settlements belonging to different tribes as well. For this reason, all the Natives along the river live in fear, especially now, after the river has opened up [thawed]. Thus, if not to forestall, then to somewhat allay their apprehensions, I decided, traveling lightly, to proceed upstream as far as I can. Therefore this day I completed my preparations for the journey and plan to leave, taking only my subdeacon and interpreter, Constantine Lukin and my nephew Vasia [diminutive form of Vasilii/Basil].

May 19: ...We were forced to find our way among the flotsam with great effort. Around noon we put in at the settlement Ikalivagmiut, but the residents were not at home. We continued and spent the night at an uninhabited place.

May 20: We continued on our way at 5:00 a.m., sailing through the entire day, at times fighting our way through driftwood and debris...At about 5:00 p.m., we reached the mouth of the channel of the Chag'liuk [Innoko] River. Here we halted for the night to give the oarsmen some rest.

May 21: At 5:00 a.m., we went on, traveling first through the channel, reaching the mouth of the Innoko by noon...I continued on to a place where the chief,

Alexander Katil'nuk and his family are staying. By 2:00 p.m., we came to his camp and here I stopped in order to talk to him about matters. He and his family are here alone. I realized that it would be impossible to assemble his people quickly in any one location. They are scattered, each family on its own, not only along this river but also along the tundra, around the lakes, and along many small streams, and I should spend a long time waiting for them. We then agreed, the chief and I, that as I proceed upstream along this river, and then plan to cross over to the Yukon at a suitable portage, he will notify his people of my presence and assemble as many as possible at the mouth of the Innoko river.

[On May 22, Netsvetov reached a permanent settlement on the Innoko River. The residents here were Athabaskan Indians, a totally different linguistic and cultural group from their Eskimo neighbors.]

May 23: ...By noon people who had been informed of my arrival began gathering here, but not all of them, since some were far upriver, and it was not possible to notify them quickly. Therefore, I commenced instructing them in their *kazhim* [ceremonial house]. It was impossible to do so outdoors because of stormy weather and heavy rain. I taught the newly baptized and at the same time preached the word of salvation to a few of those who were unbaptized. Having heard our preaching, they expressed their desire to be baptized. This very same day, toward evening, I performed the rite of baptism for seven men and four women. In spite of the poor weather, they eagerly accepted baptism in the river...Later on, when I was giving out the baptismal certificates to those newly baptized, I again taught all those present. Now I intend to leave here and proceed farther upstream, along the river, until the real Chag'liuk settlement, where the chief tells me I should meet more people, especially unbaptized ones. He himself intends to accompany me there.

[On May 24, Netsvetov with the chief in his own *baidara* spent the stormy day travelling up river to Shageluk, where they arrived about 2:00 p.m.]

May 25: By morning most, though not all, of the people who had been notified had gathered here. Many men came without their families because of the bad weather...I preached the Word of God to them, as there were many unbaptized among them. They listened to the preaching with attention, without any arguments to the contrary or any objections. The chief offered me his support, declaring to them the benefit of the preaching of salvation. In the end, those listening expressed their belief and their desire to be baptized, saying that if their brothers who had earlier heard this message had been baptized [in 1847] together with their chief, they do not wish to be separated by a different faith, but want to follow their example. After noon I began the rite of baptism, as by this time the weather had cleared. I divided them into two groups and baptized...33 men and 11 women.

May 26: Since early morning, all newly baptized persons, those baptized earlier and those baptized yesterday, came to me and I began instructing them in Christian piety. I also praised the chief for his support and diligence since his baptism in 1847. I gave him a red shirt and a certificate. Later on, I set out on the return voyage along the river.

[Netsvetov traveled down the Innoko to the Yukon, then up the Yukon toward the village of Anvik, "against the swift current."]

May 27: ...Only by 3:00 p.m. did we reach the Anvik settlement. Here I met several local residents, but many were not home, and the local chief was also absent. He is Nikolai Kakatsei who was baptized in December 1847 at Russian Mission. He arrived about 6:00 p.m., offering me generous hospitality, like a fellow Christian. I immediately engaged myself with the people as all of them gathered around my tent. We spent the evening in such pleasurable conversation, in the open, and I preached the Word of God to them, and they listened with great attention and without any controversy. The chief helped me by confirming my words and telling them that he had heard all this before, and had therefore himself been baptized. Finally, when I had preached to them about the Savior, Jesus Christ, and explained the origin of this message of salvation and how this message spread through the world and how it had reached their land, one elderly man began to speak. It was apparent that he understood the preaching very well. He was saying, obviously having been deeply moved by the preaching, "There, now, we hear true words, though we have heard similar messages before, they remained misunderstood, and now can we do anything else but turn to God? We ought to be grateful that these words, coming from so far, have reached us." To this I replied that they ought to thank God, that He, in His love and humility and through His grace and kindness sent the message to you also. Afterwards they all expressed their undoubting faith and desire to be baptized. I postponed such action until the next day, as it was already almost midnight.

May 28: In the morning, all those who desired to accept baptism gathered at my tent. Having offered them at that time necessary instruction, I baptized 19 men, 17 women, and, at their parents request, four infants, as they were baptized as entire families. Later on, I offered them final instruction and distributed the certificates.

1853

May 13: Today the Shageluk Chief, Alexander Kantil'nuk, arrived here in a *baidara* [a large, open skin boat]...He asked when I plan to come to him this season or to travel along the Shageluk River to reach the Kol'chane, who live along the upper reaches of this river, that is, to the villages whose inhabitants have come down along the Shageluk River and were waiting for me in Shageluk. Some of them had visited me here [at Russian Mission] last May and had accepted baptism. When I decided to travel there, the chief asked if I might proceed without him and depend on locally available help for travel to the settlement along the upper Shageluk River. He said I can count on his son to accompany me to Kol'chane territory. I shall need him as a second interpreter ["Kol'chane" refers to another Indian tribe whose language is distinct from that of Shageluk]. His son had helped me in this capacity on my first trip...

May 15: Having prayed to the Lord God for His aid and blessing, we left Ikogmiut [Russian Mission] about noon, traveling in two three-hatch *baidarkas* [kayaks], going upstream along the Yukon River.

May 20: Though it was my plan to travel through all the Kol'chane settlements, I have learned that on their own initiative the Kol'chane have gathered at the lowest village, Kholiachagmiut, in order to meet me. Thus I settled down to await them here. In the meantime, I was busy with those who were converted in 1851, but who had not been baptized because they had to hunt or fish. In the morning I preached the Word of God and then, according to their faith and expressed desire, I baptized 9 men and 6 women. Then I waited for the arrival of the people from upriver. In the evening they came in birchbark canoes and large wooden boats and one *baidara.* I counted up to one hundred such vessels as they converged, so that the Shageluk [Innoko] River was completely covered with canoes and boats.

May 21: Beginning in the morning, upon my invitation, all the Kol'chane and Ingalit [Ingalik] from the Yukon and the local ones gathered at my place and I preached the Word of God, concluding at noon. Everyone listened to the preaching with attention and without discussion or dissent, and in the end they all expressed faith, and their wish to accept Holy Baptism, both the Kol'chane and the Ingalit [formerly traditional enemies]. I made a count by families and kin groups and then, in the afternoon, began the baptismal service. First I baptized 50 Kol'chane and Ingalit men, the latter from the Yukon and Innoko. It was already evening when I completed this service.

May 22: I began baptizing 72 women in the morning. In the afternoon I baptized 54 older children of the parents who had been recently converted. The rite was finished by evening, a total of 126 persons, 33 boys, 93 women and girls. From this activity I became dreadfully tired and felt pain from standing so long...However, the spiritual joy at the sight of so many souls joined to the flock of the Christian Church compensated for everything, and the bodily weaknesses disappeared. That night I made a written record of the day's events.

May 23: Before noon I again performed baptism for the smaller children and infants of the newly baptized parents and chrismated the family of a Kol'chane, a wife and daughter who had been baptized by Simeon Lukin in 1846. Thirty-six more were added to the Church of Christ today...

May 24: All those newly baptized, all that are here present, attended and prayed. One must imagine the joy in my heart at the sight of so many souls gathered in one place, more than 300, praying to God, people of various tribes, formerly hostile to each other, enemies, now united as the flock of Christ's Church, offering prayers to the true God. After the service I offered them a sermon, as to the reborn children, first declaring to them why I held such a communal prayer, that is, explaining that today is Sunday. Then I taught them Christian commandments, about prayer, Christian love, and Christian virtues, but most of all about human kindness, about peaceful and cordial coexistence between all people...When I finished writing, I called the people together before me and gave out the certificates [of baptism]. Then I preached another sermon for their instruction. Thus I finished my work with them at about 4:00 p.m. and began to prepare for my departure....I left at 5:00 p.m...Traveling with the current, we moved very fast, and by 10:00 p.m. we reached the village where Alexander Kantil'nuk is chief...His son helped me very much yesterday during all my contacts with the people who were being baptized, translating whatever I said for the Kol'chane and Ingalik, and for this I am very grateful.

Appendix III

The Yukon Mission in the Twentieth Century

In about 1905, Father Iakov Korchinskii, a Ukrainian from Kiev, served at Russian Mission and probably introduced many of the folk customs of his homeland, including the "starring" tradition at Christmas time which has become a popular festival throughout the delta. Hieromonk Amphilokhii Vakulskii spent most of his adult life among the Yup'ik, serving as resident missionary early in the century and as bishop of the diocese (though remaining as much as possible at Russian Mission) for another twenty years. Capable of serving the eucharistic liturgy in Yup'ik, Amphilokhii later retired to the "lower 48," and is buried in the Metropolitan Platon chapel at St Tikhon's monastery in South Canaan, Pennsylvania. His dying wish, however, was to be buried in Alaska.

From 1906 to 1917, Father Nikifor Amkan, a Native from Bristol Bay, maintained the mission. He then retired to Kwethluk on the Kuskokwim, where he died in 1928. Another Native priest, Father Vasilii Changsak, served the Orthodox communities throughout the region from 1923 until his death in 1966. All these men continued the translation work begun by Fathers Netsvetov and Bel'kov, although these texts for vespers, matins and major feast days were not published until they were first transcribed by Fathers Michael Oleksa, Phillip Alexie, and Martin Nicolai at Kwethluk in 1972. Before then, local Yup'ik choirs sang these hymns from memory, in a uniquely Alaskan style. In 1981, the National Endowment for the Arts funded a recording project directed by Dr Richard John Dauenhauer, to document the Unangan Aleut and Tlingit Orthodox musical tradition. So loyal to their teachers were the Kuskokwim Yup'iks that they refused to alter the texts in any way, even when the vocabulary of the Yukon dialect was unfamiliar or unintelligible to them. When asked why they continued to use translations they could not fully comprehend, they answered, "This is the way we have always done it." The traditional worldview survives today.

In 1973, the Orthodox diocese published the texts of many of these translations which had circulated orally for generations, employing a new writing system devised by linguists at the University of Alaska's Native Language Center in Fairbanks. Father Martin Nicolai, whose grandfather, Paul D. Nicolai, Sr., had begun training him to serve as a church reader when Martin was still in primary school, is literate in both the Netsvetov/Bel'kov orthography and the new ANLC system. With the enthusiastic support of hundreds of Yup'ik Orthodox, Father Martin transcribes liturgical texts and chants, and composes new, authentically Alaskan music, continuing the work begun so auspiciously by Father Iakov Netsvetov, and indeed by Alaska's first Christian martyr, St Iuvenalii.

Nushagak

As early as 1819, and certainly by 1823, the Russian merchant Theodor Kolmakov had established his trading post and introduced Christianity to the Yup'ik people of Bristol Bay, baptizing seven or eight converts before Father Veniaminov's first visit to the Nushagak in 1829. When Father John arrived there, he instructed, baptized and chrismated the first Yup'ik Christians in the river itself, writing in his journal, "the Nushagak became for them a New Jordan." While forbidding him to give any gifts to the newly converted, Veniaminov authorized Kolmakov to baptize Natives who requested it. When he returned three years later with Governor von Wrangell, he discovered that sixty-two more Yup'iks had been baptized by Theodor and his Creole son, Peter. Seeing this growth and the obvious potential of the region, Wrangell decreed that the chapel which the Kolmakovs had already begun should be completed at the company's expense. When Father Golovnin visited Nushagak in 1838, he chrismated fifty-three more converts who had been baptized earlier at the outpost, and baptized fifty-two others. By 1839, the Nushagak parish had 320 members.

When Veniaminov became bishop of the diocese, he sent his newly-ordained Creole son-in-law, Father Elia Petelin, to Nushagak. The Creole Basil Shishkin accompanied the Petelins as the new choir director in 1841. Father Elia described his illustrious father-in-law as "not scholarly but diligent and skillful," and as one who "graciously bore the hardships and deprivations of the mission."

Petelin reported that in one village the Natives listened attentively to his sermons and all accepted baptism. Before continuing on his journey, he asked if there were still any unbaptized in the community, and he was told there was one blind, elderly woman who had been unable to hear any of his sermons or attend any services. He asked if she could be brought to him. Walking with a crutch and assisted by others, the woman, who was approximately eighty-five years old, soon arrived. Father Elia spoke to her at length, explaining the Christian faith and the importance of baptism. She then requested to be baptized, and the priest promised to perform the sacrament two hours later. But when the appointed time arrived, the woman did not appear. Father Elia sent a reminder to the lady that he was waiting, and the messenger returned with the news that she had suddenly become gravely ill. At first, Petelin did not believe this report, thinking that the woman had simply changed her mind. Upon further investigation, however, he discovered that she had indeed become paralyzed and was unable to speak. He could not decide what to do. If he baptized her and she died, some Yup'iks would attribute her death to the sacrament; but on the other hand, he did not want her to die without being united to Christ. He decided, therefore, to proceed with the baptism. The woman was carried to his tent, where he baptized and chrismated her. Immediately she recovered, walking home without assistance, using only one crutch. Petelin modestly concluded, "God sent her health."

By 1843, the Nushagak parish had recorded 315 baptisms and 110 chrismations of children who had been baptized by laymen, bringing the total membership to 425. Suffering poor health, Father Petelin transferred elsewhere in 1846, but Shishkin, as reader, deacon and later priest, remained at Nushagak until his death, fifty-two years later.

Hieromonk Nicholas from Kenai spent the year 1850-1851 at Nushagak, and Hieromonk Theophil was assigned there in 1853. In 1860, a new church was constructed then enlarged in 1866, when a new parsonage was also built. After the sale of Alaska in 1867, Basil Orlov, a Creole choir director and church warden, served as caretaker. Ten years later, Orlov and Shishkin were making annual visits by kayak and dog sled to all the surrounding villages, taking nearly three months to complete a full circuit. Church records indicate that, by this time, six chapels had been built in various Native communities, all maintained by the local believers. That year, 1877, Father Innocent Shayashnikov, another Creole priest who had been trained by Father Iakov Netsvetov and later served as priest at Unalaska, visited the Nushagak parish.

When American Moravian missionaries arrived in the region ten years later, they were unable to attract many converts, since the majority of the people had already accepted baptism from the itinerant Aleut and Creole clergy who had been active in the area for seventy years. Father Basil also trained local lay readers to conduct short services during the many months he was absent from the villages. This localized and decentralized leadership remains very active in rural Alaska, and explains to a large extent the survival and vitality of the Orthodox church on the Nushagak. From its beginnings, Orthodoxy became so much an indigenous institution that when the first non-Native Orthodox priest arrived in the region in 1974, Native children in some villages viewed him with suspicion: since Orthodoxy was a Native religion, how could this "white man" be a real priest?

Although there are some indications that Kolmakov and Lukin might have organized classes at the Nushagak trading post, it is certain that Father Petelin, Hieromonk Theophil and church warden Basil Orlov operated a small school before 1867, and that Orlov continued to offer instruction to Native and Creole students until the end of the century. Father Vladimir Modestov served the parish from 1895-1897. He was succeeded by the Creole priests, Basil and Nicolas Kashevarov. When Father Basil died in 1916, church reader Basil Backford assumed responsibility for the mission, and he successfully resisted all efforts by several bishops to ordain him to the priesthood. He trained his son-in-law, Basil Sifsof, originally from

Unalaska and a graduate of the seminary that functioned there until 1917, to celebrate the services. Father Sifsof transferred the mission headquarters across the river to Dillingham, where, together with his devout church warden, John Nelson, Sr. (of Swedish/Yup'ik decent), he founded St Seraphim of Sarov Church. Father Basil died in 1972. Among his immediate successors were Archpriest Vasilii (Basil) Epchook, the son of a Creole priest from the Yukon, Archpriest Nikolai Epchook, who served most of his life at Kwethluk, on the Kuskokwim, and Father Jonah Andrew, a Yup'ik, also from Kwethluk.

In the Naknek area, two Creole priests from the Aleutian Islands served at Egegik, on the north shore of the Alaska Peninsula. Father Gregory Kochergin, a prominent Unangan writer, teacher and translator, and Father Sergius Repin. Both traveled extensively throughout the region, the latter accompanied for many years by Agafangel Backford, son of the Nushagak reader Basil Backford. Pastoral visits required weeks of difficult and often dangerous sledding and kayaking, up the Kvichak and down the Nushagak Rivers. Without exaggeration, therefore, it is possible to conclude that the very existence of Orthodoxy among the Yup'ik people of Bristol Bay is due primarily to the work of Aleut and Creole missionaries who devoted their lives to the evangelization of their mainland neighbors, beginning with Peter Kolmakov in the 1830's, and culminating with Father Basil Sifsof in 1972.

By the 1980's, several young Yup'ik priests had assumed responsibility for the Bristol Bay parishes. These were Father Jonah Andrew at Dillingham, Father Maxim Isaac and his Aleut wife, at Chignik, Father Prokopii Ishnook at Koliganek, Father Alexie Askoak at New Stuyahok, and Father David Askoak at Iliamna. The oldest Askoak brother, Father Peter, succeeded Archpriest Gabriel Gabrieloff as pastor at Netsvetov's headquarters at Russian Mission, while the youngest, Vasilii, has been ordained deacon. At Pilot Station, on the Yukon, Father Stephan Heckman and his Russian Mission-born wife Anna (Kozevnikoff) serve the downriver villages with Father Andrew Meyers, stationed at Pitka's Point. All of these young priests are graduates of St Herman's Seminary, founded in 1973 at Kodiak.

The Kuskokwim

Theodor Kolmakov and Simeon Lukin introduced Christianity on the middle Kuskokwim even before Father Netsvetov arrived, and operated a school there as well; but no priest was assigned to the area until Father John Orlov established headquarters at Chuathbaluk in 1892. Father Iakov Korchinskii spent 1896 and 1897 there, and Father Nikifor Amkan resided on the Kuskokwim from 1897-1901, before relocating to Russian Mission on the Yukon. For the next two years, Father Constantine Pavlov lived at Chuathbaluk. Then Father Matthew Berezkin, a Creole from Unalaska arrived. Father Berezkin remained among the Yup'ik for the rest of his life, serving as priest from 1906 until 1926, when he left the priesthood and remarried after his wife's death. Moving to Napaskiak, near Bethel, Berezkin spent another thirty-five years as choir director and reader, promoting literacy in Netsvetov's writing system, translating many liturgical texts from Old Church Slavonic into Yup'ik, and in the process, making Napaskiak a major Orthodox center during his lifetime. Two Yup'ik graduates of St Herman's Seminary, Archpriest Phillip Alexie, and Priest Nikolai Larson, a talented wood carver, have served St Iakov parish there in recent years.

Archpriest Nikolai Epchook, originally from the Yukon, was sent to Unalaska to be trained as a priest at the turn of the century. After spending a few years at Nushagak, he returned home to serve as deacon with Bishop Amphilokhii Vakulskii, before being ordained priest and assigned to Kwethluk, near Bethel, in 1926. He remained at Kwethluk for the next thirty-six years. A distant relative of the Bel'kov family, Father Nikolai trained others to read and sing at services. Two of these were later ordained, Father Nikolai O. Michael and Father Vasilii Epchook, Father Nikolai's son. Father Nikolai O. Michael succeeded Father Nicolai Epchook as rector of St Nicholas church in Kwethluk and as Dean of the Kuskokwim Yukon Deanery. Father Vasilii Epchook, stationed at Egegik, New Stuyahok, Dillingham and Lower Kalskag, transcribed Yup'ik and Slavonic hymns and taught generations of Eskimo Orthodox to appreciate both. Another generation of Yup'ik priests has emerged from Kwethluk since 1978: Archpriest Phillip Alexie, who has served Chuathbaluk and Napaskiak, now lives at Kasigluk where he succeeded Archpriest Michael Tinker, a close friend and colleague of Father Nikolai O. Michael; Deacon Victor Nick, a talented ivory carver from Kwethluk, has recently moved to Kasigluk, his wife Elizabeth's hometown, to assist Father Phillip; Father Jonah Andrew, originally from Kwethluk, serves Dillingham; Father Martin Nikolai serves in Kwethluk, his birthplace, transcribing and composing Yup'ik liturgical music.

Both Archpriests Zacharii Guest and Michael Paul Tinker came from the "Tundra" village of Kasigluk. Ordained in 1954, Father Zacharii spent nearly thirty years traveling extensively from Nikolai and Lime Village, hundreds of miles up the Kuskokwim, to Kwigillingok and Eek, on the shores of the Bering Sea, and residing at South Naknek and Iliamna as well as at Bethel during his three decades of service. He is credited with designing and building seventeen churches and chapels, and was especially proficient in constructing traditional wooden cupolas (domes) to adorn their roofs. During his many years of missionary work, Father Guest traveled by dog sled, boat, snowmobile and airplane, crashing several times but emerging unscathed after each accident. Father Tinker was responsible for erecting a beautiful new church at Kasigluk a few years before his death in 1983. When it tragically burned during Holy Week 1990, the faithful of Kasigluk, Nunapitchuk and surrounding communities pooled their resources and built and furnished a new church within two years. Two graduates of St Herman's Seminary from the Tundra villages recently have been ordained to the priesthood: Father Zachary Guest's grandson, Father

Sergius Active of Kasigluk, now serves the Unangan Orthodox community at King Cove on the Alaska Peninsula; and Father Peter Chris has assumed pastoral responsibility for St Sophia church in Bethel, the regional commercial and transportation hub.

To summarize the Aleut contribution to the rise of Orthodoxy among the Yup'ik since 1830, statistics reveal that on the Yukon, Creoles and local Native clergy have served the mission for a total of 107 years, while ethnic Russians resided there for only 16. On the Kuskokwim, if the lifetimes of the last generation of Yup'ik priests are included, the totals are similar: Creoles and indigenous clergy have served that region for 111 years, while Fathers Korchinskii and Pavlov for only 6. At Nushagak during the same period, the Creoles Petelin, Shishkin, Orlov, Shayashnikov, Backford and Sifsof served a total of 108 years, while the Russian Hieromonks Theofil and Nikolai, only 19. On all three main rivers, the Russian presence was relatively brief, and it gave way to greater involvement of Creole and local Native clergy. Creoles not only introduced the Yup'ik Eskimos to Orthodoxy, therefore, but continued to expand the influence of the Church throughout southwestern Alaska for more than a century after the sale. Moreover, they operated schools, translated hymns, introduced literacy, trained church leaders and their own successors with virtually no outside assistance or supervision, and without any financial support from anywhere after 1917. Many served without regular income, living a subsistence lifestyle together with their flocks, as most of the young clergy continue to do today. These are the unsung heros of Alaskan Orthodox Christianity.

Selected Bibliography

Afonsky, Bishop Gregory, *A History of the Orthodox Church in Alaska, 1794-1917* (St Herman's Seminary Press: Kodiak Alaska, 1974), 106 pages.

Alexander, Hartley, B., *The World's Rim: Great Mysteries of the North American Indians* (University of Nebraska Press: Lincoln, NE: 1953).

Antonson, Joan M., and Hanable, William S., *Alaska's Heritage* (Department of Education, Alaska Historical Commission: Anchorage, AK, 1984), 197 pages.

Arnold, Robert D., *Alaska Native Land Claims* (Alaska Native Foundation: Anchorage, 1978), 367 pages.

Arseniev, Nicolas, *Revelation of Life Eternal* (St Vladimir's Seminary Press, Crestwood: 1965), 104 pages.

_____, *Russian Piety* (St Vladimir's Seminary Press, Crestwood: 1978), 145 pages.

_____, *Mysticism in the Eastern Church* (St Vladimir's Seminary Press, Crestwood: 1979), 173 pages.

Augros, Robert M., and Stanciu, George N., *The New Story of Science* (Bantam Books, New York: 1984), 235 pages

Bancroft, Hubert H., *History of Alaska, 1730-1885* (A.L.Bancroft and Co., San Francisco, CA: 1886), 775 pages.

Banks, Theodore, *People of the Bering Sea* (MSS Educational Publishing Co., New York: 1971), 101 pages.

Bearne, Colin, trans., *The Russian Orthodox Religious Mission in America, 1794-1837* (Limestone Press, Kingston, ON: 1978), 186 pages.

Berger, Thomas R., *Village Journey* (Hill and Wang, New York: 1985), 202 pages.

Bergsland, Knut, *Aleut Dialects of Attu and Atka* (American Philosophical Society, Philadelphia: 1959), 128 pages.

_____ and Moses L. Dirks, *Aleut Tales and Narratives* (University of Alaska, Fairbanks: 1990), 715 pages.

Berkh, V.N., *Chronological History of the Discovery of the Aleutian Islands*, trans. by D. Kernov (Limestone Press, Kingston, ON: 1974), 127 pages.

_____, *The Wreck of the Neva* (Anchorage Historical Society, Anchorage: 1979), 64 pages.

Bettenson, Henry, *The Early Christian Fathers* (Oxford Paperbacks, London: 1987), 310 pages.

Black, Lydia T., *The Journals of Iakov Netsvetov, The Atkha Years, 1828-1844* (Limestone Press, Kingston, ON: 1980), 340 pages.

_____, *The Journals of Iakov Netsvetov, The Yukon Years, 1845-1862* (Limestone Press, Kingston, ON: 1984a), 514 pages.

_____, *Atkha: An Ethnohistory of the Western Aleutians* (Limestone Press, Kingston ON: 1984b), 219 pages.

Blaker, Ray, *Eskimo Masks: Art and Ceremony* (University of Washington Press, Seattle: 1967), 246 pages.

Bria, Ion, *Martyria/Mission* (World Council of Churches Press, Geneva: 1980), 255 pages.

Brown, Dee, *Bury My Heart at Wounded Knee* (Holt Rinehart and Winston, New York: 1980), 508 pages.

Brown, Joseph E., *The Spiritual Legacy of the American Indian* (Crossroad Publishing, New York: 1986), 135 pages.

Brown, Vinson, *Peoples of the Sea Wind* (Collier Press, New York: 1977), 259 pages.

Bulgakov, Sergius, *Bulgakov Anthology* (Westminster Press, Philadelphia: 1976), 191 pages.

Campbell, Joseph, *The Masks of God: Primitive Mythology* (Viking Press, New York: 1969), 504 pages.

Chetverikov, Sergei, *Starets Paisii Velichkovskii* (Nordland Press, Belmont, MA: 1980), 339 pages.

Chevigny, Hector, *Russian America* (Viking Press, New York: 1965), 275 pages.

Chitty, Derwas J., *The Desert A City* (St Vladimir's Seminary Press, Crestwood: 1966), 222 pages.

Clark, Donald W., *Koniag-Pacific Eskimo Bibliography* (National Museum of Canada, Ottawa, ON: 1975), 97 pages.

Dall, William H., *Alaska and Its Resources* (Lee and Shepard, Boston, MA: 1970).

Dauenhauer, Nora Marks and Richard L., *Haa Shuka: Tlingit Oral Narratives* (University of Washington Press, Seattle: 1987), 514 pages.

_____, *Haa Tuwunaagu Yis: Tlingit Oratory* (University of Washington Press, Seattle: 1990), 569 pages.

Dauenhauer, Richard L, *Glacier Bay Concerto* (Alaska Pacific University, Anchorage: 1980), 120 pages.

Davidson, Art, [ed], *Must One Way of Life Die for Another to Live?* (Yupiktak Bista, Bethel, AK: 1974), 80 pages.

Davis, Nancy Yaw, *Effects of the 1964 Earthquake, Tsunami and Resettlement on Two Koniag Eskimo Communities,*[ms] (University of Washington, Seattle: 1971).

Davydov, Lt. Gavrilo I., *Two Voyages to Russian America* (Limestone Press, Kingston, ON: 1977), 257 pages.

Deloria, Vine, *In Utmost Good Faith* (Straight Arrow Press, San Francisco: 1971), 402 pages.

Drivers, Harold E., *Indians of North America* (University of Chicago: 1969), 632 pages.

Dvornik, Francis, *Byzantine Missions Among the Slavs* (Rutgers University Press, New Brunswick: 1970), 485 pages.

Eliade, Mircea, *Patterns in Comparative Religion* (Sheed and Ward, New York: 1958), 485 pages.

_____, *Cosmos and History* (Harper and Row, New York: 1959a), 176 pages.

_____, *The Sacred and the Profane* (Harcourt Brace and World, New York: 1959b), 256 pages.

_____, *Shamanism* (Princeton University Press, 1964), 610 pages.

_____, *Rites and Symbols of Initiation* (Harper and Row, 1968), 167 pages.

_____, *Myths, Dreams and Mysteries* (Harper and Row, 1969), 201 pages.

Elliot, H. W., *The Seal Islands of Alaska* (Limestone Press, Kingston, ON: 1976 [reprint of 1881 ed.]), 176 pages.

Elson, Ruth M., *Guardians of Tradition: American Schoolbooks of the 19th Century* (University of Nebraska Press, Lincoln: 1964).

Every, George, SSM, *The Byzantine Patriarchate, 451-1204* (SPCK, London: 1962), 203 pages.

Feodorova, Svetlana G., *Russian Population in Alaska and California* (Limestone Press, Kingston, ON: 1973).

Fedotov, George P., *The Russian Religious Mind* (Harper and Row, New York: 1960), 431 pages.

_____, *A Treasury of Russian Spirituality* (Nordland Press, Belmont: 1975), 501 pages.

Fienup-Riordan, Ann, *The Nelson Island Eskimo* (Alaska Pacific University Press, Anchorage: 1983), 419 pages.

_____, *The Yup'ik Eskimo* (Limestone Press, Kingston, ON: 1988), 525 pages

Fisher, Raymond H., *Bering's Voyages: Whither and Why* (University of Washington Press, Seattle: 1977), 217 pages.

Fitzhugh, William H., and Crowell, Aron, ed., *Crossroads of Continents* (Smithsonian Institution, Washington, DC: 1988), 360 pages.

_____, and Kaplan, Susan A., ed., *Inua: The Spirit World of the Bering Sea Eskimo* (Smithsonian Institution, Washington, DC: 1984), 260 pages.

Florovsky, George, *Bible, Church Tradition: An Eastern Orthodox View* (Nordland Press, Belmont: 1972), 127 pages.

_____, *Christianity and Culture* (Nordland Press, Belmont: 1974), 245 pages.

_____, *Aspects of Church History* (Nordland Press, Belmont: 1975), 313 pages.

_____, *Creation and Redemption* (Nordland Press, Belmont: 1976), 317 pages.

_____, *Ways of Russian Theology* (Nordland Press, Belmont: 1979), 381 pages.

_____, *Eastern Fathers of the Fourth Century* (Nordland Press, Belmont: 1987), 274 pages.

_____, *Byzantine Fathers of the Fifth Century* (Nordland Press, Belmont: 1987a), 333 pages.

_____, *Byzantine Fathers of the Sixth to Eighth Centuries* (Nordland Press, Belmont: 1987b), 292 pages.

_____, *Byzantine Ascetic and Spiritual Fathers* (Nordland Press, Belmont: 1987c), 252 pages.

Gardner, Johann von, *Russian Church Singing: Orthodox Worship and Hymnography* (St Vladimir's Seminary Press, Crestwood: 1980), 146 pages.

Garrett, Paul D., *St Innocent, Apostle to America* (St Vladimir's Seminary Press, Crestwood: 1978), 345 pages.

Gibson, James R., *Feeding the Russian Fur Trade* (University of Wisconsin, 1969), 337 pages.

_____, *Imperial Russia in Frontier America* (Oxford University Press, London:, 1976), 257 pages.

Gill, Sam D., *Native American Religions: An Introduction* (Wadsworth Publishing Co., Belmont: 1982), 192 pages.

Golder, Frank, *Russian Expansion on the Pacific, 1640-1850* (Paragon Reprint Corp., 1971), 368 pages.

Golovin, V.N., *The End of Russian America* (Oregon Historical Society, Portland, OR: 1979), 249 pages.

Golovnin, V. M., *Around the World on the Kamchatka* (University of Hawaii Press, Honolulu: 1979), 353 pages.

Gregorios, Paulos, *Cosmic Man: The Divine Presence* (Sophia Publications, New Delhi: 1980a), 265 pages.

_____, *The Human Presence* (World Council of Churches Press, Geneva: 1980b), 104 pages.

Gruening, Ernest, *The State of Alaska* (Random House, New York: 1959).

Hamman, A., *The Paschal Mystery* (Alba Press, Staten Island, NY: 1960), 227 pages.

Hanke, Lewis, *All Mankind is One* (Northern Illinois University Press, DeKalb, IL: 1974), 205 pages.

Hinkley, Theodore, *The Americanization of Alaska, 1867-1897* (Pacific Books, Palo Alto: 1972), 285 pp.

Hope, Andrew III, *Raven's Bones* (Sitka Native Association, Sitka, AK: 1982), 144 pages.

Hopkins, David M., *The Bering Sea Land Bridge* (Stanford University Press, Palo Alto, CA: 1967), 495 pages.

Hopko, Thomas, *The Orthodox Faith* [Volumes 1-4] (Department of Religious Education, Orthodox Church in America, Syosset, NY: 1981).

_____, *All the Fulness of God* (St Vladimir's Seminary Press, Crestwood: 1982), 188 pages.

Hrdlicka, Aleš, *The Anthropology of Kodiak Island* (Wistar Institute, Philadelphia: 1944), 486 pages.

_____, *The Aleutian and Commander Islands and Their Inhabitants* (Wistar Institute, Philadelphia: 1945), 630 pages.

Hully, Clarence, *Alaska, 1741-1953* (Binfords and Mort, Portland, OR: 1953), 406 pages.

Ivashintsov, N.A., *Russian Round the World Voyages, 1803-1849* (Limestone Press, Kingston, ON: 1980), 156 pages.

Jochelson, Waldemar, *The History, Ethnography and Anthropology of the Aleut* (Carnegie Institute, Washington, DC: 1933), 432 pages.

Jones, Dorothy, *Aleuts in Transition* (University of Washington, Seattle, WA: 1976), 125 pages.

_____, *Aleut Bibliography* (University of Alaska, Fairbanks: 1975), 195 pages.

_____, *A Century of Servitude* (University of Alaska, Anchorage. University Press of America, Washington, DC: 1980), 190 pages.

Kamenskii, Anatolii, *The Tlingit Indians* (University of Alaska, Fairbanks: 1985), 166 pages.

Kan, Sergei, *Symbolic Immorality* (Smithsonian Institution, Washington, DC: 1989), 390 pages.

Khlebnikov, Kyrill, *Baranov* (Limestone Press, Kingston, ON: 1973), 140 pages.

_____, *Colonial Russian America, 1817-1832* (Oregon Historical Society, Portland: 1976), 158 pages.

King, J.C.H., *Portrait Masks from the Northwest Coast of America* (Thames and Hudson, London: 1979), 96 pages.

Kovach, Michael G., *The Russian Orthodox Church in Russian America* (University Microfilms, Ann Arbor: 1981), 290 pages.

Kovalevsky, Pierre, *St Sergius and Russian Spirituality* (St Vladimir's Seminary Press, Crestwood: 1978), 190 pages.

Krauss, Michael, *Alaska Native Languages* (University of Alaska, Fairbanks: 1980), 110 pages.

Lantis, Margaret, *Alaskan Eskimo Ceremonialism* (University of Washington, Seattle: 1948), 127 pages.

_____, *Ethnohistory of Southwest Alaska and the Southern Yukon* (University of Kentucky, 1970), 311 pages.

Lantzeff, George V., *Siberia in the Seventeenth Century* (University of California, Berkeley: 1943), 231 pages.

_____, with Richard Pierce, *Eastward to Empire* (McGill-Queens University, Montreal: 1973), 275 pages.

Laughlin, William S., *Aleuts: Survivors of the Bering Land Bridge* (Holt Rinehart and Winston, New York: 1980), 151 pages.

Levy-Bruhl, Lucien, *The Soul of the Primitive* (Gateway Publishing, Chicago: 1971), 351 pages.

Levy-Strauss, Claude, *Myth and Meaning* (Schoken, New York: 1978), 54 pages.

Lisiansky, Urey, *A Voyage Around the World, 1803-1806* (Limestone Press, Kingston, ON: 1978).

Lossky, Vladimir, *The Mystical Theology of the Eastern Church* (James Clarke Co., London: 1968), 252 pages.

Makarova, R. V., *Russians on the Pacific*, trans. by R. A. Pierce (Limestone Press, Kingston, ON: 1975), 301 pages.

Mather, Elsie, *Cauyarnariuq* (Lower Kuskokwim School District, Bethel, AK: 1985), 227 pages.

Merck, C.H., *Siberia and Northwest America, 1788-1792* (Limestone Press, Kingston, ON: 1980), 215 pages.

Miller, D. H., *The Alaska Treaty* (Limestone Press, Kingston, ON: 1981), 221 pages.

Meyendorff, John, *St Gregory Palamas and Orthodox Spirituality* (St Vladimir's Seminary Press, Crestwood: 1974), 184 pages.

_____, *Christ in Eastern Christian Thought* (St Vladimir's Seminary Press, Crestwood: 1975), 248 pages.

_____, *Byzantine Theology* (Fordham University, New York: 1979), 243 pages.

Morovskoi Spornik, St Petersburg, Russia, 1818 and 1863.

Naske, Claus, and Slotnick, Herman, *Alaska: A History of the 49th State* (Eerdmans, Grand Rapids: 1979), 341 pages.

Nellas, Panayiotis, *Deification in Christ* (St Vladimir's Seminary Press, Crestwood: 1987), 254 pages.

Nelson, Richard K., *Make Prayers to the Raven* (University of Chicago Press, Chicago: 1983), 292 pages

Obolensky, Dimitri, *The Byzantine Commonwealth* (St Vladimir's Seminary Press, Crestwood: 1982), 552 pages.

Okun, S. B., *The Russian American Company* (Octagon Books, New York: 1979), 311 pages.

Oleksa, Michael J., *Alaska Missionary Spirituality* (Paulist Press, Mahwah: 1987), 416 pages.

Ostrogorsky, George, *History of the Byzantine State* (Rutgers University, New Brunswick: 1969), 624 pages.

Oswalt, Wendall, *Alaskan Eskimos* (Chandler Press, Scranton: 1967), 297 pages.

_____, *Napaskiak* (University of Arizona Press, 1968), 179 pages.

_____, *This Land was Theirs* (John Wiley and Sons, New York: 1978), 569 pages.

Otto, Rudolf, *The Idea of the Holy* (Oxford University Press, London: 1950), 232 pages.

Ouspensky, Leonid, *The Theology of the Icon* (St Vladimir's Seminary Press, Crestwood: 1978), 232 pages.

_____, *The Meaning of Icons* (St Vladimir's Seminary Press, Crestwood: 1983), 222 pages.

Pascal, Pierre, *The Religion of the Russian People* (St Vladimir's Seminary Press, Crestwood: 1976), 130 pages.

Pierce, Richard A., *Alaskan Shipping, 1867-1878* (Limestone Press, Kingston, ON: 1972), 72 pages.

_____, *Russia's Hawaiian Adventure, 1815-1817* (Limestone Press, Kingston, ON: 1976), 245 pages.

Priest, Loring B., *Uncle Sam's Stepchildren* (University of Nebraska, Lincoln: 1975), 310 pages.

Prucha, Francis, *American Indian Policy in the Formative Years, 1790-1834* (University of Nebraska, Lincoln: 1970), 303 pages.

_____, *Documents in U.S. Indian Policy, 1783-1973* (University of Nebraska, Lincoln: 1975), 278 pages.

_____, *Americanizing the American Indians* (University of Nebraska, Lincoln: 1978), 358 pages.

Ramsay, Marina, (trans.), *Documents on the History of the Russian America Company* (Limestone Press, Kingston, ON: 1976), 219 pages.

Runciman, Steven, *The Eastern Schism* (Oxford University Press, London: 1963), 189 pages.

Schmemann, Alexander, *The Historical Road of Eastern Orthodoxy* (St Vladimir's Seminary Press, Crestwood: 1977), 342 pages.

_____, *For the Life of the World* (St Vladimir's Seminary Press, Crestwood: 1973), 151 pages.

_____, *Of Water and the Spirit* (St Vladimir's Seminary Press, Crestwood: 1974), 170 pages.

_____, *Church, World, Mission* (St Vladimir's Seminary Press, Crestwood: 1979), 227 pages.

Shelikov, Gregorii, *Voyage to America* (Limestone Press, Kingston, ON: 1981), 162 pages.

Siikala, Anna-Leena, *The Rite Technique of the Siberian Shaman* (Helsinki Academy of Science, Helsinki, Finland: 1978), 385 pages.

Smith, Barbara S., *Russian Orthodoxy in Alaska* (Alaska Historical Resources, Anchorage: 1980a), 171 pages.

_____, *Orthodoxy and Native Americans: The Alaskan Mission* (St Vladimir's Seminary Press, Crestwood: 1980b), 37 pages.

_____, and Redmond Barnett, *Russian American: the Forgotten Frontier* (Washington Historical Society, Tacoma: 1990), 255 pages.

Stamoolis, James J., *Eastern Orthodox Mission Theology Today* (Orbis Books, Maryknoll, NY: 1986), 194 pages.

Starr, J. Lincoln, *Education in Russian America* (NYU Dissertation, extracts published by University of Alaska, Fairbanks, AK: 1972), 50 pages.

Stavropoulos, Christophoros, *Partakers of Divine Nature* (Light and Life Publishing, Minneapolis: 1976), 98 pages.

Tarasar, Constance T., [ed.], *Orthodox America, 1794-1976* (Orthodox Church in America, Syosset, NY: 1975), 351 pages.

_____, *Perspectives on Orthodox Education* (Syosset, NY: 1983), 79 pages.

Thunberg, Lars, *Man and the Cosmos: The Vision of St Maximus the Confessor* (St Vladimir's Seminary Press, Crestwood: 1985), 184 pages.

Tikhmenev, Peter A., *A History of the Russian American Company* (University of Washington, Seattle: 1979), 257 pages.

Toelken, Barre, *The Dynamics of Folklore* (Houghton Mifflin, Boston: 1979), 395 pages.

Trubetskoy, Eugene, *Icons: Theology in Color* (St Vladimir's Seminary Press, Crestwood: 1973), 100 pages.

VanStone, James, *Eskimos of the Nushagak River* (University of Washington, Seattle: 1967), 198 pages.

_____, *Historic Settlement Patterns in the Nushagak River Region* (Fieldiana Anthropology, 1971), 149 pages.

_____, *V. S. Khromchenko's Coastal Explorations in Southwest Alaska* (Fieldiana Anthropology, 1973), 95 pages.

_____, *Russian Explorations in Southwest Alaska*, David Kraus, trans., (University of Alaska Press, Fairbanks: 1988), 120 pages.

Veniaminov, Innocent, *Notes on the Islands of the Unalaska District* (Limestone Press, Kingston, ON: 1984), 511 pages.

Waddell, Helen, *The Desert Fathers* (University of Michigan, Ann Arbor: 1966), 209 pages.

Ware, Timothy/Kallistos, *The Orthodox Church* (Pelican Books, New York: 1976), 352 pages.

_____, *The Orthodox Way* (St Vladimir's Seminary Press, Crestwood: 1979), 198 pages.

Washburn, Wilcomb E., *The Indian in America* (Harpers, New York: 1975), 296 pages.

Zagoskin, Lt. Lavrentii, *Lt. Zagoskin's Travels in Russian America* (University of Toronto, Toronto: 1967), 358 pages.

Zander, Valentine, *St Seraphim of Sarov* (St Vladimir's Seminary Press, Crestwood: 1975), 150 pages.

Zernov, Nicholas, *The Russians and their Church* (St Vladimir's Seminary Press, Crestwood: 1978), 192 pages.